The Peacock's Eye

The
Peacock's Eye

FRANCES OLIVER

Secker & Warburg
London

First published in England 1986
by Martin Secker & Warburg Limited
54 Poland Street, London W1V 3DF

British Library Cataloguing in Publication Data

Oliver, Frances, *1938–*
    The peacock's eye.
    I. Title
    813'.54[F]   PS3565.L4/

ISBN 0–436–33997–8

Set in 11/12 pt Lasercomp Baskerville by
Richard Clay (The Chaucer Press) Ltd, Bungay, Suffolk
Printed by Billing & Sons Ltd, Worcester

I

'Well, Dr Stone.' Sir Henry Drechsler, facing me across a great expanse of polyurethaned oak, fixes upon my face cold, watery blue eyes behind steel-rimmed glasses. He gives me my 'Doctor'. With emphasis, with care. His accent, except for those treacherous *v*'s, *r*'s, and *w*'s, is impeccably English, like his tweeds. The 'Doctor' has been spreading in England; in literary journals, in reviews, we are now called by our due Professors and Doctors, almost as on the Continent. I wonder if I must address him as 'Sir', and decide, uncomfortably, unable to fathom whether it is simple weakness or simple politeness impelling me, that I will. His 'Sir' is his shield, as my 'Doctor' is mine. We come from the same country, the country where 'Doctors', where all other titles, flourish as nowhere else, but we both prefer not to dwell on it. Without his 'Sir' I can regard him as the upstart son of a small Viennese hatter, which he is; without my 'Doctor' he can regard me as a shy, insignificant middle-aged woman with a game leg, which I am; a woman whose clothes and manner his beautiful young receptionist surveys with almost open contempt. I say 'Yes, Sir Henry,' and wait. He sighs with satisfaction. Perhaps he has feared, for a moment, that I would not use his 'Sir' after all.

'You know, of course, why I have asked to see you. It is now – let me see – almost ten years since the latest book about Maria Aurora. And it is nearly – let me see – yes, nearly seventy years since the death of Hans Handelbein.'

Maria Aurora. He says the beautiful name with reverence,

with as melodious an intonation as he can muster. He would not say 'your grandmother'. He would not demean her, nor dignify me, by linking me so solidly and at once to the vanished great.

I answer flatly, 'Yes, so it is.' I know, of course, why he wants to see me. He is the third publisher who has asked to see me this year. I live in the gilded baroque shadow of Maria Aurora. I owe her everything: my work, my doctorate, my new life in England, and even my name, which is the same as hers. Maria Aurora Alexandra – but mine continues as Stein, now anglicized to Stone, as I cannot bear the inevitable mispronunciations.

'Maria Aurora von Bilderheim-Traun is becoming a more and more international figure. In America they are screaming for another book.' He leans forward; the practised salesmanship of the Mariahilferstrasse bursting through the British tweeds. And why not, I think, with sudden weariness, why not, what had any of us to be so proud about, what was it if not money that kept the carriage wheels turning and the bolts drawn on the tall wrought-iron gates? 'It's a real phenomenon, Dr Stone, one of those rare occasions when a cult figure suddenly blossoms, out of neglect – I would not say obscurity because there has always been interest, there have always been devotés – but now, you see, feminism, Dr Stone, has caught on to Maria Aurora. They are comparing her letters to Virginia Woolf's, her poems – to whom do they compare her poems –'

I say, as gently as I can, 'She never wrote any poetry.'

He dismisses this with an impatient wave. 'But anyway, all of that – the literary, the academic approach – we have from her first, from the authorized biographer. The American. Joshua Prescott. She was still alive then, wasn't she, she must have read what he wrote. And you must have known him too. I have heard nothing of Prescott in years – where is he now?' His jowls flush with eagerness. It has suddenly occurred to him that maybe a burnished, up-dated edition of Joshua Prescott would be better than some piece of half-hearted, painstaking pedantry from the rather tired horse's mouth that is myself.

'Joshua is dead. He hanged himself. It was all of twenty years ago.'

'Ah yes, I remember now,' mumbles Sir Henry. 'Strange

2

story, that. I wonder why . . . Could we not – would you not say that was part of the volcanic effect of Maria Aurora? Among her famous lovers, if I am correct, there were at least three who committed suicide.'

'Well, in Joshua's case, not really *her* effect . . . though it is true that one could write an interesting book about Joshua himself. But I would not dream of it. I don't think his family would forgive me. Nor would I forgive myself.'

'I see. Well. No matter. Although the suicide of the first biographer is a very arresting fact. That famous biographer of Beethoven – Schindler, wasn't it – had terrible headaches. There is a shattering effect that the great have on their –'

'*Nachfolger*,' I say, inadvertently supplying the German word.

'Yes.' Sir Henry looks at me as if I have stepped distinctly out of line. 'Well, as I said, I think the time has come for a new biography, and I think you are the person to do it, Dr Stein – sorry, Stone. You must have access to all the family papers – and are there not some' – his jowls flush again – 'is there not a story about a trunk that was only to be opened thirty years or so after the Countess's death?'

Now suddenly she is the Countess. 'I think my brother Felix did mention something like that to Joshua. But if there was such a trunk, no one knows what happened to it. And I think, really, that all the important papers have been unearthed. I do not think there are any startling revelations to come.' I cannot help adding, half under my breath, 'Not from the papers, at any rate,' but Sir Henry, intent on his purpose and having wasted enough time, does not bother to hear this.

'No trunk, then. Pity. That sort of thing is always good for sales. Well, as I said, a biography, then, and I think you should do it. There is no doubt of your credentials and no doubt that you can write. Your study on Oscar Kokoschka –'

'I never wrote anything about Oscar Kokoschka.'

Sir Henry, to my delight, is at a momentary loss. His mouth, just twice, moves soundlessly, his fingers twitch with impatience. 'Well then, I do have it wrong,' he surrenders at last, and leans toward me, smiling confidentially. 'To tell you the truth, I hate all the Expressionists.'

'That's quite all right. It was Egon Schiele.'

'Ah, Egon Schiele. Ah yes. The point is, we would very

3

much like a new biography of the Countess of Bilderheim-Traun. (This formality of reference, I decide, is an unconscious snub, establishing still further the distance between my illustrious grandmother and myself by using her title and surname, when we both know everyone else refers to her as Maria Aurora.) Do you think you could do it, Dr Stone?'

'What were you thinking of as an advance?'

'Well – ah – we had not really discussed that yet. Oh, something quite generous, I assure you. Something in the neighbourhood of four thousand pounds. But we should like to have the typescript in a year. And we should very much like some new material to play up the feminist angle. As has been done lately, you know, with the Brontës, Virginia Woolf and so forth – they are all being seen again now in this – ah – feminist light. And we do want something a little more intimate than what we have had before. Family anecdotes, and a little domestic scandal – oh, there was public scandal enough, I suppose, but a little of that from the inside – if you do not feel it too much of an intrusion . . .' He smiles; I do not. He goes on. 'And we were thinking of having perhaps an introduction, a preface, yes? (His impeccable English is slipping just slightly.) By some – what shall I say – avant-gardienne – (chuckle) of the 'seventies. Perhaps, you know, Perdita Blank –'

'My grandmother, Sir Henry, disliked most women, and she would have disliked Perdita Blank even more than most. She would have preferred, I'm sure, that if there is a preface it be written by a man.'

'I see. Well, still, you might think about it. It is only the preface, it does help to sell the book. We cannot always consult the wishes of the dead in regard to everything – and since we are helping to preserve their memory – they must make allowances.' (Another chuckle.)

'I am expressing my own wish as well.'

'I see, I see. But please do think about it. You would be in no way held responsible for the ideas expressed. And I do want to stress the importance of this – this feminist angle, and of being somehow a bit more . . . *personal*. But that can all be discussed. The point is – are you willing, in principle, to undertake to do a biography?'

'In principle, Sir Henry, I am willing. But I cannot promise to put into my grandmother's mouth, or find in her correspondence, sentiments she did not possess, nor can I make

4

her less a member of what your Marxist writers think of as the oppressing class. My grandmother, Sir Henry, was in fact born to oppress people. Why so many of them chose to put up with it was what makes her an interesting woman. Oh, and one more thing. You do of course realize that my English, while very fluent – I have after all been speaking and writing it for many years – that English is not my native language and that I, leading a rather withdrawn and retiring sort of life, cannot really write in the style, or with this – this *intimacy* that you seem to set such store by. I mean, that instead of the – well, rather breezy, unacademic approach which is what I feel would fit in with your ideas, you are likely to get, however hard I try – if indeed I try – what you may think a – what is the word – rather uptight sort of manuscript.'

Sir Henry, fidgeting with impatience – I have taken much time, and shown much awkwardness, in getting together this last speech – says wearily, 'Yes, yes, I think our editors could fix some of that up. It is the lack of a feminist angle that I would worry most about – and if you could just find one or two new interesting personal stories – but your credentials are impeccable, and there's no doubt you are the closest person left. But I must say, from my side of the thing – it must be clear that if you persist in presenting your grandmother only as she was seen three decades ago – please understand me, Dr Stone, it is not at all the style of your writing that is in question – but I must tell you, in turn, that just another conventional polite biography is not what we want. I must tell you also that we have other people interested in doing such a book. Dr Dawn Crump, of Columbia, who wrote – what was it – *Mary Shelley's Frankenstein; a Symbolic Quest for Female Orgasmic Freedom* – is one of them. But I doubt she is the right person. You are, Dr Stone. I hope and believe that you are.' Having made his threat, that my grandmother, if I insist on seeing her in my stubborn anachronistic lights, might be turned over to Dr Dawn Crump, he is all smile and twinkling of watery eyes. 'So please, do think about it. Perhaps you could send us a sample chapter – and we should of course see to it that you are reimbursed for your time and effort if we decide the biography is not quite what we have in mind – and you are then free, of course, to write your own sort of biography for someone else.'

'As I told you, Sir Henry, I am interested, in principle. I

5

would of course prefer a firm contract before beginning anything . . . Well, let me think it over, and call you in a couple
of weeks or so.'

'Very good, Dr Stone. And thank you so much for coming.'
He sees me to the door. My leg is bad today, and it is always
humiliating to be so slow to cross a room when someone is
eager to get you out of it. But Sir Henry Drechsler in his way
is a genius; he has almost succeeded in making me want what
I have never really wanted to do before. Which is to defend
that vampirical spectre, Maria Aurora; to lay yet another
wreath on that extravagant, truthless tomb.

Although I would prefer what I suggested, in pure irony, to
Sir Henry — to write a biography of Joshua Prescott. Or even
of the other Maria Aurora, who is myself. Have we not come
far enough for that, in this age of infinite nit-picking? (There
are, after all, only so many Ph.D. thesis topics to go around —
and only so many little lights left for the definitive biographer
whom all biographers hope to be.) We must be down to the
bottom of the barrel, far beyond new lives of the famous
biographers, the Boswells, the Aubreys — why not a biography,
a wreath for the tomb, of the unknown biographer?

But you, Sir Henry, would not like that idea. You would
cough, wave your hands about in that impatient Viennese
gesture that goes so ill with the British accent and tweeds.
'But my dear Dr Stone — what can be the possible interest —
my dear Dr Stone! Joshua Prescott hanged himself, yes, of
course. That is quite dramatic, if a little *déjà vu* — but do you
not see, Dr Stone — there must be some relevance — something
to grip our jaded readers. And that takes more than a young
Middle-Western college professor swinging from a beam. You
would have to tell us why anyone should care about Prescott,
except for his biography of the famous Countess Bilderheim-Traun. Now if you could say that it was his — ah —
his relationship with the Countess herself that led to such a
violent end, his obsession with her personality — if he had been
found, for instance, dying in some final act . . . yes, of per-
version — shall we say, wearing the old lady's stockings and
stays, the ones in that rather risqué picture by Fritz Him-
melfarth which was rumoured — only rumoured, of course — to
be of the Countess herself — if there were a gay identification
angle, say, or even a heterosexual angle, if he had been the

old lady's last great fling, in the style of – what was that old movie – *Harold and Maude* – at the end of which, in contrast to the movie, it is not the old love who bows out of life but the young lover – a good new twist that – if there were such a hidden scandal treated with warmth and empathy and *true compassion* – well, then, we might have a book.

As for a book about yourself – as for you – why *you* (in Viennese now), *Du, Mariechen, bist net amal aufghengt.*

As for me.

You, little Maria, are not even hanged.

Nonetheless. Though I may not have even that distinction (and if I had I could hardly write about it) I should like, just for once, to talk, to write about myself.

I would begin ... (And to hell with you, Sir Henry, the real reason you dislike me is because my grandmother's coachman patronized your father's little shop and you suspect that I know this. You fear that my snobbery may be as in-grained, as irredeemable as your own (it isn't), and you are aware, as I am, that while we keep up our charade of Doctors and Sirs and Being British we are, all the time, sniffing for faint whiffs of each other's antecedents, the secret hairs bristling on our backs.) I would begin ...

(But then it occurs to me that I have walked into a trap. Sir Henry does not want me to do the biography. He feels he must ask me first, especially since I am the guardian of all those papers; and when I fail, or refuse, which is his real hope and the reason for his thinly veiled rudeness, he can turn the whole thing over to Dr Dawn Crump. Or even to Perdita Blank who will fill a volume with sleazy vignettes of fornication, who will have my poor grandmother slavering, spreadeagled, eternally up-ended, a mere crested vessel of the primeval slime, exactly what the philosopher Waldmann accused her of being, in his mad ravings after she spurned him ...

It also occurs to me that my off-the-cuff remark about Joshua Prescott was a dire mistake. No doubt Sir Henry's sharp ears have picked up a reverberation of real secret scandal in the Prescott case, and he will find someone less scrupulous than I am to ferret it out. What did I say – I could write an interesting book, but his family would not forgive me, nor I forgive myself? After all these years, after all that went on in

7

my own family, I have still not learned, I will never learn, never, to be sufficiently on my guard.)

But that would be one more reason for telling at least what I really remember, about Joshua, about myself.

So then, I would begin . . .

The progeny of such lions as the Countess Bilderheim-Traun grow up like royal children dethroned – knowing the reign and the realm must end with the parent king. They are presented, at birth, with an Oedipal puzzle that admits of no solution: to break the power of their father or mother will never bring them a throne, it will only put paid to the kingdom. It is not their fault they have been spawned, often in a weak moment and regretted ever after, or born only to be shrivelled and singed in that fiery extension of egotism the lions call love. Unless they are fortunate enough to inherit the parental genius – or the parental gift for hoodwinking people into thinking it is there – or unless they are strong enough, hard enough, to escape altogether, they must resign themselves to a branch existence, to the humiliation of endless unthinking comparison, and no peace. All their lives people will expect more, or less, from them than they can do. They will be measured against an impossible standard and despised for being so wanting; or they will be fawned on, courted, caressed, because of a pale reflected glory that sticks like glue when one wants it least – but goes, when it goes, as quickly as mountain mist. They are never, in anyone's eyes, only themselves; and whatever these selves may be they are never, in anyone's eyes, worth knowing. They can of course be little cogs to the big wheels. The great virtuoso's children, if they do not become virtuosos, might make fourth violin. The Hollywood children can write about their desperate Hollywood childhoods. The literary lion's can devote a cramped life to editing and annotating Papa's works.

And the offspring of a muse – what is a muse?

A muse is a kind of temple prostitute.

The children of a muse can become whores.

No, on second thought, I would not begin like that.

It is pithy and flourishing, if a bit heavy. Not even untrue, as far as it goes. Sir Henry might like it. But just as the tomb is not entirely truthless, my splendid introduction is not

8

entirely applicable. After all, none of us did become whores, strictly speaking, not even my mother; and if I cannot end with those three terse sentences all the rhetorical effect is lost. I am running away with myself. The family tendency to dramatize everything, from which I too am not totally exempt, has overwhelmed me before I can even make a proper start.

And in any case, a proper start (if I were to write my biography – or Joshua's, or both together, because in many ways my story is also Joshua's, and Joshua's mine) – a proper start would be, in fact, to give the conventional outline of the life of Maria Aurora herself. One usually begins a life with some small reference to one or two preceding generations. So (as on the male side nothing is known for certain), some small reference to Maria Aurora.

She was born in 1867, daughter of a horse-loving, roulette-playing, handsome middle-aged noble, August von Petrolinski, and a pretty young Baroness with a much shakier title but considerably more wealth. By the time he married, Petrolinski had gambled away most of his estate; by the time little Maria Aurora (her mother's fanciful idea of a name), or 'Mitzi', was grown up, he had gambled away most of his wife's. Maria Aurora was tutored by governesses, dancing masters and priests, none of whom found her very amenable, then sent to a convent school for the last year or two of her erratic education. At seventeen she escaped from her convent and eloped with the young Count Bilderheim-Traun; a glamorous, hot-headed, dandified officer who tyrannized his men, his servants and most of all his tailors, and was killed in a duel three months later, by the brother of the equally noble young lady he had jilted in order to marry my grandmother.

So there was Maria Aurora, a widow almost as soon as wed, and barely eighteen. She inherited a large estate, but even larger debts. Somehow, she managed; she managed to lead the life of a very grand young lady. According to Joshua's researches, she had always felt stifled by an existence devoted to balls and ball gowns and the embellishment of one's drawing room; she had always shown glimmers of that rare quality, or substance if you will, that we choose to call mind. Be that as it may, there is no written evidence that Mitzi was dissatisfied with her gallants and entertainments until, some years later, with the suddenness of an angel-appearance-

9

inspired conversion, she discovered the Arts. The angel in the case was a large, hairy, low-born painter of undisputed genius, the notorious Gustav Stammlos.

From then on, Maria Aurora played muse with a vengeance. She patronized (insofar as her debts would permit), corresponded with and slept with (so it was reputed) three painters, one violin virtuoso and seven literary men. And she was as fatal as she was beautiful. She had a knack for choosing talents already infested with the wasting consumption so romantically envisioned by those nostalgic for the vanished Puccini-style Bohemia. But she never caught the disease herself. And her healthy lovers did not fare much better. One, in Shelleyesque fashion, drowned; another blew his brains out with a pearl-handled pistol in her bedroom, a messy incident which unnerved her enough to compel three months in retirement on the Riviera.

Age did not wither Maria Aurora, nor custom stale. She emerged still blooming from World War I; and though another lover had been killed in Galicia and most of her land and revenues were gone, as was the Austro-Hungarian Empire which had sheltered her and her ilk under its mothy eagle's wings, Grandmama remained undaunted, artist-loving, erratic and scandalous as ever. She continued to shuttle between Paris, Rome, Nice, Venice, Budapest and Vienna, though she could no longer always stay in the very best hotels. She was painted, yet again, by artists of the post-war period; she was acquainted with Rilke, Freud, Jung, Kafka, Alban Berg and Karl Kraus.

Rather absent-mindedly, while all this else was going on, Maria Aurora produced two children, a girl and a boy. The boy, probably fathered by one of the tubercular literati, died very young. The girl was healthy and husky as a horse, though she arrived when Maria Aurora was already thirty-six and married, briefly, for the second time, to a gouty diplomat whose title I forget and whom she divorced almost as soon as the child was born. It was said that the real father was the Countess's handsome young groom, but that of course may have been idle gossip. Anyway, it is curious and possibly appropriate that I should think of the horse simile. Whatever else, he was a marvellous groom (even my mother used to talk about this). He kept the horses superbly well. 'Their rumps shone (Joshua wrote, supposedly quoting Grandmama), like the

10

cask-hoops of the favourite *Bierstube* he repaired to when he had finished his loving currying.' Grandmama used to say that it was one of her greatest pleasures to sit on the driver's seat beside him (times being what they were, the groom also served as coachman) and watch the rhythmic motion of those splendid muscles under the polished skin. Or, to quote Joshua again, 'that polished muscled rhythm', though that was not a phrase Grandmama herself would have used.

But I am digressing. The girl had, as Maria Aurora herself wrote to one of her famous lovers, 'no wit, but much fleshy bloom, like one of those forced gardenias the florists now love to sell'.

That fleshy gardenia (we have swapped horses for flowers but really both are right, in their place) was my Mama.

No. I am getting carried away again.

That was how my brother Felix reported it to Joshua. Not entirely how it was.

Joshua Prescott, to his credit, did somewhat pare down Felix's baroque edifice. He was all conscientiousness, Joshua. For instance, he did make it clear that while Grandmama wrote to Freud, Jung, Kafka and Karl Kraus, they did not answer very often. It was her passionate correspondence with Hans Handelbein that made most of her reputation. Her posthumous reputation, at all events. As Hans Handelbein's was in turn greatly enhanced by the poems and letters found among her possessions, long after his death.

As for the rest, the many lovers, the clandestine meetings with famous married men – who knows how much Grandmama herself exaggerated in her letters and re-miniscing, or how much the gossip of the epoch was that and no more? And who could ever trace so many secret rendezvous, who would bother to grill a boozy innkeeper's daughter about whether her father, already fifteen years under the sod, ever mentioned a mysterious couple who spent a night at his inn in 1913? (Joshua Prescott actually did. He made many of the journeys involved in the great lady's escapades, visited all the inns she mentioned that still existed. And he did find one or two people who remembered someone of her description. If you talk to them long enough, people will remember any-thing.) My mother, brought up by nannies and in boarding schools, never knew where her mother went, or with whom,

11

and left home herself at eighteen . . . but I am getting ahead of my story. It was no use quizzing Grandmama herself, though Joshua tried that too. During the last few years of her life – the time during which Joshua stayed with us working on her biography – the only person who could make sense out of Grandmama's ramblings was my brother Felix. And Felix himself now lies in an obscure churchyard in Yugoslavia, near where his Aston-Martin crashed on the way to Trieste.

So, if I do choose to write about the first Maria Aurora, there is only myself to tell, or to untangle, this story. Two things which are not synonymous. And no, Sir Henry, I will not let you give it to Dr Dawn Crump or Perdita Blank or any of those silly American viragos. It is only the polyglot polymorphous mentality of Central Europe that can see so far into itself, thát can say, not that there is no truth, for perhaps there is one; but it is not for us.

Where though should the story, hers or mine, then really begin?

I think, since no one alive can be sure of my grandmother's past, with the past I know, I myself remember. With my own.

II

I could begin, for instance, with a bucolic winter scene, a scene from a Central European children's book. Winter, and snow. A sled, a hill, smiling round faces with glowing apple cheeks. One of the faces is mine; the others belong to my 'aunts' Trudi (short for Gertrude von Pokolski) and Berti (short for Bertha von Krementz-Macklburger). They are in their forties; I am five. We fly down the slope; the white crystals hissing and spinning behind our runners, we hurtle toward the forest below at a dizzying, to me unbelievable, speed, our wake of snow obscuring the battered boots of my aunts and my own little red ones braced behind theirs. The forest comes closer, closer. I shut my eyes. And as always, at the last moment they swerve; with a perfect synchronized movement they shift their weight, dig their heels in, and turn the sled in a neat smooth curve, so it only tips slightly, rights itself at once, and slows to a stop. Trudi and Berti are laughing; their laughter is loud and rich and silly and happy, against the dark-green silence of the trees.

That is one of my earliest memories. Another is of our very Aryan town's only resident Jew (there was some suspected Jewish blood among the aristocrats but those were protected, class snobbery being even stronger than anti-Semitism) tarred and feathered in the market square. This memory is more dim. A great hunched sticky bird fumbling at its face where the beak should have been, and whimpering. 'Go on, fly, you old Jewish bird,' the older children were shouting. I was much too small to know what it was all about. My mother, who had

13

had to take me out shopping as my young so-called nanny had just gone off to join some sort of female Hitler Youth organization, said softly but sharply, 'Don't look, Mitzi,' and hurried me away. But I wanted to watch the funny bird made of clay trying to take its face apart.

It is, I suppose, to my mother's credit that she told the Wehrmacht officer who was taking her out then that she thought this crowd behaviour primitive and disgusting. 'Why must they do such things in the name of the Führer?' The Wehrmacht officer chewed on his pipe, a bit impatiently (I remember that habit of his, and his nice tobacco-smell and his very blue eyes), and answered, well, they were peasants, and they must be allowed their little amusements.

Or, at least, that was how my mother reported the conversation, some years later, to Joshua Prescott. I never understood why she mentioned it to Joshua at all. But probably he had heard about the tarring, and about her affair with a Wehrmacht officer, in the course of all his intensive research. There were enough people jealous of us and our resident American, or nursing some grudge against Felix, to make it certain that Joshua would hear everything my mother might not want him to hear. So perhaps she felt she had to state her position and make her excuses. I remember her saying, too, 'It is hard for you to understand, Joshua, but in those days a woman had to have a protector. If for nothing else, for the sake of the children. A woman will do many things to give her children bread.' (She neglected to mention that when the days of need and danger came, the days near the end of the war when we did need a protector and bread was really short, her Wehrmacht officer had already been killed on the Russian front.)

But I am digressing. At all events, those are my two most vivid early memories. I present them to you, Sir Henry, because they seem to me both typical and symbolic of a country wartime childhood. Life went on, much as before. Only now and then the hideous cruelty of the human species, that cruelty to which the Nazis gave freer and larger scope than almost ever in history, burst into view.

Another instance. There were political prisoners who had to cut wood in the forest near our house. Again, they are only a dim memory to me. I remember thin shuffling men with loose grey uniforms and dreadful sores on their hands and

14

faces. I saw them once when Trudi and Berti were pulling me on the sled. Like my mother, my aunts said nervously, 'Don't look,' and pulled the sled faster.

Felix, my brother, told me years later that he and a friend once found such a man pinned under a tree, probably in a logging accident, and simply left to die; no one had even been merciful enough to shoot him. He was still breathing, but when he opened his mouth wider, perhaps trying to beg them for help, blood ran out of it but no words came. They were frightened; they ran away and told no one. But, at Felix's instigation, they did go back the next day. The man was dead by then, his body frozen stiff. The boys grew bolder and dared each other to take his watch. I never understood how he had one; I had always thought the prisoners were stripped of all valuables as soon as they reached their camps. Perhaps he was an overseer and had to bring the other men back at a certain hour. Felix said the buckle seemed stuck, so they cut the strap and then ran home, in terror again, thinking they might have been seen and the Gestapo would execute them for looting. Felix showed me the watch when he told me the story. It didn't work; he had only kept it as a souvenir, with birds' eggs and pebbles and other childhood treasures. Felix, in some ways, was a sentimental man.

I can imagine you, Sir Henry, your knobbly legs shifting impatiently in your Heal's swivel chair. This little mixed album of family snapshots and minor wartime horrors is not what you want at all. You are waiting for Grandmama to come on the scene. Though you would, perhaps, like the detail of the dead prisoner with the watch if it were an incident in the life of someone more famous than my brother Felix. In fact Felix, if not famous, was at least very notorious in our little community, and Felix also has a great deal to do with the story of my grandmother.

And it is, after all, mostly *my* story that I am telling. But even if it were, once again, entirely my grandmother's, it would be important to fill in a little of the background of her last years, of the only time I really knew her. One cannot go on quoting forever the famous love letters of Hans Handelbein. Not if it is to be the real, true to life, intimate account you say you want from me.

I will, however, in spite of myself, do as you wish, cut all this short and bring Grandmama on to the scene. I only want

15

to say that most of *my* other early memories are of empty stomachs and scratchy wool tights and chilblains. Memories of being hungry, of being cold. Memories of huddling around the tiny fires in the large tiled stove, no longer able to warm one's back while sitting on the wooden bench around it, because the little bit of heat hardly penetrated the tiles and the wooden bench itself had been chopped up and burned. By then, every twig that fell in the forest was collected almost as soon as it touched the ground, and the tree that pinned down the prisoner had, long ago, been chopped up and used as well. In my childhood, it seemed to be always winter; the summers I hardly remember at all. For the last of those winters, my grandmother lived with us. The picture of our winter evenings is still vivid in my mind. My mother is reading to me from a book of fairy tales; my grandmother is there too, my beautiful illustrious grandmother, a bundle of shawls and blankets propped up against the stove, from which sometimes emerge a patrician but runny nose and a hoarse imperious voice. The voice demands biscuits or a hot-water bottle, and my mother ignores it and goes on reading, as neither of those precious commodities, biscuits or hot water, is to be had.

And that, Sir Henry, was our wartime in the country. It cannot be said that we had a difficult war. There was privation, yes, hunger and cold, the eternal chilblains, but that was near the end, and for some time after. We were not bombed or searched, and the Russians did not occupy us. Except for the man pinned down in the woods and old Kohn who was tarred and feathered, we children saw no horrors, though no doubt there were many more than we saw, even in our quiet valley. We heard stories, of course, but I was too young to understand them. My mother, on the pretext of various illnesses, kept me out of school a great deal and fairly clear of Nazi indoctrination. When I did go to school, it was to a local convent where no one discussed politics, and Felix, who was four years older, was shipped off to be educated by the Jesuits when his antics at home became too outrageous. He did not last long with the Jesuits either, but before that first school could expel him, he got severe pleurisy and was shipped off again, to relatives in the mountains, where he had an infinitely better time than the rest of us.

The worst period was when the Wehrmacht officer was gone

and strangers were quartered in our house. There were already too many of us, packed into what had once been my great-grandfather's little 'bijou' hunting lodge, all that was left of his (my mother frequently told me) vast noble properties. It was an ostentatiously rustic and inconvenient building, never intended for year-round or servantless living. The household consisted of my mother, myself, Trudi, who was Felix's father's sister, and Berti, who was actually no relative but Trudi's lifetime companion. Also Felix, when he was there. Trudi and Berti really loved country life, and had gladly moved in with my mother when Berti had to sell her estate . . . but I realize I have skipped a generation. I must explain who my mother was, and why we were in the country.

My mother, at seventeen, had, or thought she had, a big and promising voice. The promise, alas, was mostly in the ears of the auditor, more specifically one, a teacher at the academy who gave my mother her singing lessons. 'I have to pay for some activity to keep her out of trouble,' Grandmama wrote to the playwright Friedrich Adlerhorst. 'With that enormous bosom, she is certain to appeal to the wrong sort of man and she is much too stupid to resist.' (This was one of the letters Joshua tactfully kept from publication.) The teacher, it was also said, admired my grandmother and therefore wished the singing lessons to be as frequent as possible; they were held in Grandmama's apartment near Schoenbrunn, and she usually asked him for morning coffee or afternoon tea. Since there was no hope of more than distant worship with the mother, however, the voice teacher began to concentrate his attentions on the daughter. It seems he was moved by the bosom even more than by the voice, and the singing lessons ended in my mother's first pregnancy. Fortunately for all concerned, probably the child not least, she miscarried at three months, and refused her teacher's proposal of marriage, determined to pursue her career. But even with Grandmama's help ('Though this must be said for the Countess,' Trudi once told me in an unguarded moment, 'she never used her influence to really push anything mediocre, even if it was in her own family') my poor mother never got beyond the back row of a chorus.

She did, however, marry three times. The first, following her mother's line in attracting suicides, or creating them, was a banker who went bankrupt and shot himself. The second, some years after the demise of the first, was my brother Felix's father, a handsome medical student younger than herself, with some claim to a title, or at least a *von*, and very little devotion to the pursuit of medicine. She left him quite soon, because of his constant infidelities and because she was tired of working to put him through medical school. She never wearied of telling Felix that. Though he was worth it, of course, his advent had destroyed her higher singing hopes. 'If you had not been born just then,' she would say, 'I might have sung Brunhilde,' and Felix would nod, mutter 'Thank God,' under his breath, and wink at me if I was there. We both knew from Trudi and Berti that my mother had given up trying for big roles or big recitals before Felix appeared, and that she had supported his father by doing editorial assistance work in a music publishing house. Felix's father vanished eventually in the East; he may be long dead, or a retired commissar, or even a doctor. Like Felix, I think he was the sort who lands on his feet. Or someone else's.

The third husband, my own father, was a thin-voiced tenor whose uncle was a very famous pianist. So my mother and he had that in common; they both lived under charismatic shadows, and their voices were pretty evenly matched. It should have been a magazine-story happy ending – two also-rans who embrace and live happily ever after, finding in each other those little sterling qualities no one in the harsh glitter-loving outside world had noticed before. They might have settled down to joyous domesticity – my mother was really very domestic, perhaps as a reaction to the total lack of that quality in her own mother. But this relationship lasted even less than the others. My parents parted company shortly after I was born, and by mutual agreement. Perhaps, instead of seeing each other's inner lights, they were stifled by each other's mediocrity. My grandmother's verdict on my father had been '*harmlos*', harmless, that most damning epithet of faint praise. Or it may have been (so my grandmother also said) that they simply could not bear to hear each other sing, without a surrounding chorus to drown them out.

I do not remember my father at all. He did come back to visit when I was very little; but before I was four, he moved to Prague, and died of food poisoning from the canapés at a post-concert reception. Going by the few photos I have, and the few letters, he was a wistful, kindly man, truly in love with his music and very knowledgeable about it, lost in that peculiar, innocent, almost monastic world musicians sometimes manage to live in, even the lesser talents. I wish I had known him. I even wish I had heard his singing, which might have been sensitive and warm and not nearly as bad as they all made out. I have no musical talent myself but I have always envied musicians their dedication to a realm beyond words, a pure distillation of our earthbound, sullied longings and loves and griefs, an absolute and abstract and amoral beauty, which is of course why Plato would have banned them from the Republic . . . but I am running away from myself again.

As for my mother, I always suspected that the chief reason she took up music was because there was only one musician among her mother's lovers. At all events, she gave up her singing career with no real pain, and devoted herself to her children and her domestic routine. Not without complaint; but the kind of complaints which indicated that secretly she had what she wanted, that she must have been, in her inmost soul, grateful to the circumstances that removed her from the limelight in which my notorious grandmother moved with such arrogant ease. Small wonder, after my mother's neglected, helter-skelter upbringing, that *Gemütlichkeit*, the marvellous Austrian word which means so much more than either comfort or coziness, became her guiding principle.

But alas, *Gemütlichkeit*, like the singing career, was elusive. There were not the right children to fit the respectable niches she would have liked (my mother suffered, I think, from the rumour of her illegitimacy, the coachman with the shining horses); there was never quite enough money; there was never quite the right man (there were men, of course, but not of much significance, and rather more than there should have been in a truly respectable household). It was after one of these episodes finished, and in order to escape the city before the outbreak of war, that my mother decided to move to the country, where the small pensions from her first and third marriages would go further, and she had a clear field for singing lessons. So we did move, into my great-grandfather's hunting lodge, on the outskirts of an old spa once patronized by the aristocracy, who kept their mistresses there while their wives were installed in the grander resort up the river.

*

When its war was no longer going so well, the Nazi Government decided we had too much space, although to us it seemed too little, and we had to give up a couple of rooms to a family of four; a paunchy post-office employee, just retired for reasons of health, his hefty giant of a wife and their two runny-nosed little girls. This family became the bane of our existence. So it was a very uncomfortable ménage that received my grandmother in 1944.

My grandmother sent no message. She simply arrived in a taxi, the last moving taxi in our town, and though she announced almost at once that she had lost everything, she arrived with seven pieces of luggage. The transport of those seven pieces, at that time, was nothing short of miraculous. She never bothered to tell us how she had done it, nor – except for a few vague words about her flat being bombed, or requisitioned – even from where she had come, or why. She and my mother, who were never on very good terms, had quarrelled at the beginning of the war, and there had been no contact between them since. My mother had written once to an address in Nice but received no answer.

I remember the scene very well; the taxi pulling up at the gate – we saw it from the window – my mother saying, '*Ach du lieber Gott*', and going slowly to the door. My grandmother got out of the taxi, a slim woman with high-piled white hair, wearing a long dark coat. She looked around with a momentary bewilderment, the first sign of deterioration in that gloriously self-absorbed mind, then suddenly smiled (a smile that would have moved mountains, even then, cf. Joshua Prescott) and called to my mother, 'Anna. Come to me, my darling. I have forgiven you everything. And now we can be together again,' creating, with a few deft phrases, the impression in all our minds that my mother was the errant stray to whom *she*, all noblesse oblige, was now prepared to give refuge.

My mother hesitated. My mother: a dowdy tweedy figure in a frayed skirt and sweater, her hands red and raw and chilblained, her hair escaping from her bun. Since the days of the Wehrmacht officer, she had let herself go.

By this time, our whole ménage had collected on the steps to greet the unawaited arrival, and the four warty Schweissers, our hated tenants, were leaning out of their upstairs windows, drooling with curiosity. At last, as Grandmama's arms, still held out, were beginning to tremble, my mother moved stiffly

forward. They pecked at each other's cheeks, and my grandmother gave my mother little pats on the shoulder, as one
might absent-mindedly pat a cat sharing one's armchair. Then
she stepped back. 'Anna, my poor darling, you look hideous. I
will have to do something about it. Ach, I know, I too, we all
look hideous. (She did not; she was the most beautiful person
I had ever seen.) You cannot imagine how dreadful it was in
Vienna.'

'Vienna?' said my mother. 'I thought you were still in
France.' But my grandmother did not listen.

'I suppose it is dreadful here,' she went on, 'but I will see
what I can do for you to make things better. Who are all
these people?' She gazed sternly at Trudi and Berti, whose
pink cheeks grew pinker yet. 'And my grandchildren! Dear
God, how I have neglected my grandchildren. Well, I will
make up for it. That is the girl – come, give a kiss to your
grandmama. But where is the boy? And tell me, Anna (the
Schweissers were practically falling out of their windows)who
are those horrible creatures upstairs?'

My mother, who could not of course answer all these
questions at once, decided to answer none, only gave a
warning 'Sssshhh' at the remark about the Schweissers, then
said resignedly, 'I don't know how we are going to manage
this, Mama, but let us go in and try to figure it out.'

'Wait,' said Grandmama. 'I must pay the taxi. Do you think
they (pointing to Trudi and Berti, as if their still-husky country
bulks made her assume they were navvies) can deal with the
luggage? Oh, and of course there is Janka. She is hiding in
the taxi, poor stupid little thing.'

'Janka?' My mother's voice was alarmed. '*What* is Janka?'

'Ach, Janka. Janka is my little Polish girl. I rescued her – if
it had not been for that –' Her voice dropped; the bewildered
expression came into her face again for a moment, then she
whispered something into my mother's ear.

'Oh, God. Mama, we have no room. We hardly have space
for ourselves.'

'Nonsense. She can sleep in my bedroom, on a settee, on
anything. She does everything for me, my hair, my cleaning,
she stands for me in the queues. Twice they tried to take her
away, but I managed to stop them. Dear Christ, this war,
these insane politics. (The Schweissers had shut their windows
by now, but my mother looked anxiously upstairs.) And those

21

creatures I suppose have been quartered upon you. Well, we will see about that. Fortunately I still have some influence . . .'

'Mama, you have no influence here. Not with this government. Not among these people. You don't know what we have to do to survive.'

'Of course I know. And I do have it. How do you think *I* have survived? How do you think I managed to come here when travel is almost impossible?' She turned toward me and smiled, that slow, wonderful, heart-stopping smile. 'Child, go and get little Janka out of the taxi before he drives away with her.'

Of course I do not really remember this conversation word for word. It is a reconstruction, like everything else, a report of what I *think* they said, and what my mother said they said (and would they ever have said so much when the Schweissers might have heard it, even with Grandmama's carelessness), or, again, of what Felix said my grandmother said she said (Felix, who was not even there). But I put this down, for what it is worth; it does not *seem* in any way false, it does tally with that imperial presence my grandmother is thought to have possessed and which, on this and other occasions, did really impress me as being there. It *was* an imperial presence, and I do remember it as that. But how terribly, how quickly, age and accident can mellow the keenest arrogance! And how much is my memory coloured by all the legend, all the telling, that legend which has shaped my own life until it sometimes seems there is nothing left of *me* but my scepticism – that lack of faith which can sustain an existence as surely as faith itself? (And I sometimes suspect that Sir Henry, under all the layers of money, title, success, is one of us too; that somewhere in his inmost self he knows quite well that nearly everything is – what it is. I am not prudish about using the conventional word but in this case the conventional word is somehow not strong enough. The farmyard metaphor will hardly do any more for our high-technology, media-is-message age. Never mind all that. As usual, I am digressing.)

But sceptic or not, the legend is too strong for me. Grandmama is already taking over what was to be my story, just as her legend took over my life. Or, perhaps, what is really taking over is what lay behind the legend. For

Grandmama was certainly a force to be reckoned with – only not quite the kind of force her admiring biographers would have had her be.

At all events, having dealt out that splendid opening scene, my imperial, imperious grandmother arriving from nowhere with seven pieces of luggage, I must not forget to mention what I really remember best of all; the terrified, hunted face of the Polish child I had to coax from the black upholstered depths of the wheezing taxicab.

The nuns at the convent school where I went had managed to imbue me with nagging feelings of Christian charity and guilt – though they never mentioned what would have been most deserving of our guilt and our charity, the starving men who were used to fell trees in our woods. As soon as I saw Janka, who was actually a few years older than I but looked the same age or even younger, she seemed to me a proper object for these fine sentiments.

God only knows where or how my grandmother had got hold of her. There was a vague story that she had been selected, from a group of Poles probably bound for the death camps, to work for some people who lived near Grandmama, wherever Grandmama was living then; and Grandmama had taken her on when the people moved away. 'Not that I could afford to feed another mouth, but everything I had to keep me company was gone, even the canaries, and her little pale face melted my heart.'

Janka did not respond to any of my overtures. She spoke almost no German, and did not seem able to learn more. She answered questions with monosyllables, such questions as she understood, and when she could, avoided speech altogether. She smiled sometimes, a quick nervous smile, more like a tic, but she never laughed. She did everything for Grandmama, brushed her hair, polished her shoes, even cunningly passed the food at table so Grandmama could get more than her share. No one else seemed to exist for Janka except as a source of fear.

I did not give up easily. I badly wanted some company, with Felix not home; and in my way, I could be imperious too. Since we could not really communicate, I kept trying to improve Janka's German. 'Book,' I would say, pointing. 'Stairway. Picture. Glass.' Then act out verbs. 'Look, Janka. I go up the stairs. Now I go down the stairs. I go up. I go down. Say it, Janka. Ach, Jesus Maria! All right. Don't say it. *Go* up the stairs then. *Show* me you understand.'

Janka would shake her head, and say the one German phrase that seemed to have become thoroughly embedded in her mind. '*Nicht verstehen.*' Not understand. But when Grandmama demanded a shawl or a coat or a cup of tea, she understood perfectly. She never brought the wrong thing. Whether she realized that Grandmama had saved her from death, as I have little doubt Grandmama actually did, or whether she had simply attached herself fiercely and exclusively to the one human being who had been kind to her since she had lost her parents, I do not know. Whatever the reason, she was totally my grandmother's creature, and never willingly left her side. Perhaps the children of her earlier employers – slave-owners would be a better word – had hurt or abused her. She certainly avoided me as much as she could; and remained deaf and dumb to my German lessons. After a while I did give them up. I tried simply bringing toys, and showed her how I played with them. I tried to get her to draw, to sit on a rocking horse, to hold a doll, to paste cut-outs in a scrap-book, all in vain. '*Nicht verstehen,*' she would say, hunching her dark head into her narrow shoulders and looking at me with her great frightened eyes, like some newly caged bird; and I would sigh and swear and go away again. But the next day I would try once more. It was too tempting, too frustrating, to have a child near my own age in our lonely house. It was also, as I have said, that this was the height of my religious period, and Janka was to be one of the good deeds that would get me to heaven.

I told the nuns about Janka, carefully explaining that she was a Polish orphan and my grandmother's maid, as I had been instructed to say by my mother. 'You can't understand this, Mitzi, but times are so difficult . . . and your Grandmama is so *entêtée*, she insists on keeping that child. Actually in some ways it is a blessing; if that child did not wait on her, I suppose I would have to. Or you. But we must be careful, especially with that dreadful – with Herr Schweisser in the house, who is a Party member – that is why he is here, you know, it was the best quarters they could find after their house was bombed . . . we must be very careful that he does not think – that nobody thinks that child is what she is not. I mean, they have no objection if you keep a Polish girl as a servant. But if they thought she was —'

'If they thought she was what, Mama?'

'Not Catholic. And not even Protestant. A different religion. Then Grandmama would not be allowed to keep her and God knows what would happen to the poor child. Or to us. And that Schweisser is waiting and watching for us to do something wrong. He thinks we might not agree with all his ideas . . . and he would love to have this house for himself, to get us out. I know you can't understand and I shouldn't really talk to you about it — but just remember to tell everyone that that child is a Catholic. Like the rest of us.'

I would have understood, if my mother had not been so bad at explanations. Nevertheless, I understood a little more than she thought, and I made sure to tell the nuns that Janka was Catholic. They told me to pray for her soul, poor little orphan, and asked if she had been confirmed. I said yes, of course. They tactfully did not suggest I bring her to Sunday Mass. Grandmama did not appear at Mass either. I doubt that she had gone to church since her girlhood, and my mother let it be known that her mother was often ailing. I think she was relieved that Grandmama seldom left the house; though her outspokenness was dangerous enough at home, what with the Schweissers there.

My contact with Grandmama herself was somewhat cool. She did not like children, and she probably could not entirely forgive my adulterated blood, even though she was responsible for the initial adulteration. If, that is, the famous coachman story was true. In Felix's case, his looks and charm were to cancel all that. But I was not outstandingly handsome, nor a boy.

When Grandmama did speak to me with any intimacy, it was often to enlist me in schemes for the improvement of my mother's appearance or the situation in our house; and I liked that because then she spoke to me as if I were an adult, even though I was adult enough to know the schemes held not much hope. 'Look, child, I still have some good dresses I no longer wear. Too small for your mother, of course, but such beautiful fabric. A clever seamstress could make one out of two. Don't you know anyone in the village who would do this? We could have a present for her birthday. If she would consent to a fitting . . .' Or, 'Your mother hardly invites anyone at all. I know they are terribly boring here, but one must do something to keep up one's spirits, and social abilities are like muscle, if you do not work them you lose them, the effort becomes too great. We could make a cake with honey and potato flour, as one used to do in the First War – oh, but no, it is no use. Who would there be but the von Loewenbergs and the Bruchsteins – dreadful people. No, I do not think I could bear it myself. But the mayor. We really should invite the mayor. Your mother refuses. Child, do you think you could take an invitation to him? I am sure if we talked to him he would do something to get those people upstairs out of the house.' I would say yes Grandmama and do nothing, and she never remembered it the next day.

Had I not been in my religious phase, I might have elicited, and enjoyed, all those fabulous anecdotes that Felix collected (*his* memory was quite prodigious), but I was what I was, and my grandmother froze me. I found her overbearing and selfish, sometimes even a bit absurd; and I suppose I may have been a little afraid of her. Moreover, I kept pondering about a remark one of my teachers at the convent had made, that a woman who had spent her life in *such a way* and was nearing the end of it should be devoting herself to the salvation of her soul.

What I did enjoy, and Grandmama did too, were the times she showed me her treasures. She kept saying how little she had been able to save, but it seemed to me she had saved a great deal. The good jewels, she said, were almost all gone; she had sold them to keep herself afloat, as she had sold the best antiques. But she had no end of trinkets, postcards, ball and concert and opera programmes, gloves and fans, boxes of strange buttons and beads, a silver dresser set, little ornate bottles still holding dregs of spicy French perfume. I was too unfeminine, having spent so much of my childhood running after Felix, or Trudi and Berti, and in her eyes perhaps too unlovely, for either of us to have enjoyed it if I had played at dressing up. A more conventional little girl would have been forever trying things on. It may have been just as well; Grandmama did not like her treasures handled too much, and it was Janka who had the task of getting them out and putting them away. I simply liked looking at them, and the wonderful unfamiliar sensations they gave me; the feel of a wax seal on an envelope

26

and the brilliance of its red against age-browned paper, an old gold watch ticking like a bird's heart against the palm of my hand, the touch of peacock feathers brushing my cheek, the turquoise flash of their eyes, the shimmer and rattle of sequins, the snap of a tortoiseshell lorgnette being opened, the breeze of a painted silk fan against my face. Grandmama explained where some of them had come from and what they meant to her, but alas, Sir Henry, I did not listen. I was too absorbed in the things themselves, revelling in my own feelings, my own fantasies. In the drabness of our wartime existence, I was spellbound by so much beauty, so much frivolity, by the tokens of what seemed a secure and fanciful and endlessly glittering world. The cold, the bitter wind that snaked through our rotting windows, the eternal dinner of cabbage and skimpy potatoes, even the Schweissers, would be forgotten while Janka laid things out on the bed or the table, handling them as timidly and delicately as if they were the most sacred of votive offerings. I was spellbound too by an intimation that my nuns, though I had never told them about these objects, would consider them corrupting; the shining eyes of the peacock feathers, the enamelled butterflies on wicked hatpins, the perfumes, held for me the delicious lure of sin. Wait – there is the one phrase I do remember; something Grandmama said when I was holding the peacock fan, shaking her head a bit wistfully, 'You will not be like me, child, who always saw and was seen through those blazing peacock's eyes.' But I had no idea what she was talking about; the phrase only remained because I loved the fan so much.

Sometimes my harassed, slovenly mother (I was beginning to see her, in spite of myself, somewhat as Grandmama did) would come in. 'Dear Heaven, Mama, must you take all of that out again?'

Grandmama would answer calmly, 'Janka will put it all away. It's what she is here for.'

'It would be nice if Janka, since we feed her, could help a little more in the kitchen.'

'Nonsense. And certainly not now. I need her up here. If she goes down to the kitchen, who will look after my treasures? Your poor Mitzi could never find their right places again.'

There were other times when I would knock on her door, wanting to see the treasures, and Grandmama would dismiss me with a brief, 'Child, not today, I am tired. Old ladies, you know, are often not the best of company.'

But she never refused to see Felix. Never. When Felix came into the room, even when she was older still, her grey eyes widened between the crumpled lids, her thin mouth smiled like a girl's, and there passed over her face a flash of the beauty that had led to duels and suicides. As for Felix, I have seen Felix look at many women, but never as he looked at Grandmama. 'Those two,' Trudi said once, 'they are two of a kind. That is why they put lights into each other's eyes.' It was to be many years before I understood what she might have meant.

But I am getting ahead of myself. Felix is not yet back from school or sanatorium, whichever it was. I know why I have begun, prematurely, to write about his very special relationship with Grandmama. If I am truthful, at least as truthful as it is possible to be, I must confess that Maria Aurora's fondness for Felix inspired in me – I can feel it as keenly as yesterday, after all these years – a deep and painful jealousy. It was not just that everyone favoured Felix (although Trudi and Berti, who were genuinely fond of me, took a few pains to hide from me that they preferred him). What was it I have just said about Grandmama, 'I found her overbearing, and selfish and sometimes even a bit absurd'? Did I, in fact – and even if I did, was that perhaps only defensive, and *was* it only the treasures I came to see? I do remember being indifferent to her ramblings; but I also remember never leaving her presence before she asked me to do so. We make up our lives as we write them; having cast myself in the role of precocious and unwavering sceptic, having set out to deflate a myth, must I admit that I was not immune, that those hours with my grandmother are still among the only truly magical hours of my life?

And it was my famous unconventional grandmother, with her unguarded talk and her Polish maid, who brought real danger into our little chilly Eden, our decaying hunting lodge on the edge of what had been, not long ago, Imperial forest, where the Kaiser had hunted and the Nazi flag not yet flown (my mother had the flagpole cut down for firewood early in the war – a clever move that killed two birds with one shaft of wood).

28

My mother, like many others, bumbled and schemed her way through the black years of the Reich, showing no extraordinary courage but not much malice, putting her children first, as mothers tend to do. I have never had children, so I cannot tell what I would have done. But I think of the woodcutters and the tarred man in the market-place and Janka's face in the taxi, and I know that if you have conscience, real conscience, you cannot live unprotesting next to that kind of evil and ever hold your head quite as high again. As most of our countrymen had no such conscience, however, it is an academic observation, the sort which Sir Henry will cut out in the first draft.

In brief, it was Grandmama and Janka, the mere presence of poor little hunted Janka, that led to our confrontation with the Schweissers.

Herr Schweisser was a small man whose rise, such as it was, had been entirely in and through the Party; a middle-aged post office clerk whose Party connections soon got him a better job and everyone bowing and scraping, until his building was bombed and his health broke down. There was actually nothing wrong with him that we could see, except that he wheezed a good deal on the stairs, and Felix when he came back said he always hoped the stairs would kill old Schweisser. But they never did.

When they first moved in, the Schweissers were a bit deferential, in view of our superior accents, *vons*, community standing and few remaining antiques, which (the antiques) Herr Schweisser greatly respected. 'That must be very old. That can only be genuine. From the time of Maria Theresia,' Herr Schweisser would say, caressing, with his cramped nervous fingers, some piece of 1900 oak furniture being saved for next winter's heating. 'The time of Maria Theresia' was his definition of venerable age.

We were polite to the Schweissers, as my mother had warned us to be, but we were not friendly. The Schweissers had been quartered on us. They were a gross invasion of our privacy, they were stupid and ugly and messy and crude, and their radio was always too loud. We hated them, Felix and my mother and my aunts and I, with that particular fierce hatred reserved for occupying enemies who expect you to greet them with a jolly face. How much the Schweissers sensed this,

I do not know, but they began, soon enough, asserting their rights, and encroaching on ours. There was Schweisser underwear, coarse and grey, hanging on our washing line, Schweisser wood stacked in our hallway; there were Schweisser chickens penned in our yard. They had their own stove upstairs, but they found endless excuses to use our kitchen, our telephone, our laundry room. They would bring the children down with them and absent-mindedly leave one behind on the stairs, sucking her thumb and grinning and staring. Herr Schweisser would ask my mother or aunts if they had heard the Fuehrer's latest speech. 'It looks bad at the moment, sometimes, but the Fuehrer has many tricks up his sleeve. You'll see. It may take another year or two, a little longer than we thought at the beginning, but my children will see Moscow, and Paris, and London too. We must teach the little ones early to be proud of their Reich and their Volk. I don't think (looking sternly at my mother) they learn quite enough about it in the religious schools.'

We began to keep our radio very low, so the Schweissers could not hear what we were listening to, and we always tried to reach the postman first as he came up the walk. If we were too late, Herr Schweisser would appear, engage him, as a fellow PTT man, in long conversation, and in the course of this take all the house letters and before giving us ours, carefully examine the stamps and return addresses, in hopes, no doubt, of finding something that indicated a dangerous contact abroad. 'I can always smell out Jews,' he told my mother once proudly, 'and other such obnoxious insects.' There had been an unsuspected Jew in the post office in Linz where Herr Schweisser had worked, but they had soon got rid of him. 'Up the chimney,' said Herr Schweisser with a broad smile; and then his thin, ugly nose with its criss-crossing of little red veins demonstrated its sniffing technique, as if he suspected there might be an obnoxious insect in our house too. With Herr Schweisser in our midst, though no one spelled out the danger, I learned what the tarred man and the starved faces in the forest had not yet taught me. I learned fear.

As the weeks went by, my grandmother's speech seemed to become a little more rambling, but also more aggressive. Often, when my mother was with her, there were raised voices, in spite of possible listening Schweisser ears. I must apologize for not being able to give more details of these family quarrels, but unlike the Schweisser children, I had been schooled not to listen at doors and, as I said, this was my pious phase. I can only remember an odd sentence or two. 'Child,' from Grandmama, 'you will never have another man unless you do something about your hair. And your ankles – look at your ankles! There is no need to stand over washtubs and ironing boards all the time. Let those two great oxen (she meant Trudi and Berti) do more of the housework.' Trudi and Berti, the eternal outdoor girls, managed to spend most of their daylight hours gardening or trying to get food or firewood, and their room was more of a shambles than mine. I don't know what my mother said in answer, but a minute later she fled from the scene in tears.

Another time, I heard my grandmother say, 'I told you, if you invite the mayor for tea, I will get something done about those Schweissers,' and my mother snap, 'And I told *you*, for the tenth time, Herr Allgenau, the one you knew, has been dead for ten years and the new one doesn't speak to us. He is in the Party.' Then, a minute later, my mother said – it must have been about Janka, who was down in the kitchen then – 'That child is putting us all in danger. What do you expect me to do – sacrifice my own children so that you, in these times, can keep a personal maid?'

Grandmama's reply was: 'Anna, you always were a goose. There is no danger to anyone unless you show what a frightened goose you are. And I must tell you, without that poor efficient little girl . . .' Again, I could not hear the rest.

Grandmama did not bother to show the Schweissers even the perfunctory, nervous politeness they got from the rest of us. She would pass them on the stairs or in the hall with a mumbled, French-accented 'Pardon', averting her head as if from an evil smell. When they greeted her, she did return the greeting, but always preceded by 'Ah' or 'Oh' as if she had been disturbed in the middle of a profound reverie, or was simply amazed that any creature so lacking in human dignity was capable of human speech. My mother argued with her about this too. 'Mama, he is stupid, but not too stupid to feel what you think of him. We must not offend them. Our lives are at stake.'

'You always dramatize, Anni,' my grandmother answered calmly. 'Where is Janka? I want my blue shoes. So, Anni, what do you want me to do? Curtsey to those hideous creatures? If you would only invite the mayor for a little tea, I am sure we could arrange it all.'

My mother, despairing, became extra polite to Herr Schweisser to cover my grandmother's snubs, and even intimated to them that the old lady was getting 'a little forgetful.' To which Frau Schweisser returned rudely, 'She is not forgetful, that one. She's one of those for whom humanity begins at the rank of Baron. Maybe even higher. But you know, the Party has changed all that.' Encouraged by my mother's meekness, the Schweissers spread themselves farther. Their chickens took over the garden, their loud harsh voices took over the house. And then, not long after the most recent of Grandmama's snubs, a uniformed man appeared at our door.

He was young and quite respectful, obviously embarrassed by his errand, but he said his piece as firmly as he could. It had been reported that there was an unauthorized person living in our house, a young girl, possibly an escaped prisoner, possibly even Jewish. Did she have any papers? Could he talk to her?

My mother, without a word, went to Grandmama's room to find Janka, while I tried desperately to think of somewhere for her to hide, and Trudi and Berti, hoping in their clumsy way to deflect him, made patriotic noises and asked how things were going on the Western front. It was the wrong question, as things were not going well at all. The young man became sterner and suddenly shouted, 'Bring out that girl at once.'

At that my grandmother appeared on the stairs, leading a cowering Janka by the hand. She looked at the young officer for a few moments in silence. Then she said, 'Is that what they teach the officers now, to shout at old ladies? They were not given to such manners in my father's day.'

The officer answered, stammering a bit, 'I am sorry, *Gnädige Frau*, but you have an unauthorized person here. She must be taken for questioning. She has no papers, does she?'

'Of course she has no papers. She is a Polish orphan, a kitchen girl who was kindly left to me by her last owners, Major von Lanke and his family, and whom I have trained to be my personal maid. Why should she have papers? Polish maids do not have papers. She is mine and I am keeping her. I am not well and I need her. My daughter cannot do all her work and look after a sick old lady.'

32

'It is suspected that the girl is Jewish.'

'Jewish? My personal maid is Jewish?' My grandmother's thin frame was rigid, her voice rang with fury. 'My dear young Captain, I have never been so deeply insulted. I, who am Bilderheim-Traun, would sleep with a Jewish girl in my room? My dear young Captain, in all my seventy and more years, I have never even slept under the same *roof* as a Jew. Now please be off and tell your superiors, and whatever vicious creatures have started this rumour and sent you here, that you should be put to better work for the Fatherland than listening to stupid stories and offending old ladies, especially the daughter of a nobleman who died for the Fatherland long before you were born.'

It was one of Grandmama's finest moments.

The flustered officer retreated, stuttering apologies. The Schweissers slammed their doors upstairs. My grandmother had saved Janka, and perhaps all of us, with that grand burst of put-on anti-Semitism. (Although I for one have had faint suspicions that it was so convincing because a little grain of it was true. The world that Grandmama came from was not noted for its tolerance.) The young officer did not know, of course, about her letters to Franz Kafka. But then, at the time no one did. Perhaps not even Grandmama herself.

So Grandmama saved us. For the moment. But the retreat of the young officer was not the end of it.

Herr Schweisser, having failed with his denunciation, went back to his old tactics with a vengeance.

The Schweissers now seemed to spend all day tramping through the hall, their shoes always muddy, their voices always raised. Their radio boomed forth, at top volume, its endless death rattle of Reich propaganda. Frau Schweisser would ask to use our oven and monopolize it for the whole morning or the whole afternoon – a real *tour de force* as no one in those days had anything much to bake. There was so much Schweisser washing we wondered if she was taking in other people's. There were little altercations about the woodpile. 'Excuse me, *Frau Baronin*' – Herr Schweisser always called my mother Baroness, though no one else did – 'but I think there is some wood in your stack that I myself brought in yesterday. I left it – there, you see – by the cellar door, and then it was gone. I am sure it was not meant. Maybe your child made a mistake? Or maybe the maid of Her Excellency, your Frau Mama, was stacking the wood? The Poles are so stupid, you know, you cannot trust them to do anything, and they steal of course all the time, like crows.'

Wood was like gold then, even with all the forest around, and my mother was not about to let him get away with this. 'The Polish girl never stacks wood, nor does my child. Only my sisters-in-law and I do it. And we make no mistakes. But if you think some of your wood has been stolen, please feel free to take that amount from our stack. I will not say anything, even though we have so little. These times are hard enough without quarrels between people who are forced to live in the same house.'

Or he might ask if we had not seen the turnips he had brought home yesterday – his wife had left them in our kitchen when she went down to bake bread. Were we sure we had not seen them? With so many people in our kitchen, we might easily think one of us had left them there. It was really his wife's fault, of course, for forgetting them. He could smell the soup we were having for lunch, that was what made him think of it.

'Cabbage soup,' said my mother; I could see her hands clenched under her apron. 'How strange, Herr Schweisser, with your keen nose, that you cannot tell cabbage from turnips. I would gladly offer you some soup, since your turnips are lost, but we have scarcely enough for ourselves.' Herr Schweisser would shuffle upstairs, muttering that if one did not have enough to go around one should not waste it on *Untermenschen*, on Polish slaves.

And the ugly little girls, commanded by their mother to 'go out and play', spent more and more time in our hallway instead, whispering and giggling, picking their noses, scratching their stomachs, scratching their heads. 'Never go close to them,' Trudi and Berti would tell me in solemn voices – as if I would have dreamt of it. 'They are certainly full of lice.'

The Schweissers poisoned us, as Schweissers do. It was the kind of vicious childish persecution that, when you cannot escape it, can drive you mad. It did not drive any of us mad, it did not poison us completely. But the Schweisser occupation, as we called it later, was the end of my childhood. The ugly waiting world that had been kept at bay for me by Trudi and Berti's girlish outdoor enthusiasms, by my mother's intrigue

34

and efficiency, by my pious convent-fed illusions, was now inside our very house; and only Grandmama seemed really able to face it. Perhaps that was for the unflattering reason (my mother said, before she too was gilding the legend for Joshua Prescott) that Grandmama lived completely in the past and did not understand what was at stake. (But here I support the legend; I do not think she would have behaved differently if she had. I think she would have behaved the same way in front of a firing squad.)

At all events, I was now old enough to ask more questions; and *I* could not be made to see what was at stake without also seeing how much there was to fear, how much duplicity seemed requisite for living in that adult world. In the shadow of Schweisser's tyranny and my grandmother's *panache*, my mother was a harassed drudge, Berti and Trudi two foolish ageing women pretending gracelessly to be my contemporaries. My mother, short on singing pupils and temper, was increasingly irritable with me, as I was sometimes impudent with her. She had always been heavy-handed, but not often unjust. It is at this stage that I first remember her striking me when I was sure I did not deserve it, and my resentment of it, my growing disrespect.

And there was still the problem of Janka.

Janka, though she had been saved, was traumatized all over again by the incident of the officer. The little contact I had made with her was broken. She grew still thinner and more withdrawn. She trembled when anyone spoke to her. She developed an almost phobic fear of men, especially and understandably the hideous Schweisser. When she heard his voice, she would drop whatever she was doing and scurry to Grandmama's room. She was in Grandmama's room most of the time now. When she was sent out, which was usually when my mother came and they wanted privacy for a quarrel, she would cower near the door, her hands over her ears so no one would think she was eavesdropping. But sometimes she must have heard. 'I told you that child could be the end of us, and it might still happen. For the hundredth time, Mama, why should my children be sacrificed?'

And Grandmama's voice, old and hoarse but still rich with resonance, still a voice for dismissing suitors and commandeering carriages and pronouncing titles not with envy

35

but contempt; a voice that even when querulous made my mother sound like a nagging washerwoman: 'Where do you think I could send her? And you have seen nothing happened. One must face these things with dignity, Anni, which is what you have never been able to learn.'

III

Somewhere in the middle of all this – I cannot remember exactly when – Felix came home.

Could he still have been in the mountains then? No, I think it must have been home from the Jesuits, perhaps yet another lot of Jesuits. It is curious, when much of Grandmama's past has been so avidly recorded, that there are almost no references, nothing written at all, about my own family's years with her, with which I might refresh my blurred memories. I think this time Felix had been expelled for keeping a live snake in his pocket and flashing it in the face of the priest who wanted to beat him for some other misdemeanour. No, that must have been the time before. I think what they had found in his pocket on this occasion – or was it in his desk – was a Latin poem of extraordinary obscenity, or a condom, or both. There were so many institutions from which Felix was either expelled or suspended that it was quite impossible to keep track. And I am not Joshua Prescott. A snake, a condom, a poem, or simply outrageous impudence, it hardly matters. Felix was home.

He walked through the gate, whistling, dragging his suitcase over the gravel. Like Grandmama, he came unannounced. 'As if we had all the money in the world to buy new suitcases,' my mother could not help nagging, even as she was hugging and kissing him. She did however kiss him with much fervour. She had already forgiven him his expulsion, as she forgave him everything. Felix was eternally reproached but eternally forgiven, not only by Mama (how seldom I think of her as

37

that) but by everyone in the family. Whereas I earned few reproaches; but there was a different story when I did have something for my mother to forgive.

But to continue. Felix's homecoming: Felix in the drive, my reproachful mother embracing him, the Schweissers as usual gaping from their windows, Trudi and Berti hovering, waiting their turn to hug. Then Grandmama appeared with little haunted Janka in tow.

Felix, at once, released whoever he was holding, shouted 'Grandmama!' and stepped back to look at her. Then he bowed elaborately and kissed her hand and said formally, 'My beloved Countess, I cannot find words to tell you how proud I am that you have come to grace our humble house.' Then he shouted once more 'Grandmama!' and lifted her in his arms.

Even the Schweissers were moved to smile.

Grandmama, when all this was over and she and Felix were walking into the house with their arms around each other, turned back and said to my mother, with that beautiful arrogant smile and the same mock formality Felix had used with her, 'Anna, my treasure, you have produced this. I must congratulate you. It was not badly done at all.'

'Hey, Mitzerl, I almost forgot you,' said Felix, putting his free arm tightly around me; and I trailed into the house with them, feeling only vaguely resentful that Grandmama had never congratulated Mama for producing me.

The next day, the serious reproaches began. Felix should never have come back, my mother said. They would soon be drafting mere boys, she had heard; if he was here and idle, young though he was, heaven knew what might happen, especially with that Schweisser in the house. And what school could she find to take him now? Why had he done it, whatever it was, why had he got sent home yet again, whatever was to become of him?

'What?' said Felix. 'What kind of patriotism is this, in an age when every mother must be a Spartan mother, a true Valkyrie? Do you think, Madame, that I am not old enough to fight for the Fatherland?' My mother and I stared at his grave set face, fearing he was serious. Grandmama, who was there too, standing behind Felix, went up and hugged his head against her shawl-draped chest. 'Such courage,' she said, in the same ringing tone. 'He is not only proud and beautiful, he is also brave.'

Felix was grinning, and in another moment both of them began to laugh. 'Anni,' my grandmother went on when they had finished laughing, 'what a goose you are. We will get old Dr Braunschweig to say he has tuberculosis and they will leave him alone.'

'I told you, Mama, Dr Braunschweig died two years ago.'

'Well then, whoever the doctor is now. But it will not even be necessary. They are not going to come to this bizarre menage looking for children to put into their ridiculous army. Thank God you are here, Felix. No one in this house has much sense of humour. Alas, it was never your mother's strong point.' She spoke about my mother as if my mother were simply not there. 'But on the other hand if it had been she could never have become involved with your father and then you would not be here. And for that we must be grateful.'

Felix gazed at her. 'You are still the most beautiful woman in the world,' he said huskily, and raised her hand to his lips.

'*I* have a sense of humour,' I piped up, annoyed.

'Oh, Mitzi, of course you do,' Felix said off-handedly, his fingers still enlaced with Grandmama's.

'And I, as you say, do not,' said my mother grimly. 'Mama, you do not make my life easier. My son is arrogant enough without your feeding it. How do you know they will not draft him? And how will he finish his education if every school in the country throws him out?'

'Education?' scoffed Grandmama. 'Education can only spoil him. What do you think my convent did for me or the Jesuits will do for him? He already knows enough Latin. Education is nice for the good burgers and even more for the proletariat; it makes them feel better and behave better, at least one hopes it does; but for a person of intelligence and charm and culture, Anni, it is not in the least necessary. That is why I never bothered much about educating you; I hoped you would have the native wit to manage without it.' The sigh which followed indicated that her hope had not been fulfilled. 'Even Hans Handelbein, whose poetry was full of mythological quotations, did not give *that* for his education. You know quite well that with such qualities as Felix has education is totally superfluous; they will only try to take his charm away. No, let him stay here. It will make the house much less dreary for us all.'

39

'Sometimes, Mama,' said my mother, 'I think you are the most arrogant woman who ever lived.'

'Oh, I know that,' Grandmama answered peacefully. 'It was what Hans always said to me – and that other – what was his name? But I do not remember that it drove them away. The boy knows it too, because he is like me.' She gazed at Felix. 'You see, that is what I mean. Your Jesuits would tell you that arrogance is certainly not a Christian virtue, in fact that it is a vice. Although they are much more arrogant themselves. But is not arrogance only what the humble choose to call pride? And I have never felt that pride is something of which one must be ashamed.'

Again – how could I remember this long-ago conversation, even in outline? Is it what Felix told me later, is it even something out of Joshua Prescott? I should really re-read Joshua's book before I go on. It is maddening how other people's records, true or false, tangle inextricably with what one really remembers. Just as the stories recited to bored friends by doting parents about the time when the little one did this or that clever or terrifying thing become that child's own childhood memories. Never mind. It is exactly what she would have said. It fits *my* picture, everything I really know about her, and I alone had no idealized image of her that I wished to project to anyone. No, Joshua would not have written this. He would have played down the arrogance, the cruelty to my mother, who as usual left the scene in tears.

Felix did stay, of course, and managed to injure an ankle, just in case anyone did ask why a great strapping boy like him, no longer in school, was doing nothing to help the staggering Reich. He told me years afterwards that, being still young and impressionable, he might in fact have been tempted by Nazism; 'the Nihilistic side of it, the Satanic side, the glory in destruction. But it was the Satanism of the Lumpen-proletariat. They were too ridiculous, with their goose-steps and ugly uniforms and absurd salutes. They had no *panache* at all. And anyway they were authority, which I was bound to be against. I am a man who walks alone, who can only function alone. Groups and authorities hate me by instinct as I hate them.'

'I suppose,' I said then, 'the ridiculous marching and

saluting was all that put you off. Not the massacre of Jews, or other such petty concerns.'

'I didn't know enough about that. Even Mama told us those men in the woods were criminals, she was so afraid we would say something wrong. Oh, Mitzi, you are so horribly moral, and you always think that I am a shameless monster. When I really am not a monster at all.'

But that, once more – a conversation I remember very well – is going ahead, very far ahead. At all events, Felix stayed, and did brighten the household, and he and Grandmama, in spite of the cold, the hunger, everything, flirted and bantered together like lovers. And as if Felix had not been indulged enough already by the rest of his family, Grandmama saw to it that he was indulged yet more. Handed a rare dessert or treat at the table, Grandmama would smile and say graciously, 'No, no, give it to Felix. He is the only man in this household; he needs to grow.' (You see, Sir Henry, what I do remember of Grandmama's conversation does not square at all with the feminist picture drawn of her later, let alone with what Dr Dawn Crump would make of her.) Trudi and Berti, whose big jowls, by then, were beginning to droop like bulldogs', whose skin fairly sagged on their hefty frames, would shift nervously in their chairs. But they never objected, they never complained, although, I was to find out later, it was their money that bought most of the food we had.

Even Janka came under Felix's spell. Felix, and only Felix, could actually make her laugh. But I do not remember asking him what the secret was. I was at my most pious – I suppose it was somewhat an escape from the fear and want at home – quite absorbed in my nuns and my religion. I was the star pupil, the sisters' pet, quite nauseatingly good. And Felix was busy with his own mysterious pursuits, some of which resulted in extra food appearing on the table. My mother would tut-tut, and worry, and make sure the Schweissers did not see what he brought, and forbid him ever to do whatever it was again. But we were all very grateful that he had.

Then, one evening, about three months after Felix had come home, Janka disappeared. There was no answer to Grandmama's anxious calling, nor to the rest of us. Grandmama had been asleep most of the afternoon, and we had all thought Janka was with her, but she had not seen Janka since the girl had escorted her upstairs after lunch. She

41

never went out without being told to, and no one had told her to go; nor had anyone seen her leave. We searched the house, and the garden; no Janka. No one had any idea where she might be.

Looking back now, after many years, our hunt for Janka has the blurred, jerky quality the high dramas of childhood have when one tries to picture them, the quality of an old cracked film with a fading soundtrack, running too fast, stained by too much darkness. No one else's legend or memory can help me here. But blurred as it is I remember the fear as if it were yesterday. And the hurrying feet, the sounds of all the voices, Trudi's and Berti's masculine baying; Grandmama's, hoarse and urgent but too aristocratic for the sound of despair; and Felix's, louder than anyone's. I remember Felix's face, in the dim light of our cold hallway. It was the only time I saw Felix look afraid.

It was only much later that I wondered why they searched so hard, especially my mother. Would we not have been safer with Janka gone? Or did they fear that if she had run away and was caught, caught and questioned, there were things she might tell that would put us all in danger – that she might say she was in fact Jewish, or that Felix was getting us extra food, and how? At the time it seemed to me perfectly reasonable that they all exhausted themselves looking for Janka. Janka was a child, like myself – I still did not know how much older she was – and one does not let children disappear. Also, how would Grandmama manage without her?

My own anxious thought was that the Schweissers, who were out that evening, might have done something to Janka. When by midnight they had come home and Janka was still not found I prayed, very hard, for God to punish the Schweissers, for the Schweissers to die. It was my first really wicked prayer and I felt so guilty that I whispered immediately afterwards, no God, I did not mean it. Though of course I had. But you were not supposed to pray for anyone's death, even the Schweissers.

Over breakfast the next day, while Felix was upstairs, having been delegated to calm Grandmama and bring her her morning drink of what passed in those days for coffee, my mother and aunts consulted about what to do. If they informed the police there might be more questions and more danger. If they did not inform the police Herr Schweisser probably would, as soon as he noticed Janka was gone. It was decided that Trudi and Berti, the sturdy outdoorswomen, would comb the surrounding woods thoroughly before we tried anything else. After they left, and I had been sternly forbidden to go with them – nervous though I was, I would have loved the adventure – I remember my mother sitting at the kitchen table with her head in her hands and the *ersatz*-coffee cold in her cup. She said over and over, 'Oh God, and this too. Oh God, and this too,' until I grew frightened and went up to touch her.

At that moment Felix came in. He looked very white, and swallowed and stammered before he could speak. 'Mama. Grandmama says – tell Trudi and Berti – tell them to go to the Holderland place and look in the pond.'

The Holderland place was the big property adjoining our little one, where Trudi and Berti and I used to go sledding. 'The pond?' said my mother. 'The pond is covered with ice –' Then she stopped, looked at me, and said sharply, 'Child, go out for a minute.' Soon after, I saw her with her cloak on and Felix in tow, hurrying to catch Trudi and Berti.

I waited. The house had never been so silent. The Schweissers – thank God for that – had gone to market. There was no sound from Grandmama's room. I thought of Janka with her deft little hands, laying Grandmama's treasures out on the bed, tiptoeing up the stairs with a late cup of tea – she never spilled a drop – of Janka shaking her head and cowering while I snapped, cruel with frustration, 'Say it! This is a book. That is a window.' Shaking her head and whispering, 'Not understand.'

Finally I went to Grandmama's door and knocked, and when no one answered, pushed it softly open, suddenly afraid that something might have happened to her too.

Grandmama was standing at the window, staring out between the flowered curtains. She looked slight, but very straight and dignified. She did not turn when she heard me. She went on gazing out; then she said, in a low even voice, 'That was more than I needed.' I went and stood beside her, and she put her thin hand on my shoulder. We stood like that, together, in total silence, until the little procession came out of the woods; my mother, Felix, Trudi and Berti and two old men who worked on the Holderland estate, carrying something strange and stiff wrapped in my mother's cape. My mother saw us and made angry motions to Grandmama, indicating that both of us should leave the window. I saw her mouth form the words, 'Don't look.' My childhood seemed to have been filled with that dictum. Don't look, don't look, at Herr Kohn tarred in the market-place, at the skeleton woodcutters, at whatever terrible thing was being carried away now, hidden under my mother's cloak.

Then, for the first time, my grandmother turned towards me. Her eyes were bewildered; for a moment, she did not seem to know who I was. Then she came back to herself and hugged me, and said with more warmth than she had ever shown me before, 'Come, my child, there is nothing we can do. Let us go.downstairs and try to find something to make some soup. They will all be tired and hungry when they come back again.'

No, of course I do not remember exactly what anyone said, even then, except for the stock phrases, 'Oh God, that too,' and that sort of thing. How could I? How can anyone remember conversations held that many years ago? Here I am, trying to be truthful about my own life, and constantly putting in dialogue when there is none I can be sure of. But without dialogue, it would be too wooden, it would ring less true yet, even to my own memory. We are what we say; and I think I know enough about what we were to imagine quite well what we probably said. Because these were the people I knew best on earth – or at least, knew the side they showed me, which is all I presume to write about.

Joshua was more scrupulous than I; he never put a word in anyone's mouth, he took only what was written. And in a little while I shall be putting words in his mouth too. Joshua, forgive me. Dear God, when we can hardly remember the words of the living, how do we presume to quote the words of the dead?

I talked to my nuns about Janka. I wanted to know why Janka died. My mother had said simply that she was frightened, and that things were too difficult for her, so she had walked into the pond. Or maybe she had meant to cross it, to run away. That last was very weak. No one running away goes deliberately into the middle of a pond covered by thin ice. So, she was frightened – but wasn't death the most frightening thing? What could she have been so frightened of? Why did she have to die?

I was told that no one knows why people die when they do, only Our Father who knows best about everything, and that it must have been Our Father's will. She was a poor orphan. But suicide was a sin.

Would she have to go to hell, then? I wanted to know. Oh, yes, or at least to Purgatory, but God was merciful, and I must not ask too many questions, but accept Our Father's will and pray for guidance to Jesus and the Holy Mother.

But if one's death was God's will, how could it be a sin?

Everything was His will, but one had the freedom of choice. It was a sin if one chose to die before He willed it.

But if everything was His will, so was that death . . . I was told to be quiet and pray for the salvation of my own rebellious soul.

This was not satisfactory at all. I felt the first qualms, the painful beginnings, of disbelief.

As Janka was a suicide and a Pole, she was buried in waste ground outside the cemetery. It was two *Zwangsarbeiter*, forced labourers, also from Poland, who dug the shallow grave, driving picks into the frozen ground, and this only after my mother bribed someone. She also had to bribe the undertaker to take the body and keep it until the grave was dug, a story she told later to Joshua Prescott as one of her funny stories of Hard Times During the War. 'My dear lady, it is so cold now, you could keep her in the woodshed,' the undertaker had said. 'You must remember it is wartime and we all have to make sacrifices for the Reich. However, for two pounds of flour . . . yes, I'll do it and say nothing. Although I cannot understand anyone giving up two pounds of flour to store a Polish corpse.'

Herr Schweisser, having heard through the town grapevine that Janka had drowned herself, simply observed that those Polish girls always got themselves pregnant somehow and that was probably why. Unless she had still worse reasons. Ah well, one *Untermensch* less. But he did not say this in my grandmother's hearing.

Felix – quite unlike Felix – never came out with any grisly details of the discovery in the icy pond, and Janka was hardly

mentioned again. Her death must have been a relief to everyone except Grandmama, and even Grandmama did not seem
to take it all that hard.

Janka's tasks were now divided between the four of us, my
aunts, my mother and myself, but none of us could do anything quite right. Grandmama grew more capricious and
sarcastic by the day. She demanded unobtainable foods and
impossible quantities of hot water. She nagged at my mother
to trim her hair, the local hairdresser being 'not even fit to
shear a sheep', and then complained for days about how it
was done. To me, as I remember, it was always, 'Dear child,
you are clumsy,' or 'Child, you are so slow,' or 'Oh my poor
little thing, I can see it so well. You will grow up to look
like your mother. (I didn't in fact. A worse fate befell me.)
You will have the big bovine eyes and the good thick hair
and nothing else to commend you.' So I was scolded for
looking like my mother, my mother for looking like a washerwoman, and Trudi and Berti for looking like navvies. It was
small wonder that my mother sometimes lost her temper and
snapped something back. Then Grandmama would say
simply, with enormous dignity, 'Please leave me now, Anna,'
or if the scene took place downstairs, 'I think it is time for
me to go to my room,' and walk out with a hauteur in her
frail figure that made us all feel rude and awkward and
mean.

But this stage did not last long. In April, a few weeks after
Janka's death, the weather turned abruptly bright and warm;
and Grandmama, much more cheerful ('Even a spoiled old
greenhouse plant feels the spring in all its veins'), decided she
would return the few visits that had been made to her by
whatever decayed aristocracy was still alive and mobile in our
district. She also decided to do it by the only form of loco-
motion left to her 'in these disgusting times'. She would take
up cycling again.

My mother protested that she was much too old and stiff
and would break her back. Her answer was typical. 'I, Anna,
in spite of our hardships, do not neglect myself. I exercise
every day, in front of the mirror – of course I let no one see.
An old lady in her long underwear is not a dignified sight. But
I am still quite fit. And I was always an excellent cyclist. I
used to ride for miles in the country with Hans Handelbein.
(That was another of the very few times I personally remember

46

her using the famous poet's name.) I will take Mitzi's bike and try riding it right now while the weather is so fine.'

'Mitzi's bike has flat tyres,' said my mother quickly.

'Nonsense. She was on it only this morning. I saw her. Oh, Anna, do not try to thwart me by such childish games. I know what I am doing. I always knew what I was doing, except when –' She stopped.

'Except when you had me,' said my mother. They looked at each other for a few moments without speaking and I, watching them, thought for the first time, *they hate each other*.

Then I wondered if they really did, and why. And wondered if *I* really loved *my* mother. She so obviously preferred Felix, but she took good care of me, I felt happier and safer when she was there – no, not happier. Only safer. And since the Schweissers not even always that. When I was with Felix or with Grandmama, I was sometimes happy and often furious, and I did not feel safe; I felt risk in the air, keen as the dregs of scent in Grandmama's bottles of Venetian glass, but in a way I liked that intimation of risk. The truth was that my mother bored me, as she bored Grandmama. Nonetheless, what I felt for her I had always accepted as love, as what the nuns told us to do; love and respect your parents, and all mothers are allied to the Mother of God, and so on – but I was doubting the nuns more and more, since Janka. And what did all of that mean anyway, and what did I really feel? If my mother were old and demanding, would I not hate her? And if I grew up to seem so inferior in her eyes as she did in Grandmama's (though I thought that unlikely) would she not hate me?

Grandmama finally said, again, 'I am going to get the bike,' and this time my mother did not try to dissuade her. Grandmama wheeled the bike out, and called me to help her adjust the seat. I did it, but said, 'Grandmama, don't go alone. Let me go with you. I can take Trudi's bike.'

'No, child. I do not want you to see me wobble. I will just go down the lane, and if I don't find it easy I will come straight back. I will be quite all right. Go away now, child, and don't look.' She took the bike out onto the damp road. I did look, of course, poised ready to run after her. But there was no need. She got on hesitantly, but she got on, and by the time she was nearly out of sight she had stopped wavering. She came back three hours later, in fine spirits, having visited the 'terribly boring, but at least she had decent cakes for tea' Baroness von Mandelbirken who lived at the other end of the Holderland wood. And somewhere, miraculously, she had got six eggs, which were in a small basket attached to her handlebars.

That spring, a little rhyme began to circulate among those who were daring enough to repeat it. Felix learned it, of course, and told Grandmama, who would sing it in her deep resonant voice as she rode my bicycle through the chestnut-lined avenues of the Holderland park. The chestnuts were budding, and before long they would open their creamy blossoms. The raucous propaganda voice of the Schweissers' radio could not repress the hope of spring – nor the growing rumours of defeat, which meant, for those who thought (alas, they were always too small a number), the hope that Austria would be free again.

> *Es geht alles vorüber,*
> *Es geht alles vorbei.*
> *Im April fliegt der Führer*
> *Und im Mai die Partei.*
> (All things pass over,
> All things pass away.
> The Fuehrer will fly in April
> And the Party in May.)

'If only,' my mother would say sometimes in a low voice to Trudi and Berti, nervously rubbing her work-worn hands, 'if only we do not get the Russians here.' Her Wehrmacht officer had told her a great deal about the Russians. Trudi and Berti would nod, their big faces grave, and echo, 'If only the Barbarians do not fall upon us.' In spite of my lost confidence, I asked the nuns about these Barbarians, and was told they were indeed Barbarians and Godless, but God (one hoped) would protect us and we must pray very hard. They talked sometimes among themselves, in breathless whispers, of what the Barbarians had done to convents in Russia. I could not hear the details, but I had visions of wild Cossacks with sabres in their hands and daggers in their teeth riding down helpless shrieking nuns. We were getting no accurate news, except by hearsay, and the hope of that spring was mixed with terror – for those who did come under the Russians, a terror justified. Often, thinking about the Barbarians and chafing under the strain of not being rude to the Schweissers, I lay awake at night, my body rigid, my heart beating, almost listening for the hoofbeats of the wild Cossack ponies, while Trudi and Berti snored in the room next door.

And the Reich, in last orgies of blood and horror, took down with it whom it could. We heard volleys of machine-gun fire from the end of the valley; someone said later the last prisoners had been shot. And one day – this was of course a minor and trivial incident, but I shall always still look on it as part of the war – while Grandmama was riding her bike downhill past the hedge on the lane, singing her little song in spite of my mother's warnings, someone behind the hedge thrust a stick into her front wheel.

It was Trudi and Berti, coming back from market, who saw her. She was unconscious, her legs tangled in the bike, her white hair matted with blood. We guessed what had happened because a bit of the stick was still caught in the spokes; and Felix, who knew these boys' tricks – though in Grandmama's case the culprit was probably not a boy – found the rest of the stick behind the hedge.

At first, it seemed Grandmama might recover. Only her shoulder was actually broken; and though she had hit her head quite badly, our old doctor said the damage might not be permanent. Her daily exercise had stood her in good stead; any old lady less fit, the doctor said too, would probably have been killed. She would be confused for a while, but it might pass; one would have to see.

And immediately after her fall, we were preoccupied with something else. For the little rhyme had been correct. In May the war ended. And we did not get the Russians. We got the Americans.

The Americans, the beautiful young Americans, bursting with health and good food and good spirits and generosity. They thought we were a country they were liberating, as in fact we were; they could not understand the dour Hitler-moustached burgers and their potato-faced wives who glared at them in the streets. (Although, this being Austria, most people, whatever their sentiments, soon turned on the expected Austrian charm.) Oh, the Americans – the world is so much down on them now, everyone has forgotten that it need not have been their war but they fought it, that some of them actually volunteered to help save humankind from an age of total darkness. For me, they were knights in shining armour, most of all the tow-haired, freckled, gum-chewing soldiers, looking hardly older than Felix, who bustled Schweisser and his family out of our house so their Lieutenant could move in.

They had given Felix and me K-ration chocolate, and we watched, chocolate and happiness bursting out of our mouths, the Schweissers bundling their belongings into a cart, the little girls sniffly and tearful, starting a long trudge to relations in Linz. How unchristian, you might say, how inhumane, to rejoice so gloriously in the downfall of one's enemies. But it was a justified downfall, and I think I have never known a more delicious moment. We know how to hate, in my family, and the rare, sweet triumphs of hate are as keen as the triumphs of love. Let those who have never tasted them, who have not sat for two years, cold and hungry, with the Schweissers like a Damocles' sword over their heads, who did not see Janka drowned and my beautiful imperious Grandmama made helpless and senile (for I am sure it was a Schweisser child – or adult – who put that stick through the hedge), condemn me. Is it any wonder that I did not offer those pig-tailed, piano-legged brats a piece of my superb K-ration chocolate to speed them on their way? No; if I had known a curse, if I were as thoroughly heathen as I am now, I would have cursed them, I would have wished them sorrow and bitterness to the end of their days.

At this point I should add (there you are, we are getting to what Sir Henry would call the story line) – I should add that the young officer the Schweissers made way for was a shy Middle-Westerner named Joshua Prescott.

However, the rest of the story will have to wait.
There is a grave and major interruption.
Dr Dawn Crump.

At eleven o'clock this morning, the doorbell rang. I was expecting no one (I am not very sociable any more, perhaps I never was – I go through the necessary motions, to the requisite faculty parties, but with some reluctance, and I have no close friends), so I went to the door braced for Seventh-Day Adventists. Before me stood a squat woman – large but squat all at once, an attenuated toad; that was the image that leapt at once to my mind. The toad impression was accentuated by her somewhat pouting lips, painted a vivid red, and the shingled greying hair which did nothing to soften her features, the thick jowls, the heavy-lidded eyes, at once sleepy and predatory, reptilian, behind big glasses whose pale plastic rims were visibly dirty. She was wearing an open quilted jacket, a red shirt, and a cream-coloured skirt too tight over her stomach . . . (Yes, this is a subjective description, but that *was* how she looked to me before I even knew who she was. But I will try to write dispassionately.) And track shoes, expensive ones, whose red stripes matched her mouth.

'Dr Stone?' Right hand jerked quickly forward, determined smile.

'Yes?' I say, bewildered.

My hand is swallowed in a soft but insistent grip. 'Dr Stone, I am Dr Crump. Please forgive me for not telephoning you first, but I was in the neighbourhood, I've been looking at some things in your library. Are you busy right now? May I come in?'

'Well, yes, of course,' I say, knowing I will have to face this sooner or later and preferring to face it sooner.

When Dr Crump has finished pacing over my Hamadan with her wet track shoes, saying that she adores this room, she admires this striking combination of starkness and coziness, and it's wonderful to have just those few relics of the past because that way they get the prominence they deserve, and that striking young man in the photograph – is he Maria Aurora's grandson? (Not 'your brother', Maria Aurora's grandson, she says, but I am used to that.) 'He looks so much like her' – she plonks herself on the couch holding aloft the little blue crystal glass of pale sherry I have given her (yes, Dr Crump, another souvenir of my old home) and gets down to business. It is not Sir Henry who has sent her. Especially since I am late, perhaps too late, in accepting his offer, I would not put it past him to have started negotiations with Dr Crump and dispatched her here as a scout, and/or a stick to go with the carrot of my suggested advance. But no, someone has jumped the gun on Sir Henry. She is doing a book for her own university press.

'I hope, of course,' Dr Crump looks demurely down at her track shoes, 'I hope there'll be an English publisher too.

51

Eventually. But now – Dr Stone, I'm a very direct person. I know I offend a lot of people by being as direct as I am. Well, really, I think that's their problem, not mine. I think – do you mind if I smoke, Dr Stone?'

'No, not at all. There's an ashtray on the little table.'

'Oh, yes. Thanks, Dr Stone. What I mean is – I hope I won't offend you by coming right to the nitty-gritty.'

'Not at all. The nitty-gritty is what I am waiting for.'

'Good. Nowadays I guess they'd say the bottom line, wouldn't they? Or am I using it wrong? I guess you don't have that phrase so much over here. I don't know if you've read any of my stuff. I'm not nearly as radical as people make me out to be. But I do have my own particular view of things. And I guess I will always do my best to make it a more general view, I mean, to get people to see it.'

'Indeed,' I say, still waiting for the nitty-gritty.

'Now, the biography of Maria Aurora that's been most read – the definitive biography, I guess you might say – and I want you to know right away how much I admire her, what a glorious character I think she was – I really do have the greatest respect for her – but that biographer, the one that everyone refers to, was a man, and he wrote from a man's point of view. He saw her as a man would and he saw her in terms of her cultural context.'

'Yes. That was how she saw herself.'

'I'm not sure what you mean,' says Dr Crump.

'Well, simply this. My grandmother was completely a creature of her time and place. She was very confident, very proud, very conscious of belonging to an elite, however much in decline that elite may have been.'

Dr Crump holds up both her hands. 'No, no, Dr Stone. I disagree. I'm sorry, but I really do disagree. I think there's quite another side of her that comes out in some of her letters, and that's what I want to write about, the side that Prescott and everyone has missed. You see, I'm convinced that inside – behind all that pride, behind that beautiful aristocratic face, inside that image of perfect femininity, that flirtatiousness, that ideal mistress image – oh, tempestuous, passionate – but that's part of the image, isn't it, a man doesn't want the ideal mistress to be just a shy violet, he, macho man that is, wants something to conquer, he wants that passion and tempestuousness, that pride to overcome – inside there is a person trapped in that beautiful feminine image, a full, warm, independent person, not an ideal woman but a *person*, crying to get out.'

I am at a loss for words.

'Oh, I know what you're thinking. Here's this stranger rushing in where angels fear to tread. But believe me, Dr Stone, I'm not just talking casually. I have been fascinated by Maria Aurora for a long time. I've read everything by her and about her that I could find. I'm convinced that Joshua Prescott never got close to the real woman. I won't ask for your help now. I realize you may not want to give it to me. I also . . . realize . . . well, that with the Handelbein anniversary coming up you may be working on something of your own. I just thought we should have this talk. I'd like to know how you *see* her.'

'Well, I certainly do not see her as a person struggling behind an idealized image. And I have already said that I do not feel Joshua Prescott's picture of her, whereas somewhat exalted, was as incorrect as you seem to believe.'

Dr Crump holds up her blunt white hands again, like an orchestra conductor. 'Wait. I'm just remembering. Just bear with me while I try to think how it goes. There's something that shows exactly what I'm trying to say. You know the Handelbein poem – I can't quote it in German but there's that wonderful translation – well, maybe you won't agree but I always thought it wonderful – by Gregory Barnum, I think – the poem that was found among her papers, in her handwriting – you know that poem?'

'I'm trying to think,' I say, suddenly seeing not Dr Crump's intense painted reptilian face, but Felix, Felix with his dark curls and his slow guarded smile, Grandmama's smile but more deliberate, colder, holding a sheaf of papers out to Joshua Prescott.

'There are eagle's wings beating inside my breast,
The beak tears at my vitals. I am my own
Screaming victim, the monster fused with Andromeda,
I am the Spartan boy dying with the fox under his coat.'

'That was rather a free translation. And not one of Handelbein's best. That was –'

'Yes, exactly. I don't think Handelbein wrote it. I think Maria Aurora wrote it herself. I think that poem was the desperate inner cry of a person forced to play muse and mistress to a group of artistic talents that would maybe have turned out to be inferior to her own if she had been allowed to develop it, if she had been allowed to live not just as a woman but as a person.'

I think of Felix pushing the wheelchair with its frail silent burden down the gravelled avenues of the Holderland park, talking, talking to Joshua Prescott who walks beside him. 'Surely, Dr Crump, there was not much, even in 1900, that stopped a woman from writing poetry. And you forget that my grandmother, the Countess, had all the time and leisure and independence in the world. I do not think anyone, ever, stopped her doing anything she wanted. Or even tried.'

'But do you know what it means,' Dr Crump is swelling with indignation, 'to have nothing wanted from you except your beauty?'

'No,' I answer quietly. 'Do you?'

All right, yes. That was cheap and unworthy, below the belt and in the case of Dr Crump also above the neckline. But the good doctor did not even notice. There was no indirect way, however crass, to get rid of her. I finally interrupted her endless monologue about the Handelbein poem and Maria Aurora's secret self (oh, Felix, how you would have loved this, what hilarious grist you would have found for this mill) and said I had work that had to be finished and must ask her to leave. But she will come back. The Crumps of this world do not give up easily. Twelve feet of barbed wire would not keep her out. She is so anxious, she says, to have my further opinion, on the travesty she is about to perform. She would be really grateful for any childhood recollections of my grandmother that I might be willing to share with her. 'I'm afraid you'll find I'm a pretty tenacious character, Dr Stone. When I feel I'm on the track of something that's really vital, I go for it all out. Just like war is too serious to be left to the generals, scholarship is too serious to be left to the scholars. I mean of course your conventional male academics . . .' She is still firing as I see her to the door.

Having penned down Dr Crump, at least to this extent (why is it some people, as soon as one meets them, invite a splutter of paltry puns, of snide wisecracks, bring out the meanest of one's literary sides), I am no longer annoyed, I can go on with my memoir. Having met Dr Crump, I know that I must go on with it. Somewhere, published or not, there should be a record of what really happened to the muse's offspring, in the course of which may be revealed, if not who the muse was, at least a bit of who she was not.

But where was I, then?

Ah yes. Joshua Prescott.

He was different from the others. As Trudi and Berti said, one could see immediately that he was an educated, a really well-brought-up young man. Moreover, he came from a Catholic family, and had been to Jesuit schools, like Felix – but not, like Felix, expelled. Joshua was doubtless a model pupil, as he was doubtless a model officer, at least for what he mostly did, which was something concerned with supplies. He must have lived in our house about six weeks before he was posted elsewhere, but he was so shy, so deferent, that it is mostly his shyness I remember. That and the incredible meals my mother was able to produce with his contributions. I also remember his painfully practising German and saying how much he loved the language, what a rich and deep language it was, marvellous for song and poetry. Trudi and Berti and Felix all helped and encouraged him. And I remember his boundless admiration for everything, our little faded hunting lodge, the sad neglected Holderland park with its decayed pseudo-Gothic pile, now being converted to a T.B. sanatorium, the mediaeval altar in our village church, our baroque market square, the few swans on our river that had not been eaten. Felix, who remained at his most polite and struck up a great friendship with Joshua immediately, explained to me that Joshua saw America as a sour green apple and Europe as a rich ripe cluster of beautiful grapes. 'That's what he says himself.'

But why? I wanted to know. Europe was poor, hungry, fearfully damaged, perhaps beyond repair. 'Trudi and Berti say nothing will ever be the same again.'

'Because there is *culture* here. That's what he says. Because there is an old civilization, and that, he says, means more than anything. America he says is a cultural desert. And he will send us a CARE package every month when he goes home.'

*

55

I should, at this point, for Sir Henry's benefit, be able to re-
collect some electrical first meeting between Joshua and my
grandmother. But the truth is that Joshua hardly saw her then.
During the weeks he was with us Grandmama was much too
ill and weak, with her broken shoulder and injured head, to
receive new visitors. The women of the house took turns
attending to her, and Felix looked in often to see how she was.
For a long time, she hardly spoke, except to demand necessities
in that same deep imperious voice. And she called, often, for
Janka; it was weeks before she seemed to understand that
Janka was dead, and the next day she would forget and call
again.

It was not only Janka's death that she kept forgetting. She
forgot most things, almost as soon as they were told to her.
She forgot who Trudi and Berti were, and sometimes asked
me too who I was. But she always recognized Felix; and one
thing she did always remember was to criticize my mother's
appearance, even if her harsh remarks trailed off into ramblings. 'Anni, you are too fat to wear that blue skirt. It is a
disgrace to dress like that. You must set an example for your
children. Poverty is no excuse for such slovenliness . . .' My
mother would smile a tight-lipped smile and say nothing.
She showed exemplary patience, but I do not think much
of it was kindness or affection. Even senile, Grandmama was
a formidable person, and one thought twice about crossing
her, especially with Felix as her undeviating protector. Any
sign of irritation with Grandmama was met by a display of
Felix's temper, which was a temper to reckon with. How Dr
Crump would have hated that household! Felix was cock of
the roost; they all loved him, and except for Grandmama,
they were all a bit afraid of him, his rage, his sarcasm, the
abrupt and terrible way he could turn off his charm and
bare his teeth.

It was of course easier for Felix to be patient. Being the
man of the house, he was not saddled with the more sordid
tasks of caring for Grandmama. It was not Felix who escorted
her to the toilet, who bathed her, who changed her sheets.
She did get better, a bit more mobile, a bit more coherent,
before she got worse again, but that is taking this narrative
too far ahead.

I wish I could remember more of her ramblings; or that I
could honestly say they were profoundly revealing. But like

most senile people, she told the same few stories over and over. They were mostly stories of her girlhood and childhood, for in senility some of the distant past may remain fresh as yesterday, while yesterday is forgotten.

There was one story about having tripped on the stairs in a ball gown and danced all evening on a sprained ankle, until she fainted from the pain and had to be carried 'out into the night, to revive me. And that night was full of stars, and the young man who carried me out and could not resist waking me, like the Sleeping Beauty, with a kiss, was the young Count of Bilderheim-Traun. And when I was recovering he came to visit every day, with boxes of liqueur chocolates and those very powdery truffles from Hasenblatter's. Oh, they were marvellous! There has never been anything like those chocolate truffles since Hasenblatter closed. And once, I opened the box of truffles and stuck upright into one of them was a diamond ring.' The story usually trailed off at this point, or I do not remember how or if it went on. It was the stuff of operetta rather than great literature, and has therefore been given minimal space in Joshua's biography.

There was of course the tragic sequel to the truffles and kisses and diamond rings – the duel in which the Count was killed, by the man whose sister he had jilted. But Grandmama talked less often about that. She did say something like, 'On the day when Nicki went out to shoot Bobby (our aristocracy always have these diminutive nicknames, and someone with a mile-long title is usually Bobby or Pumpi or Popsi or whatever to his or her intimates; persons referred to by their full names in this circle are nearly always of an inferior class), it was all Bobby's idea, he always had stupid ideas like that. When we were children he tied my cousin to a tree and told him he was St Sebastian and shot an arrow into his leg. I don't know why he wanted to fight with Nicki. Nicki would never have married Dolly anyhow. She had crossed eyes and a large rear, two things Nicki could not stand in a woman. It was all a story she invented and told Bobby because she was so angry that Nicki married me. Oh, I was so young then! I was wearing a silly blue dress with a sort of bustle, and when he went out he touched me and said, "Don't hide that under a bustle, it is the most exquisite arse in the Empire." (Grandmama senile said a few things she would not have said before, and there were times when my mother sent me out of the room.) And then he

57

said, "Mitzi, it is possible that I will be late for breakfast."
And those were the last words he said to me.'

The story would get stuck at this point, and she would
repeat the 'Mitzi, it is possible that I will be late for breakfast',
and shake her head wonderingly, and lapse into silence. Sometimes one had the feeling that she told these stories, which she
would begin abruptly and even in the middle of someone else's
quite unconnected conversation, not to us at all but to an
imaginary listener, who knew the faces behind all the nicknames, knew the Popsis and Rudis and Dollys and their due
places in the Almanach de Gotha.

Mostly, her stories went all the way back to childhood. It
was a childhood that I with my wartime one could hardly
imagine. The stories were of pet baby donkeys going astray on
the family estate, of night-time sleigh rides to Christmas
parties, of tricks played on governesses and teachers, like the
dancing master whose shoes they had waxed on the sole, 'So
he fell on his head, and was really hurt, and Papa was very
angry.' A fairly-tale childhood, with some of the cruelty of
fairy tales. And of 'Papa', having lost nearly everything at
roulette, 'He managed to do that not once but several times',
coming home and putting her on his knee and saying, 'My
darling, let me give you a piece of advice. Cold nerves and a
steady hand, like virtue, do not always win.'

I rack my own memory; that is all I remember. Where are
the painters, the poets, the suicides, the literary aspirations,
where is Hans Handelbein? They were later, of course; the
obsessions of senility, as I have said, are usually concerned
with early youth. It may even be that the blow on the head,
having wiped out her recent past – she was never again to
know when she had come to us, or from where, and the war
years had gone almost entirely from her mind – wiped out
much of the less recent past as well. Although it seems that
snatches of it, extraordinary snatches, sometimes emerged in
her hours with Felix during the later stages of her decline.

There, Sir Henry; I fear that is all I can offer you. It does
not quite tally with Joshua's image of a literary lioness. It is a
picture of a woman who had remarkable strength of character but equally remarkable vanity and not much time for those
who neither served nor entertained her, a woman of little social
conscience or philosophical bent, a woman perhaps more like
Marie Antoinette than like Lou Andreas-Salomé. And yet at

some mysterious point the one metamorphosed into the other. We shall get to that. But before we do I must leave poor Grandmama and concentrate on myself. As was my original intention. For these next few years, which meant nothing to Grandmama except increasing vacuity and discomfort, were for me, the second and lesser Maria Aurora, the most critical of my life.

IV

After Janka's death, as I said, I began to question things. At
first it was very tentative. There was still the war and its fears,
there were still the Schweissers; God was there because one
prayed to him to let one survive. But after the war we began
to hear about endless horrors, which God had allowed to
happen; the mass graves where Polish and Jewish prisoners
were buried, in Mandeldorf at the end of the valley. The gas
chambers, the death camps. My mother had tried to keep us
like Hansel and Gretel, dodging through the wicked wood;
but without telling us how wicked it was. Now it was no longer
necessary to say 'Don't look'; it was also no longer possible.
(Although you will find in our town, to this day, people who
think all those prisoners at the end of the valley were real
criminals, and others who regret those days of law and order
when 'old ladies could walk home at night unmolested, when
crime was kept off the streets' – because it was almost a
government monopoly. 'Public execution,' I have heard
someone say in the local *Weinstube* on one of my rare visits
home, 'and a good bloody one. That would stop all this hijack-
ing. Say what you like, the Führer had some excellent ideas.')
    She is digressing too much into politics, I can hear Sir Henry
grumble. Dear Sir Henry, you know as well as I that life is
politics. When one has lived under a totalitarian government,
even young, even briefly, one knows forever that everything is
political. And Sir Henry does not want me anyway, he wants
Grandmama. But I must stop worrying about the biography I
may be commissioned to write.

So I asked the classic question of wavering faith: why does God, if He is good, if He is omnipotent, let these things happen? And I got the classic answers. There is evil because man is wicked, but it will all be straightened out in Heaven. Man is free to sin, to listen to the blandishments of the Evil One. If there were no such choice, there would be no freedom. And has not the war shown us what a precious thing freedom is? But wait a minute, I said. God is all-powerful and every-thing is His will. Then it must be His will that we choose evil. So is He not playing a cruel game, and if He plays cruel games, can He be a good God? Of course there never has been nor will be an answer to this question, except perhaps the Manichean concept of a Divine Essence trapped and sullied in the material world, which our virtue can help to free. So my confessor got angry then, as the nuns had when I asked too much about Janka, and said that those who had suffered would be rewarded in Heaven and I must be patient and wait to understand more when I was older. Also that all this doubt was dangerous. I must be especially careful now not to stray from the path because I was approaching what was, for young girls, a 'dangerous time' of life. Why was it dangerous? He would not say, he dismissed me, before I could even ask him how the Jews, who had suffered so much under the Reich, would be rewarded in a Christian heaven they were not admitted to.

Felix, who had lost his faith (if he'd ever had any) long ago, bolstered my doubts with books. He also helped to shake my dwindling faith in the family. I had already begun to see my mother and aunts with critical eyes. Now Felix told me that '*die Alte*', the old one, our Mama, had slept with more Wehrmacht officers than one and always had an eye out for new male protectors. 'I don't mind that, she has to live. But she shouldn't moralize about what *I* do.' And one day, after they had been telling another American officer invited for tea how terrible the 'Nazi occupation' was (welcomed by a majority of the population with open arms, it was now referred to, at least publicly, as a conquest by force), he told me the scandal about Trudi and Berti. Before they came here, they had led groups of Hitler Youth girls on hikes and sports events. 'But they are not really political. I think they just liked looking at young girls. They had a falling-out about that with one of the other leaders, that's why they retired and came here.'

61

'What do you mean, looking at young girls?'

'Why, they're "warmers", of course. Don't you know what Trudi and Berti are? Why do you think they live together? They are not really related at all.'

But what did *'warmers'* mean? 'Oh, Mitzi, you little goose, don't you know anything? They are women who go to bed with each other and not with men.'

I hardly knew then, except in a vague way, even what happened when women went to bed with *men*. There was that thing – I had seen it once, when a friend and I happened on some boys bathing in the river – and it went in between one's legs and babies were produced, but it was something one did not talk about, except very occasionally, in giggly whispers; and I could not imagine what women would do with each other. Horrified, I put my hands over my ears, and said, 'I don't want to hear any more.' But when I thought about it later, the idea of their being involved with the Hitler Youth was the real horror; though to this day, I do not know for certain if either of Felix's stories was true. Whether deliberate, whether conscious or not, it was one of his favourite activities, the destruction of faith, the dropping of a hint which blooms into obsession, the offhand remark which breaks friendships, destroys marriages, dethrones gods.

I don't know why he was intent on guiding me down the path of disillusion; to understand that one would have to understand Felix, something very difficult for my own cast of mind, which is undevious and, however sceptical, free of gratuitous malice. (I do emphasize the gratuitous.) I think part of it was simply that Felix enjoyed the effects. He took, I think, a strange aesthetic pleasure in disharmony, in watching just how far the ramifications of his casual revelations or inventions would go. Just as, at other times, he took an aesthetic pleasure in building up myths. Among the unpublished Handelbein poems found in Grandmama's effects, there is one that begins:

> It is power I love, the puppet threads
> Taut in my thinking fingers.
> As far as I move them, God
> Can never move me.

True or not, the stories coloured my relationship with the family from then on. I was, by turns, provocative and rebellious, sullen and abstracted. As I was at the 'dangerous age', I might have been like that anyhow, without Felix's help; but perhaps not so soon, while I still needed the props and fables of childhood. At all events, I told my mother that her Wehrmacht officer might have been a war criminal, and Trudi and Berti that we should all be ashamed to be Austrian, and waited for reactions, for signs of whether what Felix said was true. They ignored the contents of my little speeches. 'She was always such a good girl,' Trudi said grimly to my mother, as if I were not there, 'she had to become difficult sometime.' And my mother would snap that if I had been in her place and had two children to look after during the war, I would not talk such nonsense. Sometimes they did lose their tempers, and my mother would hit me, though not as effectively as before, and tell me to get out of her sight, which I would do with great dignity, imitating Grandmama as she had been before her fall.

Grandmama was too senile now to participate much in these controversies, if she happened to be there. Sometimes she would shake her head and say, 'Children, children.' Sometimes she would interrupt loudly, 'Yes, I remember. There was so much blood. There was so much blood, when they brought him in.' These recollections, whether of the Count's death or a lover's suicide, interjected a note of surrealism into the scene and usually quieted us all.

But soon there would be another row. And my marks at the convent were slipping, and the nuns beginning to complain of my impudence. 'There is a devil in her, all of a sudden,' my mother would say to Trudi and Berti, 'a little devil, a goblin. And we all know where it is inherited from,' looking at Grandmama, away in her own world, humming to herself.

'Who knows, Mama. It might even have been my dear father. Or perhaps it was coachman's blood.'

After retorts like this, there would be hushed conversations between my elders about the possibility of sending *me* away to school. They did not worry me much. We were poor as ever. They might have been willing to scrape the school fees together for Felix, who was a boy. They would not for me.

Meanwhile Felix, who was past school-leaving age and could not be forced to attend, began to spend more and more time away from home. He went to visit old schoolmates in Salzburg or Linz; sometimes he simply announced he 'had an invitation' and vanished for days on end. No one knew what he did when he was away, and my mother soon gave up asking. He also made friends with more American soldiers, and set himself to learning English, announcing he wanted to emigrate, 'to America or Canada or Australia, some new continent, where there's a chance to make money and to live. Here, everything is dead, and what isn't dead is dying. Except for those idiots who were Nazis and still are, they are all still stuck in the days of the Empire, sitting around waffling about their vanished glories. I've had enough of it, Mitzi. As soon as I can get the money together and get a passport, I'm going. And if you want, when I get established, I'll send for you. There's nothing for you here either.' This would be privately, to me, but he would say more or less the same to my mother and aunts.

'And how,' my mother would answer, her voice heavy with sarcasm, 'do you think you are going to get this passage money together when you are hardly adult and have no *Matura*, no qualifications in anything, when you are too lazy to do an apprenticeship and every school I have ever put you in has thrown you out?'

Felix would grin. 'That's just it. I'm no good in institutions. When I am out of institutions, I can always find a way to wherever I want to go.' And if the old lady was in the room, muttering to herself, he would add, 'Am I not right, Grandmama?' and go over to hug her; and no matter how far away she had been, she would smile and hug him back and her face would light with that extraordinary radiance.

'One heart and one soul, those two,' my mother would say bitterly, and shake her head. But I guessed, even then, that in the end she would try to help Felix emigrate, that she would find a distant relative or a secret source of funds to get him what he wanted. Sometimes this too filled me with resentment, although Felix, wanting a young ally in the household, was doing his best in those days to be nice to me. It was so unfair; the indulgence he obtained so effortlessly from my mother and his aunts, only because he could charm them and was good-looking and a boy. The resentment did not make my impudence less. Whatever he did, Felix was forgiven in the end. Even when my mother caught him taking money out of her purse. On that occasion, she slapped his face, and wept, and gave him a long lecture about the terrible end he would come to, and threatened to deprive him of all funds for a year. Finally she told him, as she often did me, to get out of her sight. Felix, leaving the room, winked at me – to my horror, as what he had done seemed to me a real crime.

My mother went upstairs to cry. After half an hour, I passed Felix tiptoeing towards her room. 'Opera,' he whispered to me. 'She has to do Verdi once in a while. It's actually very good for her.' He tapped gently on her door, and went in. I have no idea what he said to her, but after another half hour they came out of the room with their arms around each other.

When I was alone with Felix later that day, I told him how disgusting I thought he was – but I could not help asking how he had got round her. 'I said it was only to buy her a Christmas present,' Felix said.

'But Christmas is months away.'

'Yes. But I saw something I knew she wanted, and I had to get it now, because I knew it wouldn't be there later. I meant to put the money back as soon as I earned it.'

'If she believes you, it can only be that she desperately wants to. You're not only a thief, you're a filthy liar.'

'How do you know I'm lying?' Felix bridled at last. 'Just because *you* don't really care about the old girl doesn't mean that *I* don't.'

'But you winked. I saw you. I know you're lying. And what do you mean, I don't care?'

'Well, remind me, Mitzi, that you are too much of a naïve little convent mouse to even be winked at. I am not lying at all. You'll see when Christmas comes. Mitzi, don't be so moral. None of *them* are. You will never get anywhere with so much morality.'

'I don't want to get anywhere, if it takes being like you.'

'What, not to America? Not to all the places I'm going? Oh yes, you do. But believe what you like, do you think it matters? And I know our dear mother is poor, but not as poor as she claims, and she gives us a lot less than she could. You'll find out when you're older. The present is an enamelled brooch. You will eat your words when you see it.'

In the end he almost had me convinced. That was typical Felix. When he invented a lie, he persuaded himself it was true and even lived it out. My mother did get an enamelled brooch for Christmas, a very odd and beautiful one, but not so expensive that we needed to suspect Felix of another theft to pay for it, though I have no doubt at all that he did take the money from someone else. Perhaps Berti, who was very careless about her handbag. But if anyone else had suspicions, they did not voice them.

And that was always how it was. Felix led them around by the nose, while he schemed and plotted for his 'emigration'. I, meanwhile, grew more irreligious and restless and resentful. But then I was, as the priest had said, at the dangerous age.

And, like my mother, I was what the Austrians call 'frühreif', ripe early. Boys in town began to look at me, began asking to walk me home, thinking I was older than I was. I refused them, of course; for all my rebelliousness, I was still shy and frightened with anyone strange. But sometimes when the adults were all out I would sneak into my mother's room, undress in front of the gilded baroque mirror, and stretch, and pile my long auburn hair up on my head, like the girls in the magazines Felix used to get from the American soldiers, and run my hands over my body, shivering with cold and a feeling of shameful but delicious wickedness. Very innocent wickedness it was, really; the nuns' prohibitions, like my last vestiges of belief, could not be shaken all at once. But I began to daydream about a man, a lithe elegant man with indistinct features – with our few acquaintances, I had nothing to base them on. The only really handsome boy I knew was my brother Felix.

One day, I was alone with the mirror, when to my horror the door was flung open. I almost shrieked, 'Mama,' desperately searching for what to say, how to explain . . . it was not my mother though. It was Felix.

For a moment I wondered absurdly if Felix had come to seek out the only large mirror to do what I did, if boys did it too. Felix simply stood and stared at me, with an odd half-smile, his hand still on the door-knob. I looked frantically for something to cover myself, and seeing nothing else, pulled the bedspread off the bed; I was too confused, too humiliated, to speak.

Felix walked in then, closing the door behind him. He said softly, and in a tone of relief, 'So that's what you come here to do. I have been wondering. You just come in here to look at yourself.' He came over to me and put his hands on my shoulders and turned me so that we both faced the mirror again. Felix was tall, but I was now up to his chin, and I could not help being fascinated by our two faces close together, so different and yet somehow alike. We both had the high foreheads, the large wide-set eyes, of the Petrolinskis, and Felix's face was all in the pure Petrolinski vein: the cleft chin, the neat close-set ears, the superb arrogant mouth with an incisive upper lip and a full sensuous lower, a mouth that did not seem quite all of one piece but even more attractive for being that way. I, on the other hand, had been gifted with my father's too pointed nose and my mother's slightly too wide jaw, and my mouth was too quirky, a mouth made for irony. But all these lines had then the softness of youth, and, framed in a mass of wild auburn hair, they did not look bad at all. And Felix, as if reading my mind, addressed our reflections. 'And you are right to look at yourself, Mitzi. Because you are becoming really – quite – pleasant to look at. Do you know – I never thought it would happen.' He moved his hands on my shoulders so some of the bedspread came off again.

'Stop it,' I said sharply, and pulled away from him, then in a rush – 'You won't tell Mama, will you? I don't know why I do this – Oh God, why did you have to come in?' After a moment, getting more courage, 'And anyway, what the devil are *you* doing here?'

Felix answered without a second's hesitation, 'I came to see what you were up to, that's all.'

'You couldn't have. You didn't know where I was. You weren't here when I went upstairs,' I said, my voice rising, though it was fear that was making me attack him. 'You didn't. You came here to steal again.'

Felix smiled that same odd smile. 'All right, little Mitzi. Think what you like. And don't worry, I won't tell the old one that you come in here to stroke your stomach and admire you nice new apples – and they are very nice indeed, you are quite right to admire them – if you don't tell her that I come in here too. Or anything else that I ask you not to tell her. Is that a bargain? Are we agreed?' He took hold of the bedspread and pulled me towards him. 'Say yes. Or I won't let you get dressed. I'll keep you like this until Mama comes home.'

'Let go. You're a swine! I hate you,' I cried, struggling.

'Sssshhh,' said Felix, still keeping hold of his end of the bedspread. 'You'll wake up Grandmama. You haven't said. Is it a bargain or not? Would you want me to tell Mama about your little games with her distinguished old mirror?' Then he added, as if exasperated, 'Really, Mitzi, there is nothing wrong with it, you know. No matter what the nuns have told you. Those horrible dried-up witches, how can they know anything? There's nothing wrong with it, even if you – there's nothing wrong with anything you do with yourself, or with anyone else. Ever.'

'Shut up and let me go,' I almost screamed. But Felix whirled me round in the bedspread till I was wrapped up like a mummy, and suddenly in spite of my fear and shame, in spite of everything, we both began to laugh. Then he did let me go, and we both stood breathing hard; I was no longer laughing, I felt tears in my eyes. Before I could stop him, Felix caught hold of me again, pulled the bedspread down a bit and kissed me hard on the shoulder. Then he ran out of the room, while I got dressed with frenzied speed, but not before – oh, Mitzi, what is happening to you? – not before glancing again into the mirror, and thinking, with terrible blushes and shame and disgust but nonetheless, thinking, of what he had said about me, about my body, about my breasts.

Neither Felix nor I mentioned this episode again. Only once in a while I would catch him looking at me with the same expression that had been on his face when he stood with his hand on the doorknob, motionless and smiling, studying my naked body, and I would blush and turn away, or find some reason to leave the room. And in spite of myself, the mysterious words he had said would echo in my mind. *There's nothing wrong with anything you do with yourself. Or with anyone else. Ever.*

I did not go back to my mother's mirror. But I began, sometimes, in the dead of night when I could not sleep – and there were many such nights now – a furtive process of self-exploration which would leave me weak and tearful, more with self-disgust than pleasure, dreading the hideous damnations that might yet befall me, even though I no longer really believed in hell, nor in God. But then, the fears bred by a religious upbringing often last longer than the faith . . . (I see Sir Henry's swivel chair grating with impatient turns. Sweet heaven, we want a feminist biography of that exalted old witch and instead we are getting Mitzi Junior's first attempts at . . .) All right, I will not go on much about it all. I am, anyhow, still too shy. I will skip as much as I can, the giggly conversations with other girls, the reading of forbidden books borrowed and lent and borrowed again, the fierce study of cinema kisses (is that how they do it – do anyone's mouths fit together like that, so neatly?), and all the rest. Everyone knows it, it has been told so often before, better than I can tell it. The sexual awakening, and the spiritual, and the confusion of the two; the desperate nameless yearning that is suddenly aroused by the flight of a bird or a snatch of music or the glimpse of a face through a window; the electrical excitement of a new idea (there were not many in our educational system, but I had made friends with the local book-shop keeper, and now there was no more Nazi censorship, the works of the writers and thinkers who had made pre-war Vienna a great intellectual centre began to circulate again). All of that, the self-questioning, self-glorification, self-abasement, the abrupt alternation of impulses of saintly altruism and sensual desire, the waking at night to the sound of a train whistle and asking oneself out loud, 'Where shall I go, what do I want, will I ever find it, will I ever even know what it is?'

Yes, I will try not to dwell on all that, having merely stated it. But in spite of the shyness, I abandon it with reluctance. That time was for me, as it is for many, the time when I was most myself, and most, more than ever later, alive.

Of course, other things were happening – gradual changes in the country, the town, in our lives. Slowly, our diet improved. Joshua Prescott faithfully sent CARE packages from America and nylon stockings for my mother and for me, and there was real coffee again, and cakes in the *Conditoreis*.

The big Holderland house, where evacuee families had lived during the war, became a T.B. sanatorium, and in summer there were thin men in striped pyjamas wandering listlessly on the neglected lawn. Trudi and Berti told me not to go near there because of the bacteria. But in fits of defiance and pity, I would sometimes sneak something out of Joshua's packages and leave it where the patients would find it, with a delicious sense of doing something forbidden and terribly virtuous all in the same gesture.

My mother still gave her singing lessons, had her hair done in a new style, and wearing Joshua's nylons, began to go out with a local manufacturer of wrought-iron gift-items for the growing American tourist trade. I understood from Trudi and

Berti's low-toned conversations what I would have guessed anyhow, that he was very much our social inferior. But 'Anni was always like that,' they would say, sighing, 'she can't bear it for too long without a man.'

The ironmonger, as Felix and I referred to him, was very polite and awkward on the first, few, occasions we saw him. But he had coarse hands and a Hitler moustache and both Felix and I snubbed him in that oblique, instinctive way which puts up insurmountable and fiercely resented barriers by its very lack of deliberation. It is your tainted blood, his friend Werner said to Felix once, that makes you such a snob; and perhaps that is true of me as well – or was. Anyway, I was never able to stomach the self-made or those in the process of self-making, particularly when I suspected them of being ex-Nazis; though I can be irresistibly drawn by the unmade, by those who stand, defiant and self-assured, on the bottom rung. It is the climbing that makes us monkeys; and Herr Kropetschka seemed to me very much an ape, with his eternal agreeing, '*Ja, ja,* I meant that too,' or 'I say that too,' and 'Exactly, gracious lady,' and his covert but hungry glances at my mother's sumptuous rear when she bent over to pour him a cup of Joshua's American cocoa laced with local Slivovitz.

Herr Kropetschka was part of another change; the refugees who had poured across the eastern borders in advance of the Red Army. Like many immigrant minority groups, they were more enterprising than the locals. 'One thing you must say for them,' our townspeople would grudgingly observe, 'they really work.' Work they did; market gardens, poultry farms, small manufactories, began to spring up on our sleepy Imperial outskirts. The magazines Joshua sent us still showed pictures of occupied Vienna, with old women scrabbling for cigarette butts in the street at the feet of the big Russian statue Felix told me the Viennese (Felix always knew these things) called The Unknown Rapist. Austria, the magazines declared in pitying articles, was a heap of ashes from which no phoenix could rise. But we in our secluded valley had the Americans and the thrifty ambitious Sudetens, and though times were still very bleak, the *Wirtschaftswunder* was beginning in our midst.

Grandmama, who did realize the war was over, began in her more lucid moments to ask my mother when she could go back to Vienna. 'Even if everyone is dead, they cannot be so dead as in the country. I had two apartments – I think one was bombed – but the other – in the nineteenth district – no, was it another – how stupid, I cannot remember the address. Anni, will you go there and see if it is fit to live in? I have imposed on you all long enough.'

'It is impossible, Mama. Much of Vienna is occupied by the Russians and you can no longer live alone. I told you that yesterday.'

'Oh, is it still? I must have forgotten. When do you think they will leave?'

'No one knows. And as I just said, you cannot live alone any more.'

'Nonsense, Anni. I can have Janka back. Janka does everything for me, and is much more efficient than anyone else.'

'Mama, for the hundredth time, Janka is dead.'

Sometimes this went on several times a day, like a litany. It is to my mother's credit that she never, even when we could have done it, thought of putting Grandmama into what is, in both German and English, with horrible ironic euphemism, called a *home*. Perhaps hatred, with the guilt it brings, is as binding as love; perhaps she derived some bitter satisfaction from having her autocratic mother so dependent on her. Last but not least, I think it was because Felix would not have forgiven her. Felix – to *his* credit, I suppose – was as tender and flirtatious with Grandmama as ever, and they still carried on their little *conversations galantes* – the one function of Grandmama's mind that seemed totally unimpaired.

But for me, absorbed in the private world of my crumbling faith and growing sexuality, most of this went on as if somewhere else. I had embarked on the voyage of emotional self-discovery that shuts out the universe, and afterwards leaves one with nothing to record except such fantasies and obsessions as the reader had best be spared. I went for long walks in the woods, I read a great deal, mostly in English – Joshua was sending us books as well as food – and for the first time, I failed some of my exams at school. I began to sometimes linger in town, having a coffee at the *Conditorei* or just sitting on a bench by the river, with a dark, vivid girl named Helene, who laughed a great deal and looked quite boldly at passing men and who, though she came from the best circles, had been expelled from the convent the year before and was now going to the secondary school in town. Sometimes we chatted with boys from the grammar school, and sometimes they walked us home. I longed to go to the grammar school, the *Gymnasium*, too, since it was a mixed school and the brighter lights went there, but my marks were now too bad for a transfer and my mother would not have let me. As my mother grimly said, 'You are sitting with your head in the clouds all day, in the clouds or in the wrong books, and if you fail again you will have to spend the next two years in cooking and sewing, which you hate. I do not think you could even keep up at Helene's school.'

'There are no wrong books,' I answered. 'And if there are, it is the ones the nuns give me, because they are so boring,' but my mother walked out, threatening mechanically to box my ears, old as I was, if I kept on with my 'shamelessness'.

Nonetheless, I decided to be more polite to the nuns, and try to bring my marks up again. It occurred to me that I might want to go on studying, in another country. Felix's restlessness was beginning to affect me. And Joshua Prescott, writing glowing letters about his German Literature courses – he was going to university on the G.I. Bill – made me wonder what it would be like to study in America.

It was during this time, and by mail, that Joshua and I really became friends. Before that, he had written to all of us; now, in answer to my enthusiastic thanks for the books he sent, he began to write separately to me. It was he, more than anyone, who guided my reading, even in my own language; and he passed on to me the best titles from his university courses, the most thought-provoking comments of his professors. Through Joshua – and had he done nothing else for us, for this alone I would be eternally grateful to him – I saw, at that 'dangerous' age when I was turning away from it, that learning could be something more than stultifying cramming for state exams.

That summer, while I was in fact cramming hard to retake what I had failed at the end of the school year, Felix vanished on a mysterious visit to Italy. 'I am adult now, Mitzi, she can't stop me doing anything. Anyway, the people I'm going to are as titled as Grandmama, there is nothing for *die Alte* (our mother) to complain of. I can't stand it here another minute, with that ugly example of *Lumpenprolet* coming here to ogle her. Do you know what he had the nerve to say to me the other day? He took me aside, blew his stinking cigar smoke in my face, and told me that I should stop idling around and finish my education or do an apprenticeship like a normal person. A normal person! If he is normality I would rather be dead. The future of this country, he said, will belong to the people who can produce something. I almost hit him, the smug stupid shithead! I would have hit him, if I hadn't needed some money from *die Alte* to get myself as far as Naples.'

The day after Felix left was dark and rainy. My mother was out for a singing lesson, Grandmama asleep, Trudi and Berti off on a week's hiking tour with a group of girl scouts. I sat over my maths books, trying to concentrate, but my eyes kept wandering to the window; it seemed as if the whole land-scape, green and fecund and fresh with the rain, throbbed with my own half-understood longings. I put my books down, and for the first time since Felix had found me there, went stealthily to my mother's room to look in her mirror.

The door opened to a smell of stale cigar-smoke, not at all like the normal air of my mother's room. Why would she – but of course. She had been out the night before with Kro-petschka.

I looked for the cigars. I found them, two cigar butts in an ashtray under her bed. What a pig he was, to smoke cigars in her bedroom. And she to let him. Then I noticed that her bed was stripped and the sheet, all crumpled, thrown into a corner. But the routines of our household went like clockwork, and we never changed sheets on Monday . . . With a kind of disgusted fascination, I began to pick up the sheet – then I flung it back and without even glancing at the mirror I had come for, ran downstairs and out, not even checking whether Grandmama was still asleep.

How classic and Freudian, how predictable, that on my walk through the rainy Holderland woods that day, when I was filled with revulsion and contempt for my mother's affair, I should meet Stefan.

But here I am going to digress again. I realize, all at once, that I have written pages and pages of action on an empty stage. I have written about sledding with Trudi and Berti but not about the hills; the prisoners in the forest, not the forest itself; Janka's death in the icy pond but never the pond in summer, when midges danced over it in dotted clouds and swans floated on its unruffled surface as if absorbed in their own vague reflections, and I sat hidden and happy on a branch of the weeping willow on the bank, trailing my toes in the water among the willow fronds. I had thought the pond would become a place of horror for me but, surprisingly, it did not; it seemed as beautiful and peaceful as before. It was Felix who could never bear to go there again.

It is not merely that Sir Henry does not want my meandering landscape descriptions, that I am constantly imposing prohibitions from the biography I should be writing onto the memoirs I am. It is also perhaps that I find it hardest to write about what I have lost that I loved most, the hilltops reached after a hard climb, breathless and freezing, through the bitter valley mist, the sudden break into blinding sunshine, the sky like an Advent calendar heaven, the mist rising like fairy smoke from the brilliant green needles of the trees below. Perhaps one does not know how much one loves a landscape until one is exiled from it; that mine was a self-imposed exile, that I could not bear to go back and live among the ghosts that walk for me in that landscape, brighter and taller than the living, that I could not bear the narrowness, the malice of the living themselves, does not make the exile less truly an exile or my love for the landscape any less. Maybe when I am very old and odd and self-contained, I will go back after all, I will forsake kindness and neighbourliness and ease and a freedom as innate and natural as breathing, the freedom political institutions cannot give, only reflect, and go back to where every stretch of grass in the parks has a Keep Off sign and almost every citizen will turn you in for disobeying it.

That I have not written more about the landscape is perhaps because I love it too much; precisely because to think of the dreadful human things that happened in it is so much worse when one remembers how beautiful it is, that it was a fairy-tale, Hansel and Gretel forest, with secret hollows and tall spreading beeches and mushroom fairy rings, where the prisoner lay crushed under a tree; because one wants to keep one's memory of that landscape somehow separate from the ugly dramas of the past. If one knew it would be there long after us – that it would go back to itself one day, cleaned of pesticides and acid rains and memories – but one does not know that, there is far more reason for thinking the contrary;

74

that the woods will be stripped and replanted, one single fast-growing species of conifer, the deer farmed like cattle, every hill gashed to make a quarry or a ski run, perhaps even before I am dead.

Still, imagine then, this pre-Alpine landscape of forested hills and valleys and a sleepy town with gingerbread villas on the bend of a grey, glacier-fed river. Here and there a crag, a tall dramatic limestone outcrop, jutting up through the trees; here and there a mouldering baroque chapel on a cleared view-point, a field of wild flowers, a pasture, an isolated chalet with its cut winter wood neatly stacked against the shingled façade. Imagine the spring when the snows melted, the grey water churning and tossing, rushing with a sound like thunder against the piers of the bridge, and the white cups of the snow roses opening in the forest, the pale green tufts of new needles on the larch trees, and later the purple crocuses pushing through last autumn's fallen leaves. (I could go on in this vein but I can hear Felix saying, Mitzi, stuff the romanticism; and I am haunted by a new suspicion. Perhaps I am now taking refuge in the landscape, as I did in actuality at times of stress, to postpone what is still more painful to write about, the episode of Stefan.)

All right then, simply imagine the Romantic landscape of Central Europe, that restless landscape of heights and depths and swift waters, dark forest and naked stone, lush rainy summers and bitter winters. It is a landscape and climate ill suited to some of the Classic Revival idiosyncrasies of the baroque that abounds in it – though admirably suited to ochre walls and marble curlicues, to baroque trick fountains and grottos and rock theatres and onion-tower churches. Hans Handelbein wrote – my own pedestrian but I think correct translation:

> The fountain gods, once half believed
> Are now more alien with every season
> And most in winter; in the marble cold
> They stand bewildered,
> The fountains in their open mouths
> Frozen, like human cries.

Yes. And there I met Stefan.

He was working as an assistant gardener and handyman at

the Holderland place, cutting grass, raking gravel, painting benches, chopping wood. It was Helene who noticed him first, one day when we were walking into town together, and he was filling potholes on the long desolate drive that began near our house. 'Not bad,' she said to me in a low voice as we passed, and I turned and saw a tall fair-haired boy with bold eyes and a perfect elfin face. The glimpse of that face brought an immediate, painful blush to my own. I was learning Greek and still had hopes of a Classical school degree, and I was just then obsessed with one of those absurd adolescent fantasies, in which a kind of Marsyas figure, unflayed of course and armed with a magic melodious flute (though there were some elements of the hairy devil one of the more hysterical sisters swore she had seen once in the doorway of her room), would come to me in the night; and I would wake to feel his strong but delicate musician's fingers on my thighs . . . and here was a real faun, young, husky, straight-limbed and beautiful, with no seeming elements of the hairy devil at all.

After that, whenever I could, on any pretext I could find, I cycled, whistling, past the drive, I trespassed on the Holderland grounds. I only want to look at him again, I told myself. I only want to see if he really is as beautiful as he first seemed. He was; and I had to look at him again. The first time he spoke to me – a tentative, almost shy good morning – I stammered an answer and almost fell off my bike. The next time I saw him was inside the grounds. He asked me, very politely, what I was doing there, if I did not know the place was a sanatorium and full of contagiously sick people.

This time, I babbled on and on in answer, unable to stop. I said yes I knew but I was looking for wild garlic, no one seemed to gather it here and it was so good for my mother's rheumatism. I was quite proud of that detail, not having learned yet that lies are best kept simple. He said, smiling, that he had not seen any wild garlic in the park. I said 'Oh,' and blushed dreadfully, then gasped, 'But there was lots of it last year.'

He smiled again, and looked down at the ground, and then up at me once more, his eyes bolder now, as I had first seen them. Neither of us moved to leave. And when he went back to work and I did leave, a half hour later, we had arranged to meet again the next day.

Stefan was Hungarian and like Janka, an orphan of the

war. His parents had been taken away by the Nazis when he was quite young; he supposed they had been killed. He said it tonelessly, with no emotion. The aunt he lived with after that had fled with him from the Russian advance, hoping to reach friends in Vienna, but they had been separated on the way, and he had not found her again. He supposed she was dead too. He had wandered on alone, 'It is too long a story to tell you now, and much of it I never want to tell,' and finally ended his wanderings here and got the gardening job. 'I am very lucky. I like it, I like to work outside.'

I was deeply impressed by his laconic manner, by the lack of drama, the brevity, with which he told his story. I took it as a sign of mature stoicism and manly courage amazing in one so young, for Stefan was only a year or two older than I. I lied to him about my own age, adding two years. 'Do you miss your parents?' I asked, in a voice taut with tenderness and pity and admiration.

Stefan said he hardly remembered them, they had left him mostly with a nanny, and that he had not liked his aunt very much. He was sorry of course that she was dead – if she was dead – but he would not want to live with her again and for himself, personally, he did not care if he ever found her, he felt much better on his own. 'I have learned not to miss people. But if you do not come back to the park, I know I will miss you.'

This gallantry sent my heart soaring. It seemed to me quite worthy of one of Grandmama's lovers. Who knows what his parents were, I thought, with the ingrained snobbery I was too unaware of, yet, to wish to outgrow; maybe they were terribly distinguished people. He might even be noble. He might be anything. And whatever he was, my changeling prince, the gardener's boy at the T.B. sanatorium, I was head over heels in love.

But this scene too is a reconstruction, perhaps even more than others, because I was so overwhelmed by his physical presence that it was hard for me to register anything else, even the things he said. And now even my remembrance of that marvellous physical presence is blurred. I have a poor visual memory and though I could describe him, I could tell you the exact colour of his eyes and how perfectly proportioned his features were and the way his hair curled on his forehead, I can no longer actually picture him in my mind; so writing this I realize with horror how even that is now lost to me. What will never be lost is the way that seeing him, being with him, made me feel.

Your mouth says everything without speaking
All the old bloodstained ghosts, the exhausted histories die,
And are laid to rest by a single glance from your eye.

(Hans Handelbein, supposedly to Maria Aurora, though I myself am certain it was meant for a gentler and more serene mistress – if for anyone specific at all. It is a bad translation and one of his worst poems, and does not entirely fit, but . . . dear God, how imprecise everything is; and why does one even attempt to describe being in love, whatever that charged phrase truly means, when it probably does not mean the same to any two people, even those ostensibly in love with each other?)

But never mind. In the presence of Stefan, I did feel something like that very romantic poem of Handelbein's. I felt that, although he himself was a child of the war, and far more marked by it than I, when he was with me both the black ugly past and the grey present were wiped out; that he had escaped and always would, to be with him was to be in a magic circle, that nothing could touch such beauty. What is unattainable, or not yet attained, has a touch of immortality; how bitter that once attained it always turns out to be vulnerable as ourselves, made of the same mortal clay. At the beginning, I never worried that anything might happen to Stefan, only that he might meet someone else, that he might tire of me. Though I might have had snobbish fantasies about his mysterious antecedents (knowing how the family would react if they heard I was meeting a gardener's boy), I had no false pride. I never thought that, coming from where I did into the hut at the back of the toolshed, which was where he lived, I might really have seemed what he tritely called me – a visiting angel.

I cannot remember what we talked about after that first meeting. I must have told him silly incidents of my life at school or my brother's escapades, and about the Schweissers and Joshua and Grandmama, and he taught me the names of flowers and complained about the grouchy old head gardener, whom we had to keep an eye out for in our clandestine rendezvous. In fact, we talked very little. He did confess to me his life's ambition; like Felix, he wanted to go to America – to the far West, where there was lots of space and not many people – 'For me, the fewer the better.' Perhaps California. An American soldier he had made friends with had told him about California. He wanted to have a farm there, or a nursery garden and grow exotic plants. In California, you could grow anything. And maybe there he could study botany. Here, there was no chance for him to study. He had not enough schooling to go on, and in Austria he would never earn enough to go back to school. But in America everything was possible.

We met a total of eleven times. I marked each of them on my calendar with a code sign, so that number is not lost to me. The last five times, we made love, and on only the second of those times I learned what ecstasy is. I know that first sexual experiences are presumed to be unsatisfying and embarrassing, that it is not supposed to go right – go perfectly right – so quickly, but mine was not, and it did, and those hours with Stefan have kept me alive through years of spinsterhood and loneliness, for they were the most unalloyed joy I was ever to know. And that is not supposed to happen either – that a few nights – or days – or hours of love, can last someone almost a whole existence. Not in real life. Not even in supermarket novels does this happen any more. But in my generation such romanticism was still – just barely – possible, and in my case it was a particular romanticism, the romanticism of perfection. I had had that, and wanted nothing second-best.

But where then is the scepticism on which I so pride myself? Cannot all this be an excuse, a story one tells oneself to cover an inability to form mature relationships, an inability to accept others, that may in turn be a Freudian mask for some basic rejection of oneself? Is there not something deeply wrong with anyone who remains fixated on a first lost love? I will admit the possibility; I know only too well, coming from the family I do, how many possibilities must be admitted, how passionate a virtue one can make of the dark necessities of the soul. And yet all of that is irrelevant. I, who live by the dissections and speculations of my mind, still know that I *know* only what I feel to be true, and I know that Stefan was the only human being I have ever wholly desired or wholly loved. Puppy love, we say, calf love, adolescent nonsense, and sweep it away. We regard childhood as critical, but adolescence, which is still half childhood, we consider like the state of the Austro-Hungarian Empire in its last throes, desperate but not serious – a time in which nothing that happens, except catastrophe, ever happens in earnest. The adolescent now escapes through drugs, some of which can be fatal. In my youth, there was often no escape from adult pressures and adult restrictions but suicide direct.

So there it is, the banal romantic story, the brief adolescent episode which was so central, so decisive in my life. I will not write about it in more detail, for that would be travesty. Dear God, I have exposed myself too much already. I could not describe it, not I, not now, a lame greying middle-aged woman with a severe face and a thickening figure. It was another I to whom all that happened. Dwelling on it now, I would feel ludicrous, agonizedly aware of what Orwell called 'the terrible deterioration in oneself'. Just as I have not described, cannot really describe, Stefan. He may have been far less than I saw in him, but he was beautiful and sensuous and tender like no one I have ever known, and the idyll was too brief for any illusion to be shattered. That alone was the mercy – the fatal mercy – of its brevity. I am old, but Stefan is young, as young as on the last day I saw him.

> Who has abandoned you is longest-lasting
> A clear-eyed ghost untainted by decay
> Green and unbending to your dying day.

So runs the first verse of the only poem Joshua himself published; he sent me a copy of the college magazine in which it appeared, and I still have it, and I still love the poem, but again it is not entirely apt. Stefan did not abandon me, nor I him. Fate and malice wrenched us apart. For alas, the story ends in the banal romantic vein in which it began. Rash and happy and naïve as I was, so full of my happiness I wanted to share it (or was there just a hint of triumph in my confidences?), I told Helene, who had been the first to see and admire him – told her not much, only that Stefan and I had become friends, and saw each other sometimes, and that he was indeed a very nice boy and 'quite different from the boys around here'.

Helene, to my surprise, said contemptuously, 'But he's only a gardener. And he's from the East', and was very cold to me

80

for the rest of the afternoon. I never realized she might be jealous, and certainly never – pretty, flighty, popular Helene – so vicious and so sly as to spy on us. But that was what she did. She saw where I went, and when, and told my mother; and the next time I came out of the park, my mother was waiting at the gate.

My mother reacted, as Felix said when he heard about it much later, 'just as you might have expected, Mitzi. In times of crisis, people always show what they are made of, that is, they usually show they are either degenerate or coarse. No one on earth is more moral than a reformed whore.' To which I answered, hating her enough by then to say that, 'She is not reformed.'

I began by denying everything. She went wild and tried to beat me with a clotheshanger, which I tried, in vain, to wrest away from her – I was old and strong enough now to defend myself, but not strong or defiant enough to win. My mother, physically, was a very formidable woman. At last I screamed that she of all people had no right to call me the things she was calling me, and if I did have anything to do with anybody at least it was not an ex-Nazi nouveau-riche with a face like a rotting potato whom one could only want for his money. Love and righteous anger had made me eloquent as never before; I did not know, any more than she, that I would ever dare to talk like that to my mother. The effect was terrifying. Her face grew so red I thought she would burst a vein; forgetting everything operatic, she gave an animal shriek and me a final sharp blow with the hanger.

I fled to my room – oh, stupid and fatal move! Had I run out of the house, tried to find Stefan before they could, it might all have been – but no, it would not. I was a minor, so was he, and we were penniless, without help, without friends, and Stefan for all I knew still stateless; we were at the mercy of our terrible adults. She ran after me and locked my door, then went to attend to Grandmama, who was calling imperiously from her room to find out why her afternoon sleep had been so loudly interrupted. Then she let herself into my room and went on at me again. 'This is not the century,' she said grimly, 'for Romeo and Juliet.' I was not even sixteen, a delinquent minor, I could be sent to a state reformatory for what I had done, and so could the boy, and if anything was said to his boss he would lose his job at once and I would not see him again. But if I would agree to go away to school for a term – she had been considering that anyhow, with my marks as bad as they were – and not see him before I left, she would report nothing, and he would be safe.

I knew she was counting on what adults always count on; that a few months apart would destroy our love. I asked her if she would try to stop me seeing him again when I came back. She hesitated, then said no. But I did not trust her. I told her I must write to Stefan and explain what happened, and if I could not do that I would kill myself. She told me I could write from the convent where she was sending me. At that I burst into such wild hysterics that, frightened at last into thinking I might mean it, she left me alone to write, and walked with me to the corner to post my letter. There was no way, I thought, for her to stop the letter reaching Stefan, and I would write again from school. I could do no more; I could not risk losing him his job, and I knew if I did not give in my mother would do what she threatened.

She was kinder then, and gave me a cup of tea – to which I realize now she may have added a sedative; and exhausted with shock and misery, I sobbed myself to sleep. The next three days, I was not allowed to leave the house, and the day after that, Herr Kropetschka, who was almost the first person in our town to have a car after the war and already had one then – Herr Kropetschka, to make my shame and horror complete, appeared, to drive my mother and me to my new convent school, fifty kilometres away in a town called appropriately Steingarten, the garden of stones.

We hardly spoke on the drive, my mother grim and braced for impudence from me, I determined to freeze both her and Kropetschka, answering his jovial talk with monosyllables or not at all. I do not know what my mother had told him, but the thought that he might know why I was going away made me dizzy with rage. I was not in the least ashamed of what I had done, but I was bitterly ashamed that a man like Kropetschka should have so intimate a connection with my mother and so with me. When the car stopped at a tall wrought-iron gate set in high walls I got out and walked through without a backward glance, past the old gatekeeper and the nun who met us, leaving Kropetschka to take my suitcase, and my

82

mother hurrying and apologizing in my wake. My mother kissed me on the cheek and whispered, 'Be good. Maybe you can come home very soon.' I suffered the kiss as if I were a statue; I hardly breathed an answer to my mother's farewell. But when the gate clanged shut behind her, leaving me alone in the cold echoing hall with those wing-wimpled nuns in their raven black, a little girl's terror took hold of me and I clenched my fists against my sides to keep from crying aloud. I fought my tears and thought desperately, I must bear this, I must bear this for a while to keep Stefan safe, while a certain Sister Theresa looked at me through her little round glasses and said sternly that I must unpack my things at once and then come to the chapel, where she would say an Act of Contrition with me.

I do not need to describe the convent. It was no worse than many other boarding schools; for me it would have been a prison, no matter what it was, because Stefan was not there. 'If you are good,' my mother had said, 'maybe you can come home very soon.' I was good. Reserved, unbending, but good. I rose at dawn, washed in cold, and it seemed to me, slimy water, chanted communal prayers with my eyes shut, only occasionally giving in to the temptation to just mumble wordlessly instead, went to Confession and even confessed that my head had been full of venial thoughts which I hoped God would help me to dispel. I did not however confess more than that. Nor did I manage to choke down much of the horrible food, and I could not make friends with the cowed, childish girls who surrounded me. Whatever my mother said, I was no longer a child. And I felt I did not want girlfriends, that I would never trust one again. My mother had told me what Helene had done; and even had the gall to say that Helene was very grown up and sensible to wish to save me from the danger of pregnancy and disgrace.

I was good for a week; then I asked Sister Theresa, who was in charge of my dormitory, if there had been any mail. She said no. She added that I would receive no letters except from my family, that one of the conditions here was that all mail was vetted by the Mother Superior and only delivered with her approval. Was that, I asked, my voice trembling, a condition that my mother had made for my admittance? The Sister said no, it was a convent rule, but my mother probably

83

knew about it. 'Maria, we do not wish to be unduly hard with you, but our girls may be exposed to dangerous temptations if we allow them to get letters from anyone. There are already some who have not always behaved as decent Christian girls should. These rules are for your own protection. When you are old enough you will thank us for what we have done.'

I said nothing, and turned away. This was my mother's final betrayal. If Stefan wrote me and got no answer, would he not think I had given in, had forsaken him? For a moment, the cold room with its military row of iron beds – iron beds, such as the old Kaiser had slept in, one of the older nuns told us almost every day – rocked and swayed, and I thought I was going to be sick; for a moment, I gave in to a sensation of total despair, total abandonment. Then I took a deep breath and lifted my head. Now I *had* to see Stefan, to find out if he had got my letter and if my mother had, against her word, reported him. Now my only hope was to escape – but how? The doors were locked at night, the gates were locked, no one went out unsupervised – and I slept in a room with eleven other girls and not a moment's privacy.

Or perhaps if I behaved badly enough, they would send me home – and then surely I could escape and find Stefan. Or if I was ill – really ill – but what illness could I sham or get that would be too bad for the school infirmary – and if it was, it would mean hospital, not going home.

I said, trying to hide the tears in my voice, 'Then, if that is so, may I phone my mother?'

Sister Theresa said firmly, 'No. Not now.' Phone calls were for illness or emergency, and there was no illness, there was no emergency, was there? She asked this rhetorical question impatiently, her thin red spinster's nose quivering between her tight glasses. Sister Theresa, sniffing out sin; she made me think suddenly of old Schweisser, sniffing out Jews. But we had been a family when the Schweissers threatened us; we had been, however shakily, united. The thought of my mother's treachery choked me, and I could not say another word. The sister looked at me once more, urged me to pray to Maria our merciful Mother after whom I was named, and left me, adding from the doorway that all newcomers found the hard discipline of the school difficult at first but in time I would be grateful, and merciful Jesus would give me strength.

During that next week, I tried it all, hoping at least to force a phone call home. They did not believe the illness; they punished me for the bad behaviour by making me kneel on dried peas. There was a nun with a ruler who was supposed to hit my hands if I tried to get up. This sounds a trivial punishment, but it is very painful. At the end of the hour, I was almost fainting, but I neither cried nor asked for mercy. 'You have a hard heart, Maria,' said my tormentor with something like respect. 'Yes,' I answered, 'as hard as these peas.' For that she made me kneel another ten minutes. 'And the next time,' she warned, 'there will be something worse.' I did not risk a next time; the pain inside me, the fear of losing Stefan, was greater than anything I thought they would do, but I was afraid they might weaken or injure me, confine me yet more, and make it even more impossible to escape. During that week too, my mother wrote; she hoped I was behaving well, and studying diligently, and my first report would be good. Not a word about Stefan.

I had one hope – the apple tree, a single tall, neglected apple tree that leaned against the convent wall on the far side from the gate. If I could get up that tree and down on the other side, somehow or other – on foot if I had to – I could manage the fifty kilometres to home. And one dark rainy night, I managed to linger in the chapel, then to hide in an archway – or no, I do not remember it that clearly – but somehow, by some miracle, in the little space between last prayers and bedtime, I was able to sneak to the door, turn the great key, and slip outside.

The courtyard had a light; I knew I might be seen from the windows, and when I reached the tree I saw the door open again and heard someone call, asking who had gone out. There was a forest beyond; if I could reach it, if I could run, only run fast enough, the forest would hide me. I fought my way up the old tree, moaning with fear and the despair of my exertion; with my last strength and branches beginning to snap under me, I hauled myself up to the top of the wall. Then I looked down and saw, as if in a dream, the ground far below. On this side it sloped, much more than I had guessed, and the drop must have been more than twenty feet.

I swung my legs over, and pressed my hands against the stone. This was my only chance, and if I died it did not matter. I thought, I will kill myself anyway if Stefan is gone. Once this thought had been formulated I felt a strange peace.

The space below seemed to become vaster and still darker but also safe; it was as if I had really commended myself to the God of my childhood, the God they were always preaching about, the God in whom I had stopped believing after Janka died. The sounds and lights behind me were part of another existence, my mother, Felix, everyone, everything, far far behind; there was only the waiting darkness, my element, to which I was going. I shut my eyes, and I did, I think, say his name only once, like a prayer. 'Stefan,' I whispered to the darkness below, and then I pushed myself off the wall.

V

When I awoke, I was in a white bed in a white room. There was a plain wooden crucifix on the wall opposite me. I stared at the crucifix; then I whispered, 'Take it away. Take it down.' Someone next to me moved and murmured, but the crucifix stayed. I thought, they do not even know what I mean. Then I said louder, 'Stefan. Where is Stefan?'

My mother's voice said tearfully, 'Don't try to move.'

I was not trying to move, but when she said that of course I did, and realized that my right leg was in plaster and my head covered in bandages, and that my head ached and my face ached and there was a gnawing pain in the helpless leg.

Someone else – perhaps Trudi or Berti – said, 'Thank God she has come back to herself again.'

I thought, come back? But I do not want to, I do not want to be conscious again. I asked once more, 'Where is Stefan?' and shut my eyes, wanting to return to the painless darkness that had been so kind to me. I did not expect an answer; I knew already then, without anyone having to tell me, that I would never see Stefan again, not ever in this world, and I did not believe there was any other.

The next time I came to, my mother was sitting by the bed crying. She took my hand; I pulled it away, but opened my eyes wider and watched her sitting there, a large woman growing dumpy, with her permed hair and a new but seedy fur-collared coat Kropetschka had got for her, probably on the black market.

'You lied to me, Mama. You never told me. You never told me I could not get letters or send letters or telephone. You left me there without a word. Where am I now, how long have I been here?'

'In hospital, in Salzburg. You have been here, unconscious, for three weeks. Oh, Mitzi, why did you do that? We thought you would die.'

'I wanted to. I wish it had happened. I want to die now.' I turned my face to the wall, and waited for the pain inside me to grow and rise in my throat until it choked me, as I thought it must, and took me back to the darkness again. But the pain dimmed, the voices blurred, the room turned gently. Once more, I fell asleep.

When you are young and intrinsically healthy, it takes a great deal of will to die. I had risked it once and now my body rebelled, battered though it was. The same constitutional toughness which had made Grandmama survive her accident pulled me, almost in spite of myself, through mine.

When I was thought to be out of danger, my mother confessed to me that Stefan had been sent for by an American soldier who had befriended him, and that he was gone, probably to America, leaving no address and no message. She swore this story was true and that she had had nothing to do with Stefan's leaving. She had even gone to ask his boss if there had been any word from him. 'Humiliating though it was for me to go to that drunken old man and ask about his gardener's boy. I can only tell you what the old man told me. When you are well enough you can ask him yourself; but I think maybe you too will feel we have all been embarrassed enough.' She took my hand. 'I was too harsh with you, Mitzi, I did not know it was so serious, I did not know they would treat you so badly.'

'They didn't. They treated me the way you knew they would treat me. You knew what sort of place it was when you sent me there.'

'I was trying to protect you. You are still a minor, still a child. You don't understand what you were risking with that boy. In my place, if you were a mother, you would have done the same.' Then suddenly she got up and added, half to herself, 'And why must I justify myself so much to you?' Her self-righteousness being, after all, stronger then her contrition.

'It doesn't matter. It is all as you will.'

She came closer to me again. 'What is? What are you talking about?'

'You've had your way. I have lost Stefan. What does anything else matter to me?'

'Mitzi, please do not be dramatic.' Exactly what Grandmama always had said to her. 'You are young, you will recover. There will be other men in your life. This was too soon. And he was only –'

I said, in a voice that startled both of us – though it was not raised, there was something in it stronger than shouting – 'There is one thing I do not have to bear. Your talking about him. Ever.'

She drew back. Her mouth moved to speak, then stopped. After a minute she sighed and said, with her old, everyday exasperation, 'Life is such a gift, Mitzi. You must, you must be glad you are still alive.'

I answered more calmly, 'Oh, I'm alive, yes. And maybe I will even be glad of it. But there will be no other men. No one like Stefan. And I will not recover. Not as you think.'

And I did not recover. My broken leg, after years of inadequate food, did not knit properly; I was very lucky, my doctors said, not to have caught bone T.B., which was rife then among the young. As it was, I was left with a slight deformity and a limp that would not right itself, not for the rest of my life.

And now I must interrupt myself and make a terrible confession.

I have spoken much of deflating myths; in the last few pages I have indulged in a myth of my own. No, not about Stefan. Stefan was real; Stefan was, and will always be, the realest thing in my life. And not the waking in hospital, the conversations with my mother. That was as accurate as I can make it. But just as one cannot remember an accident, the actual collision, any loss of consciousness lasting for any real length of time wipes from memory the events immediately before; and if the loss of consciousness is long, as mine was, days or weeks, even more, can be lost forever, again as they were with Grandmama. In my case, the first week in the convent, the waiting for a letter, the despair on discovering I could neither write nor hear from Stefan, is only a hazy memory; and after that I actually *remember* nothing at all. I shall never know how or with what intention I jumped from the wall, whether it was a devil-may-care attempt at escape, as seems to me most likely and as I have told it here; or at suicide pure and simple, or even at injuring myself so that I would have to be sent home.

I have based the story on what I know about the convent; kneeling on dried pulses was a standard punishment, and the prohibition of letters except those from relatives was standard too. And I do really remember Sister Theresa's spectacles and nose, and the dark arches in the chapel, and the dreary courtyard with the apple tree and the royal iron beds; and if I try very hard I can remember the face or the voice of one or two other nuns or pupils, but there is no name, no character, to go with the voice or the face. I have also based the story on what Trudi and Berti told me I said to my mother when I came to in hospital. I do not remember this either, but I believe what they say they heard, and it fits with the feeling of total abandonment and betrayal that I had at the convent, the last feeling I remember before the blank.

Why then, after all my careful disclaimers about other passages, have I continued my story here without a break, a bit sketchily perhaps, not dwelling with due ironic care and attention on those grim details of institutional life so beloved of autobiographers – I couldn't, since I remember it so little – but continued heedlessly nonetheless? I can only answer that the temptation was irresistible, the blank cried to be filled. It is what I think must have happened; it is also the one space into which I can write myself, unashamedly, a high dramatic role. Compelled to spend my life in the shadow of other legends, why must I be denied my own, when it is so plausible, so simple, so brief? It has been a great comfort to me, all these years, the blank space, the *tabula rasa* on which I can draw forever a girl with streaming auburn hair leaping blindly to love or death. No one has ever belied me. Adolescent suicide is all too common, especially in Austria, especially in schools like the one where I was sent, for anyone to doubt that I would have taken that jump. And the moment on top of the wall is so real to me it is as if I did remember it.

I am too scrupulous, as always. I should have had my small indulgence and left the story as it was; in fact, I should have embroidered on it, *à la* Jane Eyre, the cold refectory, the stern confessor (even better, I could have made him into a dirty old man, who wanted salacious details of sins he did not even know I had committed), the cruel nuns, the basins of icy water filled from a cracked dirty pitcher for morning wash, the dark hushed chapel where I had to kneel, stiff and aching, muttering endless hypocritical Hail Marys. But even if this were all commonplace and real, as it would be, no one would believe me if I had gone a step further than I have – simply because I do not in fact remember it. Those who attempt to be generally honest are never believed when they fabricate. To do it well, you must be born to it. Like Felix. And it is difficult now to picture myself as that young tragic heroine, just as it is to picture myself as Stefan's lover, to imagine that this ageing body once held such an amazing capacity for giving and taking joy.

No, let it all go, let the larger dead crowd in on me again. For what I said to my mother was true in another sense as well. Whether I meant to or not, I did in a way kill myself when I jumped from the wall; and partly it was she who killed me, sending me away. Or perhaps I spent, like Andreyev's Lazarus, too long in the darkness. I got well in the end, yes, almost well, but from that time I ceased to be a willing actor in our family drama; I strove to become the observer who writes this now. Some motive spring, some inner warmth, was no longer there. And, like Lazarus, ever since then I am always cold; my toes, my fingers ache and stiffen at the first sign of frost, I huddle over fires, I cannot put enough sweaters on; only brisk exercise – difficult with my leg – gives me any relief; and perhaps this physical cold is only a reflection of the psychic, of the iron in the soul.

But I have not told the worst of it. I have said the blank space is a comfort. One aspect of it is; another, a torment, and that far greater. A thought began to haunt me when I was, as they said, well – had it haunted me before I think I should have died of it. Since I remember nothing of those last two weeks before my fall, is it possible that Stefan did somehow get a message to me (I would have destroyed a letter at once in case it was discovered), that his story about going to America – which should have meant months of waiting for visas, unless he had already applied and not told me – was a ruse – that we had planned to meet and run away together, and it was to escape with him that I jumped from the wall? This is a thought which, even now, steals into my dreams and wakes

91

me, my heart wildly beating, stops me dead in the middle of a lecture, a conversation, even laughter. I have learned, after these many years, to drive it away, to bear it when it will not be driven; but the effort has made me colder still.

After several more weeks, I went home. It was already clear that my leg was permanently damaged. I would always walk with a limp, but I would walk; I would never ski, but I could still hobble, taking my own time, up the easier and safer mountain paths, leaning on my great-grandfather's sturdy ashwood cane, which he had preferred to the carved bamboo, the one embossed with silver, and even the most elegant one whose handle was a lean greyhound's head carved from buffalo horn.

At first, I had to be very careful, and did not walk much at all. I still had frequent headaches, and was allowed to remain out of school for a little while more. I studied as much as I could, determined to get my *Matura* as soon as I could, though I knew I would already have to repeat a year. The *Matura* was and still is, unlike the English 'A'-levels, the gateway to almost everything. I wanted it because without it I feared I would never have a chance to study abroad, which was now my only dream.

With my mother, I was a model of distant politeness, but I made it clear that affection was not welcome. I must confess that it gave me a not unpleasant sense of freedom and power to know that these three quite daunting women, my mother and Trudi and Berti, were now afraid of me, as they had been of Grandmama and still in a way were. Though with me it was for quite other reasons. They were afraid of my coldness, afraid of my headaches, afraid of the judgment my near-fatal accident had somehow passed on them – for Trudi and Berti had done nothing to stop my mother sending me away.

I was a bit more disposed to be kind to my mother, as her own affairs were not proceeding well. She had given up Kropetschka, but the American major who replaced him had soon found himself something younger. 'That will always happen now, she is getting too fat and worn-looking. She should stop,' I heard Trudi say to Berti, and Berti murmured, 'I don't know – maybe a music professor, an old one but not too old? The music professor at the *Hochschule*? He seems quite nice.' They discussed the possibilities for my mother's waning love-life as matter-of-factly as they would have discussed the mating of the dogs they had owned before the war. 'She is always so restless without a man,' one would say, and the other sigh, 'Thank God that for us all this is irrelevant.' Whether this was a confirmation of Felix's remark about their lesbianism, or a reference to their age, which was little more than my mother's, I do not know. In those days of greater reticence, it was still possible to live in the same house with people for years and know nothing about their sex lives – in fact, know whether they had any at all. Not many women were as like the proverbial ostrich with his head in the sand as my mother was – and even my mother seldom kept a man in the house at night.

As for Grandmama, she had deteriorated still more in my absence. She hardly ever got up from her chair now, and she spoke very little, even to herself; but she would still make demands in that hoarse imperious voice, and she still criticized her daughter's appearance. 'Anni,' she would say, looking sharply at my mother, *'Du schaust heute wieder grauenhaft aus.'* ('Anni, you look gruesome again today.') Then she would turn to Trudi and Berti, who nearly always, even in those days, wore trousers, and say sternly, *'Wie Strassenarbeiter. Grauenhaft!'* ('Like road-workers,' and again, 'Gruesome!')

She had moments of weird and touching lucidity. (How dreadful and humiliating for that proud woman that one should have to describe any of her behaviour as touching!) Once, for instance, when I saw her looking through the frosted window at the birds that came to our bird-table, I rubbed the frost-flowers off so she could see better. She sighed and said suddenly, as if she had just realized my condition, 'Poor Mitzi, you are walking badly too.'

'Yes,' I answered, with a bitterness that, from her, I felt no need to conceal, 'now both Mitzis are crippled', but she was no longer paying attention to me. She began to name the birds, one by one, pointing them out to me as if I were still a little girl, and she herself had a little girl's pleasure in doing so. 'Grandmama,' I said, 'I never knew that you know so much about birds.'

'Hans taught me all that.' She smiled. 'He was most dreadfully fixated on nature, like most poets.' The remark was so like her old self that I gasped; but in another minute she was gone again.

There were other times now when she would smile at me, and pat my shoulder or touch my hair. These vague senile gestures were somehow acceptable and comforting, while my mother's dutiful solicitude set my teeth on edge, and it was only a mutual strained forbearance that kept us from quarrelling more than we did.

It was some months after I left hospital when Felix came back.

What he had done and where he had been he would never say, except obliquely. He had crewed on a yacht, he had worked in a bar in Monte Carlo, he had sailed round the Cape, he had worked in South Africa. Or, so one might presume; he never actually said he had done any of these things, he simply dropped names, high and low, and native lore, and little stray bits of experience. On being asked, 'Where was that, Felix, and what were you doing then?' he would say vaguely, 'Oh, that was in Cape Town,' or 'That was on the *Elefteria*, you know, Manoli's boat.'

'But who is Manoli?' Trudi or Berti might ask, and Felix answer, 'Manoli? He is a Greek ship-builder. Quite a well-known man in Greece. Getting the boat-building industry back on its feet. But a very jolly man, quite fun. Not your typical tycoon at all.' Or, asked about another name, he might say, 'Oh, a friend of mine. But not one I could introduce you to,' and laugh.

Trudi and Berti ate it up – though in private they expressed doubts and worries, and would sometimes say darkly, shaking their heads, God knew where he *really* had been. It was a marvellous technique; the lie indirect, the casual, offhand lie, is much harder to spot or pin down. And for all I know, knowing Felix, a good half of his stories might even have been true.

My mother did not seem so enchanted. It was a measure of the shame she felt that she never told anyone what Felix's friend Werner told me later; wherever he had been before, the place from which he contacted her was a Munich jail, and she had bailed him out and paid his fine. It was nothing serious, a minor theft or smuggling offence, but now both her children had really disgraced her and it must have seemed, with her slippery hold on respectability, a hard cross to bear.

However, Felix got round her with time, as he always did.

Sensing the travel stories did not please her, he stopped telling them; he began to outline schemes for making his fortune, if only he could get some capital, manufacturing this or that with cheap labour from the East. He said he had ideas for gadgets and toys, 'All you need to get rich is a new kind of zipper.' (Soon after that someone did invent Velcro, but it was not Felix.) My mother was still suspicious, but she liked this line of talk better, and she thawed. Soon, we were back to old times, and even I felt very glad, scoundrel though he was, to have him home. Whatever else he did, Felix made everything come alive.

And he was charming as ever to Grandmama, and Grandmama still recognized him. Sometimes when he spoke to her and she smiled, her face had the old radiance; but it was dim and flickering now, like a film running down.

That spring, I was considered well enough to go back to school, and I went. To the local *Gymnasium* this time; they were giving me a trial. It was a trial, in all senses. The classical *Gymnasium* took a truly classical attitude to handicaps such as mine. If one could not keep one's marks up, one fell by the wayside. Mitigating circumstances did not exist. The girls, some of whom I had known slightly, treated me with a coldness I did not try to break down. Helene had moved away, but it was a small town, and everyone knew my story. Perhaps everyone had known about Stefan and me, all the time. I was something of a pariah; and the animal instinct which turns against physical weakness had been fostered by the Nazi propaganda of their childhoods. My limp did not make me forgivable, it made me less so.

The professors, except for one ex-concentration-camp inmate, whom the Occupation Government had reinstated, were crabbed and dull, intent on getting their students through the mill of the exams, as discouraging as the nuns to anything that resembled independent thought. The ex-prisoner spoke in a breathless squeaky voice and was given to occasional epileptic fits. When he was well and could teach, his class, which was history, was the one interesting course in the school. The students took notes on what he said as doggedly but with no more interest than they took notes in the other classes, and did outrageous imitations of him behind his back. No one noticed that not only his physical state but his teaching was different from that of the others. I would have liked to make friends with him but he was too eccentric and forbidding; he did not treat the students with much more kindness than they treated him. It was the loss of my last adolescent illusion, that suffering makes people desirable acquaintances. I should have known better from myself.

I tried to keep to myself and do my lessons well, but the strain was great, and before long I had 'flu and was home in bed again – and no sooner up than I had a relapse.

My mother sat and wrung her hands. Now they might have to get me a private tutor, which would cost even more than boarding school. What would happen to my education if I went on and on being ill? But Grandmama, in one of her momentary spells of lucidity, declared loudly, 'Anni, you are a goose. The child does not need more education. This proletarian education does nothing for them, they become more and more uncultured. The child is sick, let her stay at home.'

I did stay at home, for quite a long time. I lay feverish in bed, listening to everyone's complaints, especially Felix's, when he was there – for Felix was going out a lot again, participating in any festivity to which he could get entry. 'I just have to have people to drink with, if I don't drink here I go out of my mind. We have to both get out of here, Mitzi. It will destroy us. Look at us! You are always sick and I am going crazy.'

'You've only been back two months.'

'That is two months too long. I tell you, if I can't get out, I will do something really awful. Well, maybe that would be good. Maybe then our old Mama would scrape the money together to send me away.'

And he did. A few nights later, he went to a party in one of the grand old villas, got very drunk, and tossed three Biedermaier chairs through a stained-glass window. The only thing that saved us from a court case was that the drunken son of the family, inspired by this, began to throw furniture out of the windows himself. But there was a grand row at home, and the next night Felix went out again and came home as drunk as the night before. Lying in bed, I heard the door slam shut, the raised voices downstairs, then my mother crying. But the fever muted everything, made everything unreal; I myself was unreal, nothing touched me but the high

96

fretful singing of my own blood.

Half-awake, I remembered Joshua's last letter. I still have that letter, like most of Joshua's. 'My dear Mitzi, I do not want to intrude on your private life. But I know the pains of adolescence can be really awful and we adults (We adults! Did he think me still a child?) forget them all too soon. You say so much about what you read, so little about yourself. I know from something your mother wrote that you have been going through what my wisest old teacher would have called a time of trial and tribulation. (Dear Joshua, how pompous he some- times was!) She did not go into details, just that all has not been well in the household. I would only like to say that if ever I can be of any help . . .' I thought drowsily, I must get myself together, I must write Joshua that I want to leave here, why haven't I done it yet? Was it because I dreaded his saying that he could not help me, the closing of my best avenue of escape? But even this was remote, and when I shut my eyes there were brilliant colours, there were Oriental caravans crossing dunes that glittered in a red unearthly light. Then the room filled with whispers, and I was bound down to listen to them; bound like Gulliver, there were little spidery beings walking over my burning body. I half rose to shake them off, but the pain in my head was so blinding I fell back again. I must not move my head, I told myself, not now, not ever, it hurts too much. Oh Stefan, I said aloud, but in the daze of my fever it was an empty name, the way I would say God.

They were still shouting downstairs. I could have died alone up there, they would still have been shouting. They were still at it when I fell asleep. I don't know how long I slept. What woke me was the sound of my door opening, and a cold hand touching my cheek.

I said irritably, 'Mama?' and turned my face away. I did not want her to touch me.

Felix whispered, 'It's *me. Die Alte* is crying in her room. We've had a terrible scene. She wants me to get a job with Kropetschka, though she's not even going out with him any more – Mitzi! My God, you are hot. You are like a tiled oven. I will get Mama. I think we should have the doctor, not tomor- row morning, now.'

'*No*. Just leave me alone. I don't need anyone.'

'Are you sure? Are you sure you are not being brave and stupid? I worry about you, Mitzi. You seem so unhappy, and you are taking so long getting well ... and you and Grandmama are the only people who really matter to me.'

'Liar.' In spite of myself, I was smiling. 'Only Felix matters to you.'

'Everyone thinks that about me. But it is all a cover. I am really a very sensitive person. I am terribly hurt when someone I care about thinks badly of me. Because I'm aggressive, and when I'm not aggressive I joke a lot, people think I have no feelings ...'

'That's what I mean. I'm lying here half out of my head with fever and you are talking as usual about yourself.'

'Of course I am. You don't want to talk about you, do you? You want to pretend I don't know what happened. I do, of course. I've been wanting to tell you, to try to comfort you. You know, Mitzi, something about being in love – and I have already been in love many times – but in a way it is always the same person, and that person, the first person, you look for in others, and I think somewhere, somehow, you find that person again. It may take centuries and many lifetimes, or it may be in this life. But no true lovers are separated forever. No one and nothing that matters is ever totally lost to you. You were meant to find Stefan, you will find him again.'

I wanted to say, in my habitual ironic tone, 'Is this your new Eastern religion? Do you believe in reincarnation now?' I started to say it, but my voice broke and I found myself whispering instead, with tears running down my face, 'Do you really think that? Do you think I am meant to find him?'

And to explain why this happened, why all my guards should so easily have come down, I would have to explain Felix, I would have to capture a quality that cannot be captured in words. Felix, like my grandmother, can never appear in this memoir except as the palest shadow of himself. Felix had the rare gift of saying the most banal or contrived or unreal thing in the world as if it had never been said before, as if it were a glorious revelation meant for the hearer's ears alone, coined from profoundest experience and saved for this particular moment, stained with his heart's truest blood. No one else had talked like that to me, everyone else had said, it will pass, but Felix was saying the words that hummed in my own feverish veins: It will not pass, it is forever. And that animal instinct for touching one's most vulnerable, most secret spot, that flawless timing, was part of the gift.

'You know that yourself,' answered Felix softly, and though I did not at all, now, at 103° Fahrenheit, I was sure that I did, and that Felix for all his faults and cynicism and selfishness was the one person who understood.

Before I fell asleep again, I cried more openly still, not bitterly but with a sense of release and relief. I seem to remember that Felix stroked my face and my hands (or was I dreaming then, or did I imagine it; how many memories are in fact the visions of hindsight!), and licked my tears off his fingers in a way that would have told me, had I been well and a little wiser, not only what he was after but that he was sure of his prey.

The next night, I was better, and he came again, in pyjamas and robe, later still, after everyone else was asleep. He brought me a hot drink 'with a little alcohol in it – don't tell them, they'll disapprove. Poor little Mitzi,' he said softly. 'I will just sit with you for a bit before I go to bed.'

We exchanged confidences, as we sometimes had when we were children; and, as then, his were far more spectacular than mine. He confessed that some of his 'work' when he was away had been smuggling – nothing wicked, he said, just cigarettes; and the most money he had made on his wanderings was when he was kept by an Italian Princess – 'a little too old for me, and a little too thin, but still beautiful, with violet eyes and a *Jugendstil* face', but her husband had found out and Felix had had to flee. I was incredulous and shocked and amused, by turns or all at once, and he made me laugh so much my fever went up again. While I was still laughing he suddenly said, 'Mitzi, I am so cold, my teeth are chattering. I can't go on staying here unless I can get warm. Let me get into your bed.' And before I could protest, he had his robe off and dressed only in his thin pyjamas, he was in the bed beside me, and I was caught between him and the wall.

'Felix, you're crazy. I'm sick – you'll catch it – Felix, there isn't room –'

'I've already caught it. Don't be so nervous. It's just Felix, your brother. Mitzi, look at me.'

My lamp was still on, the light of the weak bulb yellow and dim through the parchment shade. He leant on his elbow, very close but not touching me yet, gazing intently at my face. 'Mitzi, do you remember when we were children and we used to play that game you liked, that game of seeing which of us could outstare the other? Let's play it now.'

'Felix, this is ridiculous. I don't want you in my bed. If you don't get out, I will –'

'Look at me, Mitzi. Let us just see who can stare the longest. *Look at me*. Don't lower your eyes. If you do, you will lose.' Then he said in a still softer voice, 'But only your half-brother. So it is not the same.' His eyes did not move from my face. 'It wouldn't be wrong, you know. The Egyptians married their sisters. And there are native tribes who do it all the time. It is what you need, you need it so much, you will be so much better. It will make you well. And don't worry – I have something with me so nothing at all can happen to you.'

I do not know if he hypnotized me, or if I was simply too unhappy, too feverish, too weak to resist. I only know that soon I *could* not take my eyes away from his face, that there was a great heaviness in my body and my head was buzzing and I could not move; I know that, looking at him, I was suddenly spellbound by how beautiful he was, as beautiful as Stefan. And spellbound like that I listened while he went on talking, whispering, cajoling, exhorting. If he had kissed me, if he had put his mouth on mine, I might have awoken, I might have felt the shock I know I should have felt and pushed him away; I know too that he would have drawn back at the first sign of real revulsion. But he was too clever, he did nothing to wake me, he knew that mouths are too personal and that what he did to me must stay impersonal, elemental, direct, almost like the sex games of children, or I would revolt. So he talked and talked and then he told me I had won and could close my eyes, and he turned out the light.

I do not remember what I felt, if my body responded, but if it did my mind was elsewhere, my mind said firmly this is not real, this is not happening, I am dreaming this, I am sick and in bed and dreaming. Everything merged with the dreams and visions of my delirium, and the rhythmic motion was that of the glittering caravans crossing the purple darkness, going over the horizon in a blinding shower of stars. What happened was only another dream. I have one last vivid memory of the light going on again and Felix standing pulling his robe on, looking down at me, his beautiful face ascetic and bemused, with a sort of kindly academic interest;

he had conducted another of his experiments, and it had been a success.

I fell asleep at once, and awoke in the morning feeling light-headed but cool, quite free of fever, and with the sense that some great weight had been lifted from my body and now I could get well. Then the memory came back. I sat up and said aloud, *No*. No, you could not have done that, it was not real, it did not happen, it was only a dream.

Felix came in a little later that morning, in the same robe, red-eyed and unshaven, his face thick with sleep. 'I really have got it, your 'flu,' he said hoarsely. 'I've come to get some of your aspirin.' Without a word, I took two aspirins out of the bottle and put them on his palm. Then I said, 'All right. And now get out of my room.' Felix shrugged, smiled, and we looked at each other for a moment, then he went. If I did not dream it, I thought, he would tell me I did.

That night, I locked my door, but Felix did not try it. In another two days I was up and about, and not long after we were back to our edgy, bantering relationship, though the bantering was careful, more restrained than before.

It is bizarre with how much calm I look back on this, that I cannot write much about Stefan but I can write about sleeping with Felix, my half-brother, with almost less restraint. Incest is only a word, Felix would have said, what you commit is what you feel you are committing. (This was when he was reading Nietzsche – or was it Kierkegaard – a stage that did not last long.) I did not feel I was committing anything, I was passive and spellbound, the thought that it was *incest* did not really occur to me till afterwards. I was only amazed that Felix should desire me, and amazed at the ease with which this act could be accomplished without love. And it may have been this very amazement that made me comply. I have put it down here as a curiosity. I did not get pregnant, I was not traumatized, I was not harmed. I did think, near the time of my next period, if I get pregnant of course I will kill myself, in the matter-of-fact, emotionless way one might think if it rains I will buy an umbrella. My life, then, seemed hardly more important. It is all much easier to write about than the brief indescribable happiness that Stefan gave me, which I will keep to myself. Had I not lost so much, had I been happy, Felix I think could not have come near me. But still, should I not have felt, after so religious an upbringing, at least a little

101

guilty; is my indifference a sign of how much of myself was dead?

No, Mitzi, you are lying, you have not told the whole truth. I was not so dead, and it is not so easy to write about. All right then; I have said I do not remember if my body responded. I do remember, and it did. And it was only on the fifth night, and not on the second, that I locked my door. And on each of those nights our bodies joined, almost without preliminaries, as easily as if we were two halves of a perfect whole, and on each of those times we came together, as synchronized as two watches, and not once did we kiss, and we hardly said a word – only once Felix, 'Ah, Mitzi, you do have a talent for it.' I did think, each night, this must be the last, and I still did it all like a sleepwalker, like someone in a fevered dream, as I had done it first. Perhaps after the fourth time I was well enough, or afraid enough, to stop, and it was as if Felix knew, because he went out that night and did not come back till morning. A few days later, he vanished again, after another family battle royal. I gathered that it was Trudi or Berti who lent him, this time, enough money to go.

VI

'What I would be so grateful for,' Dr Crump is sitting stolidly forward, elbows on her knees, hands clasped (she is trying not to smoke), a hank of the greying hair falling across her Neanderthal forehead, 'what would be so helpful to me is if you could remember any of the Countess's own stories. She *must* have told you stories about her own youth, when you were a child.'

'All the stories of any significance are in Joshua's book. Actually, she did not tell many, and when she did she usually broke off in the middle. She was too impatient, and then too senile, to do more than just make passing references to things. Most of what I remember, to be truthful, is her telling my mother how dowdy she looked.'

Dr Crump sighs. 'And the unopened trunk – the trunk full of papers – you say that's a rumour? With no foundation?'

'None that I know. I've told you, Dr Crump, there is really not much I can say to help you, and there is no material I have access to that you do not.'

This time, having aired her particular views at our last meeting, vaunted the delusions of her own brain when she came ostensibly to pump mine, she has remembered that information is what she is after. She can do without my blessing, but she must at least make a final effort to quiz me, must be justified in pointedly omitting me from her list of acknowledgements or including a polite damnation, 'Dr Maria Stone, the Countess's grand-daughter, kindly gave me a few minutes of her time . . .'

We have been sparring like this for half an hour, and I am tired of it. 'I can understand,' Dr Crump is saying, 'that you might see my work as conflicting with yours. I'm not worried about that, and I don't think you should be. I just thought I might find your impressions stimulating, and I had hoped that might be mutual.'

I find myself unable to reply. Sometimes it chokes me, the academic intrigues, the politeness to inquisitive strangers, the painstaking efforts to correct false interpretations of things that may never, in the first place, have been real at all. And what a monstrous edifice they have left me with, to shore up against the diggings of moles like Dr Crump. Then I think, Dear God, why am I so uncharitable? Dr Crump is only doing her job. It is not her fault that the character of my grandmother would be completely incomprehensible to her even if she – or I – had infallible evidence of what it was. Those smug and naïve creatures who tell us that human nature is the same in all times and places – well, nature, perhaps, but beings, never – have not even measured the gulf that divides them from their own kin. I watch her moving around the room, restless and exasperated, picking up photographs and gazing at them sullenly, pausing again over the one of Felix. It is not snobbery that prompts me to write like this; please believe me, it is not that, though I do confess I am irritated by pretensions to a culture that sits so ill on the pretender. No, even Grandmama's daughter, my own mother, was quite alien to her, though not admittedly as alien as Dr Crump; but possibly Dr Crump is a nicer person than either of them was.

'I do see such a strong resemblance, Dr Stone.' Dr Crump is still gazing at Felix. 'I mean to your grandmother.'

'I knew what you meant, and there was. There was also a certain resemblance of personality, the same greed for experience, the same flamboyance . . .' She is watching me now, her forehead knitting, a half attentive, half sceptical smile on her mouth.

'. . . the same absolute conviction of superiority.' I am going on talking in spite of myself, maybe to drown my unkindness, my dislike. 'No, that is not quite true. In my grandmother's case it *was* inbred and absolute. In Felix's case, it was not, it was something he had to keep demonstrating to himself, since he had neither means nor assured ancestry nor a title, nor any particular talent. No, that is not true either. He had –' She is tapping the photo lightly against her other hand, and I realize that although she has been urging me to talk, she wants to hear nothing except food for her theories, the idea that what I say about Felix might possibly shed light on his illustrious ancestor is totally strange to her.

'Yes, Dr Stone? A talent for what?'

Fornication (like you, Mitzi, what a pity you have had so little of it), lying, laughter, the creation of havoc, the creation of myth? I say, of course, none of these. I say, 'For keeping his own counsel', in my usual prim way, and then a demon seizes me, perhaps the demon of Felix himself. 'Curious, there was that rumour about the trunk, but also another one. There was a rumour that Felix had some letters not even Joshua had seen – they were supposed to be particularly scandalous, those letters – and Felix's first wife somehow got hold of them when she was in our house. The story was that Joshua found out about this – I don't know how – and there was some correspondence between this first wife and Joshua about it, but she refused to let him read any of them in the end. She was waiting, it seems, for 'the right person' to come along and it wasn't Joshua because by that time she hated us all and she knew he was a friend of ours. This first wife was the American one – he had three, you know. Mind you, there may be no foundation to all this either. But I remember, I think, where she lives now, and you could try to find her address.'

Dr Crump is a little suspicious. 'Scandalous letters? Could they have been more scandalous – I mean for the time – than the ones already published? I mean – there's that famous letter from the painter Stammlos –'

'Yes, yes,' I say, fearing she will quote it. *My darling, yesterday with my head between your thighs, the final scene for* Proserpine in Hades *came to me in a blinding vision, complete and perfect.* It was actually one of the longest letters Stammlos ever wrote. I cannot help smiling, imagining Stammlos, that great shaggy lion of a man, in his cluttered studio on the Pilzgasse, dishes and bedclothes and half-finished drawings everywhere, wild sketches of lowering harpies with arched folded wings; and Maria Aurora in a lace-trimmed hat and buttoned kid shoes stepping over the threshold as she would step over a puddle of muddy water, saying, 'So much genius is very amusing, but

105

where may I sit down?' Lost in this fantasy, I hardly remember to answer until she asks again.

'I'm sorry – the scandalous letters. I don't know, of course, what their contents were, and as I said, if they exist at all. But if anyone had kept some of the letters for future publication, they might well have kept the most scandalous and revealing, mightn't they?'

'Yes, I suppose they might.' Dr Crump puts down the photo of Felix, in the wrong place. 'Have you yourself ever checked this out? Are you in contact with this ex-wife of Felix's at all?'

'No. As I have already implied, it was a rather acrimonious divorce. If I wrote to her about this, or about anything, she wouldn't even answer.'

'Then you're really not interested in following this up? Would you mind if I did? I don't want to leave any stone unturned.'

'No Stone indeed, Dr Crump.' A bad pun, but she is too fatuous to register it anyway. 'As long as you realize it's a long chance. In cases like this, there is always a lot of idle gossip about vanished papers. But if you will promise not to use my name –' Dr Crump's broad face is concentratedly bland, but I can sense the eagerness, and I am almost sorry. However, it is now too late, and the demon drives me on. 'If she's still married to the same man, her name is Mrs William Benderley, and if she hasn't moved, she lives in Chicago.'

Felix met her in Salzburg.

She was attending a Summer Seminar as part of her college courses in the States. It was her first time abroad, her first venture out of the boating, riding, dancing debutante set in which she grew up. She was a little older than I was, but she had lived, in her Middle-Western upper-crust suburb, in a world of mindless security, hardly aware there had been a depression, hardly touched by the war, though one of her uncles died in it. The security was particular as well as generic, for she was the sort of girl who is always in the right place at the right time, and more important, is seen to be there. Felix showed me, once, the album which Betsy sentimentally took along on her trip; Betsy as a little girl in dancing class, with a puffed-sleeve velvet dress and white bobby socks and patent-leather shoes; Betsy winning the red ribbon at the Hunt Club

Show ('we'd have got the blue but he shied just before the last jump') in her neat black cap and vented tweed jacket from Abercrombie and Fitch; Betsy on her Daddy's sailboat with white shorts and a spectacular tan. ('Gosh, Felix, I didn't smile for years, 'til I had my braces off. You should have seen me then, all freckles and barbed wire. You wouldn't have liked me at all.') And Betsy at her 'Coming-out Party'; 'Miss Betsy Coolwell,' the newspaper clipping said, 'made her bow to society in a dress of eggshell taffeta, wearing the cultured baroque pearls given her by her grandmother, Mrs Quentin burgess of Waterside Drive.' Yes, Betsy too had a grandmother, who lived in an even bigger house than her parents' house. ('She's all alone there with fourteen servants. I don't know how she stands it, except she has a lot of bridge parties. I guess that's her main distraction. We used to call that house the Mausoleum.') The deportment and education of girls like Betsy is entrusted, I discovered, to institutions whose names are always prefaced by the words Miss or Mount (Miss Jameson's Kindergarten, Miss Hill's Dancing School, Miss Tutnell's Academy, Mount Pleasant Junior College); and even at the age of nineteen, Betsy was still using, instead of swear-words or conventional euphemisms, the clique-invented expletives of her high-school days. ('Oh, bork! Oh, that's really fritzy!') After which last, she once looked around and said, in breathless apology, 'I'm sorry, that's a local expression, from my home town. It doesn't mean anything anti-German.'

It was impossible to tell whether Betsy was really embarrassed by this gaffe, because she pretended to be embarrassed so often, as a gambit to keep people entertained, and at ease. It was part of being *popular*, which was the most important thing to be. In the same vein, she could not go around the corner without having a little adventure to tell her friends. ('The first time I took Daddy's new Lincoln out, there was this spider that suddenly came down from the windscreen on its thread and landed right in my lap, and I drove right up on the sidewalk and nearly hit a fire hydrant and jumped out of the car screaming and this man came running out of his house and wanted to call an ambulance . . .' and so forth.) It is what a sociologist whose name I forget has called the 'Our Hearts Were Young and Gay' syndrome. Life is a series of jolly pranks and mishaps, gloves forgotten in fraternity houses, dinner-

107

jacketed beaux leaping, or falling, into the swimming pool, and a belated case of chicken pox just before the Senior Prom. Perhaps it is because real adventures do not happen to the Betsys of this world and when they do, like most real adventures, they are terrible and best not thought about (the time when Daddy's Lincoln actually crashed, the time when the boyfriend caught polio). But barring such events, the Betsys of this world go on as they began; and when the society columns mention her as an established matron, when the face packs and massages will no longer keep wrinkles from the face or flabbiness from the body, when there may be nothing left but the whiskey bottle to shut out those sudden views of the abyss that yawns under even the greenest of suburban gardens, Betsy is still luckier than you and I; she can drink enough to put a Bowery bum under the sod and come back for more, sobered and slimmed, bright as a button in new couturier clothes, from the best drying-out farm in the country. And there is always the psychoanalyst, the weekend in Rio, the cruise to the Cyclades. It is one of the outrageous myths foisted on the poor that the rich are as unhappy as they, a myth the rich, and the media that make some of them more so, do nothing, of course, to dispel.

I am being uncharitable again. We think of the rich generically, as they think of us, and Betsy was also (to some extent) a person. From Betsy there emanated a thoughtless *joie de vivre* which, when we put aside snobbishness and envy, warmed our decadent European hearts. (Well, mine not quite.)

And for Felix, Betsy was a sitting duck.

Or so he thought.

I do not mean to imply by all this that the Coolwells were the sort of Americans my mother and her acquaintances, over coffee in the *Conditorei*, would categorize as Barbarian. (Joshua, to my mother, was not even American but a sort of honorary European, perhaps because until we got onto first names he always called her *Gnaedige Frau*.) Betsy's parents patronized the local symphony, went to the theatre when in New York and subscribed faithfully to the Book-of-the-Month Club. They even (Betsy told Felix) read the book-of-the-month aloud to each other in bed, for half an hour before lights out.

108

Well, sometimes they did. There was not much time for this because Mr Coolwell worked very hard. He owned various enterprises, among them a dog-food factory; and I have often thought of the miles and miles of tripe which must have been processed, spiced, coloured, emulsified, to support the environment that produced Betsy's air of total wholesomeness, a wholesomeness so perfect I could not regard it but as a veneer, a coating as laboured and unreal as French polish. Here again I was wrong, for those who grow up in a suburban Garden of Eden, with eyes blinkered and ears shut, must of nature be wholesome, just like Adam and Eve. Betsy loved horses; did she ever find out, or think it incongruous, that some of the last mustangs of the golden West were being hunted by helicopter, gunned down from the air, as grist for Daddy's mill? (The labels on the dog-food cans did not of course say this but a certain magazine did, a year after Betsy and Felix separated, and it had been going on for a long time.)

But all this is by the way. At all events, had they not been people of some culture, or at least an awareness that culture exists, the Coolwells would not have sent their daughter to Salzburg and Felix would have pursued his devious course to South America or wherever he was thinking of going then, and not returned three weeks later, with Betsy in tow, announcing they were going to get married.

They met in a café. Felix saw a group of American girls and, with his unfailing instincts, chose to concentrate on the wealthiest (he said she was also the prettiest but I am not sure that was true). He asked her out for that evening. She made a charming little moue and pointed to her cashmere-covered bosom. (Felix, with glee, told me all this later.) 'I'm pinned,' she said. Felix, gazing intently at the bosom, said it was very attractive and the pin was nice too. Had it been anyone but Felix she would have taken offence (I have watched Felix in operation, and one thing I must hand him is that he did take risks), but she only blushed, and said, 'You don't understand. I'm *pinned*. That's a boy's fraternity pin. It means I'm, well, almost like engaged. It means I'm going steady. I'm going out with only that boy.'

Felix – his English was very good by this time – said, '*You* don't understand. I want to take all three of you out. I want your girlfriends to come too. Surely your boyfriend couldn't object to that. But if you think it's wrong, I'll take the two others out without you.'

So of course she came, and he blew a good deal of the money Trudi had given him taking them on a tour of Salzburg wine cellars and cafés. He took them out three nights running, then he began to take Betsy out alone. He took her to have *Eiskaffee* at the Café Bazaar, and they gazed at the river and he told her that he had spent all his money taking the other girls out because he had to see her again. He took her down into the catacombs of the Peterskirche, and put his arm around her when she shivered. He took her to Hellbrunn (Jesus Maria, said Felix to me later, it was terrible, all those noisy fat Americans among the *Wasserspiele*) and they wandered among the half-believed fountain gods, and she marvelled at the giant carp, and all the tricky things that could be done with fountains, and gasped at the golden crown lifted high on a shaft of clear crystal water; and she blushed when he explained to her that the little ochre castle on the hill above the park was built by the Prince Archbishop for his mistress and is called the '*Monatschlösschen*' because the mistress only used it a few days out of every month; and, in the baroque rock theatre, she let him kiss her for the first time . . .

Felix had decided on his image before he even approached her. It was his natural one; the decayed aristocrat, down on his family luck. (After all we were in war-wounded Europe and many of us had had to give up our family estates. Not only that, but we'd had to renounce our titles.) And Grandmama, of course, who had been a real Countess, figured largely in the airy ancestral castle that Felix constructed in Betsy's mind.

It was Berti who answered the phone when Felix called with his news. 'Felix? You haven't gone abroad? What – you want to bring your fiancée?' Berti cried, and at that my mother took the phone away from her and began to yell into the receiver. 'If she had come over as strong in *Fidelio* as she does on the telephone,' Felix once said, 'our fortunes would have been made.'

'Felix, you have no money, no job, and if you come back here now the von Trommels have threatened to take you to court. How can you get married?' I don't know what Felix told her, but she stopped shouting, though the anxiety and suspicion did not leave her face. 'Well,' she said, when she put the receiver down, 'he says she's American, and not quite twenty, and completely in love, and he had to assure her his intentions were honourable. Which means . . .' She shook her head. 'He says he will invite us all to America for the wedding and pay the fares. Nonsense, of course. And her father, he says,' she was trying to control her face muscles, 'her father makes dog food.' We looked at each other, and then we began quite helplessly, all four of us, to laugh.

Felix arrived a day early, 'to get the house ready. We have to make it all look very noble. I had already told her that I am not sure how my family will react to my wanting to marry a commoner.'

'What is it?' asked Grandmama from her corner. 'Who is marrying? You, Felix?'

'Yes, Grandmama. And she is very pretty and very rich. The daughter of a big industrialist. You know how it is, we have come down in the world, we have to marry into trade.'

'Be careful what you say in front of her,' Berti cautioned. 'You know she repeats things now.'

Felix gave the old lady a quick kiss. 'Nonsense. The Countess has a much better head than any of you. Except perhaps Mitzi. And she will make a marvellous impression on my fiancée.'

'It is not necessary any more,' said Grandmama, who, though hard of hearing now as well, seemed to be able to follow Felix's conversation when she could follow no one else's, 'that I impress anyone. *In meinem Alter muss auch das Imponieren aufhören.*' At my age even impressing has to stop. 'Though I was always told that it was the one thing for which age is an asset.'

Felix kissed her again and said, 'But you do, Grandmama. You were always my trump card.'

The whole of that day, Felix rushed around, hanging family portraits in prominent positions, insisting that everything be dusted, swept, polished as never before. 'One would think the Kaiser was coming,' said Trudi grimly to Berti, as they struggled to help Felix move the piano. 'I do not see why the piano has to be in a different place.'

'Of course you don't my darling,' said Felix cheerfully, 'you never understood anything about décor. But it gives the room a certain something to have the piano over there, with a vase of flowers on it. And now I can have crossed sabres on that wall.' He had discovered the sabres in the attic. 'I knew they were there, Rudi von Trommel and I used to fence with them in secret when we were boys, that was how I got that cut above my eye. It's a wonder we didn't blind each other. For the rest, it's fine. This place is basically *Bauernrustik* (peasant rustic); and that shouldn't be hidden, the way Mama tries to, it should be emphasized. My friend Werner says (friend Werner, a young writer in Salzburg, was quoted often of late) real style is like existential freedom, choosing to be what you are. Only please remember, all of you, that we only came here temporarily and are still hoping to reclaim one of our large estates near the Czech border when the Russian occupation ends.'

Did it need all that, to capture poor Betsy, when she was already head over heels in love? No, of course it did not. But Felix was something of a perfectionist, and the scenes he set, the images he projected, would not have satisfied him if they had comprised only what was necessary for their practical ends. In Felix's conning, there was always an element of baroque. And there was also that love of risk, of flirtation with disaster, that impelled him to overplay. Trudi and Berti and my mother, even sometimes I, watched hypnotized and did not question what he was so magically juggling with. And my elders genuinely hoped, that time and every other, that Felix might really be on the road to success. They had worldly, practical views on careers, position, marriage; and they all thought that Felix was a prize this little gormless Middle-Westerner should be delighted to catch. There was no doubt either that it would have made their own lives easier. They scoffed and grumbled and warned, but in the end they played along.

   I must also confess that there was, in all of us, who had been long hungry, a twinge of glee at seeing something so well fed landed so easily in Felix's net. I did anticipate her arrival with a certain guilty sympathy; but when I met her, I had an immediate distinct impression that Betsy, for all her fresh-faced college-girl airs and raptures, could take care of herself.

In my mind's eye, as I write this, I see as if they were two

leaves of a diptych, slim rosy young Betsy in a pink New Look
cotton dress with a tiered skirt and white collar and cuffs, her
dark hair escaping from under her little straw hat in the softest
of feathery waves, walking through our front door exclaiming,
'Oh Felix, I've never seen anything so darling as this house –
it's like Hansel and Gretel – I don't believe it's real,' and
Betsy as she may be – must be – now, Betsy in kid mules and
a robe of mauve chenille, cracked polish on her toes, still not
dressed though it is nearly twelve o'clock and she has to go to
a Junior League luncheon at one, her face swollen and puffy
with sleep and shiny with dregs of night cream – Royal Jelly,
Moon Drops, Vitamin E – lifting the telephone receiver,
holding it slightly away from her ear to mute the strident
tones of Dr Crump. I can imagine her own hoarse voice,
'Felix? We got divorced years ago and Felix is dead. Felix's
grandmother? Oh my God, what is all this? I have no idea
what you want,' and the way she will beckon impatiently to
the Philippine maid to bring her a cigarette and another cup
of coffee. (The whiskey bottle she will fetch herself, later – no
Betsy, you promised yourself, not before lunch.)

Yet for all I know, Betsy is dead too; and my only reason
for thinking that if she is not she is drinking herself there, is
what Joshua said after he saw her, and that was a generation
ago. But the picture is so vivid I can hardly believe this future
scene is not as real as the past. Is this, I wonder, how things
sometimes went on in Felix's mind, did he dream up such scenes
and then set forces in motion to create them? If so, perhaps it is
one of the demons that inhabited Felix which made me set Dr
Crump on Betsy. Or is it a small belated gesture of malice, was
I more jealous of Betsy than I ever admitted to myself? Not
because of Felix. At all events – I trust – least because of Felix,
but for being what she was, or what she seemed; buoyant,
bursting with wealth and health, untouched by war, untouched
by pain, standing free and easy and totally confident on her
two perfect American legs?

My mother and aunts moved forward to greet her. Everyone
was improved for the occasion. My mother had piled her
greying hair neatly, for once, on top of her head, and was
wearing a snow-white blouse and a dark skirt and a brooch
Felix had carefully chosen from among her jewels, a big

113

glowing topaz ringed with irregular natural pearls that proclaimed long-ago money as discreetly but definitely as Betsy's appearance proclaimed money being made. Trudi and Berti, even for Felix, could not quite achieve a *fin de siècle* look, but their shingled mannish cuts were combed and properly parted, they had put on skirts and their most feminine shoes and they too were bejewelled; precious stones gleamed on their coarsened, capable fingers, gold on their lapels. It was like a kind of stately dance, the approach to a cotillion, Felix with Betsy on his arm, the three smiling middle-aged ladies, gliding toward each other with measured steps, Betsy offering her box of chocolates and with the prettiest gesture leaning over to peck my mother on the cheek. Grandmama wheeled in then and said loudly, 'What have those two done to themselves?' indicating Trudi and Berti. 'They look like stevedores at a *Fasching* (carnival) Ball.' 'Navvies in drag' would give more the flavour of what she said. Fortunately Betsy's German was not yet good enough to take in this remark, and Trudi and Berti, displaying the breeding which in fact they had, simply ignored it, but I choked and had to leave the room.

When I was enough in control of myself to return, they were all seated in our rustic salon, and Betsy was explaining that it reminded her of her uncle's hunting lodge in the Adirondacks, which she adored – 'the antlers, and all this dark wood panelling – some people find it gloomy but I love it and it never goes out of style.' And we were so lucky to live here where everything was so beautiful and so old. The only old thing in the suburb where she lived was, and it wasn't even really, a sign that told you a lot of French and Indians had massacred each other on that spot. 'Or was it the French killed the Indians – I can't remember. But anyway,' she added modestly, 'my mother was from a French family that came with those early settlers, though that wasn't anything very grand, they were just trappers who went up the river and founded this place. (I saw my mother's ears prick up at this casual talk of old settlers and wondered if Felix had coached Betsy in turn – though it wasn't much, it was better than mere dog-food manufacture.) And I'd love to hear more about the place you used to have, the castle in Schwanenfeld.'

'Schwanenfeld?' said Trudi dubiously, and Felix coughed. 'Oh yes,' my mother said quickly, 'castle is a little exaggerated, it was . . . but we all lost a great deal during the war.'

'It must be just awful for you,' Betsy cried, 'to think of the Russians there. Felix told me they've made it a batallion headquarters. And he told me all about the room which is all blue and gold, where you used to have banquets, and the deer park, and the big bed where the Empress Maria Theresia slept when she came to visit . . .' Our elders exchanged worried looks; this castle in the air was taking too definite a shape. 'But I think it's great, the way you've adjusted to living in such a different style, and how really darling you've made this house. You know,' she leaned forward, twisting her cultured pearls in her hand, 'My father says we should never have let the Russians get so far into Europe. He says maybe we should have let the Germans take Russia first and then try to make a deal.' Everyone nodded approvingly at this piece of political acumen, except me, and Felix winked at me over Betsy's head. I was about to remark that of course the Russians should not have been let so far into Europe, but even we, who had an easy war, might not have survived another year under the Schweissers, but I contented myself with murmuring 'No,' which no one paid attention to.

'I mean of course,' Betsy went on hastily, 'if they'd have stopped the concentration camps and all that. My father says Roosevelt was responsible for the Russians getting where they are. He hated Roosevelt. I grew up very Republican and I guess I still am but since I've been to college I've tried to be more objective.' They were still listening intently, with a mixture of approval and bewilderment. 'I'm sorry, I can't say all this in German, but Felix says your English is good enough to understand anything I might say, because I'm such a featherbrain.' She laughed, tossing her head back, showing the neat little teeth perfected by five years of orthodontia. Then, in German, 'Tell me please, are you going to the *Festspiele*? Felix is going to take me next week.' Trudi and Berti and my mother exchanged discreet looks again; they knew who would have to pay for the tickets. 'I've already seen *Jedermann*. We all had to; it's part of our course.'

'Did you like it?' I asked.

'I thought it was thrilling,' Betsy said earnestly. 'It really gave you a feeling of being right back in the Middle Ages. And I loved the costumes.'

'In English it is *Everyman*,' I said, in English. She was so pretty in her pink dress, and her eyes looked so wide and interested, that all at once I wanted to swallow my envy and doubt, my impression of shallowness, and make friends. I gazed at my elders, with their unfashionable clothes and tense guarded smiles, their bodies thickened by the starchy diet of the last years, and thought of Felix saying, the old world is injured and tired and sick, I want to be part of the new.

'We have a friend in America who is sending me books from Everyman's Library, and I always like so much the quotation inside the cover. *Everyman, I will go with thee and be thy guide, in thy most need to go by thy side.* It means the books are your guide, of course, it means knowledge, and I think it is ...' I could not think how to explain in German, let alone in English, why this quotation moved me so much, so I finished clumsily, 'I think the word *Everyman* is sounding much better than *Jedermann* and I would like to see the English *Everyman*.'

As soon as I stopped speaking, I realized I had made a mistake, that it was silly to think Betsy might respond to the sort of thing I knew from his letters Joshua would respond to. There was a silence. Felix, with an impatient gesture, lit another cigarette. Since my accident, and except for my brief periods of *Gymnasium* attendance, I had hardly talked to anyone outside the family, and when I was not withdrawn and ironic, when I tried to be warm and open, I must, I thought, sound pompous and graceless and raw ... Betsy's face was blank. At last she smiled, and gave me a small vague nod. 'Well, I – I haven't seen it either. I didn't know we had an *Everyman*.' Then she turned to Felix. 'Your sister has the most fabulous hair. If I had hair like that I'd do all kinds of stuff with it.' She turned back to me. 'Mitzi, would you let me put your hair up for you once? I bet you'd look wonderful.'

'Well, yes, maybe sometime,' I murmured, though I did not really want her to, but she had already switched her attention to Trudi and was saying in German, in a raised voice – she had somehow got the impression that it was Trudi, not Grandmama, who was a little deaf – 'I hear you did a lot of skiing before the war. Where did you go?'

They were off then; Betsy and Trudi and Berti discussed skiing, then still a minimum-equipment sport and little practised except by inhabitants of mountain country. Betsy's skiing in those days was another mark of high privilege. They

116

went on to other sports, and Betsy, with her etiquette-book politeness, tried to include my mother and me; but my mother had never been a sportswoman and I was not likely now to ever become one, so Betsy eventually tacked about. 'Felix tells me,' to my mother, 'that you sang at the Vienna opera. That must have been so glamorous. Tell me about it. I'd love to hear you sing.' Felix raised his eyes towards heaven. My mother, just then pouring tea, spilled a little and answered in awkward English, 'Well, you know, I only had the not so very big parts. Please take more *Kuchen*.'

Felix reached over and heaped whipped cream onto Betsy's plum cake. 'My mother is much too modest about her singing. You cannot get her to sing in public any more. And she is a wonderful *Hausfrau*. Thank goodness that in our aristocracy the ladies all learned how to do all the domestic things, and even the ones with high titles, when they lost their servants, they could manage.'

As in our aristocracy this was not true at all and what a good many upper-class girls did manage to do, even now, was grow up without learning how to boil an egg, I wondered what Felix was leading up to. 'You see, I will expect a lot from my wife. I will expect her to be as good a housekeeper as my mother, to wax the floors every week, to polish all my shoes –' Betsy was looking at him with a dubious little pout; he laughed and leaned over and kissed her.

'Oh, Felix, you're such a nut,' she said, relaxing again. 'I never know when you're serious. Do you know when he's serious, Mrs von Lenauer?' (Felix's father's name, not that of mine, who was my mother's last husband; I smiled, and Felix frowned warningly back.)

'It is hard to tell,' my mother said, passing yet more cake to cover what she thought Felix's *faux pas*; but I knew it was not one at all. He was sure of Betsy now. He was beginning to test his power, to see how much he could ask of or tease her, how far he could go before she bridled.

Occasionally, Betsy smiled in Grandmama's direction. Grandmama was humming faintly, lost in one of her reveries. Betsy said softly to Felix, 'I'd love to talk to the Countess but I feel so shy – and you say she wouldn't understand me?'

'No,' said Felix firmly, 'she would not.'

Grandmama, who was beside me, stopped humming and pulled gently at my sleeve. '*Harmlos, die Kleine.*' Harmless, the

117

little one – that most damning piece of faint praise. 'Tell me, is she his wife?'

'No, Grandmama, but he says they will get married.'

'She is not his wife then. I hope he marries her before she is pregnant. The Americans are very puritanical about such things.' Fortunately, Betsy missed this interchange.

Later that afternoon, the young lovers went for a stroll in the woods. When they returned, Betsy was leaning heavily on Felix's arm and her eyes were wet and shining. She broke away and ran to embrace my mother.

'Oh, I've just got to hug you. I'm so happy! Felix says this is one of the oldest rings in the family, and it's meant for the first bride in every generation. It's the most beautiful piece of jewellery I've ever worn. Oh, thank you so much for letting me have it – because of course – wasn't it – it was yours.'

On the fourth finger of her left hand was one of Maria Aurora's rings, an emerald set with tiny diamonds. I had never seen her wear it; we had little such jewellery left and during the war had worn none, especially with Schweisser in the house. But I did remember seeing it once among the 'treasures' Grandmama used to show me. I did not believe that Grandmama had given it to Felix – my mother certainly had not as she had never owned it – but Felix was probably relying on Grandmama's senility to cover for him. I wondered what else might be missing from the treasure boxes, how much Felix had pocketed during his long flirtatious bantering sessions in the old lady's room. Saying it was my mother's gift, which my mother could hardly deny now without destroying the new engagement, was a way of preventing what might after all have been an embarrassing scene with Grandmama, if Betsy ran to thank *her*. Felix had learned the rule that works in personal relations as it does in politics; if you behave outrageously with an air of behaving well, you are quite likely to get away with it.

My mother did not blanch. I think she had decided that Betsy was quite a good match, and she would put the best face on this new effrontery that she could. She would tear into Felix later, when Betsy had left. And of course she would, as she always did, forgive him in the end. 'I am so glad it pleases you,' she said stiffly in German. Felix stood beside Betsy,

118

solemn and innocent as only Felix could appear, holding her hand.

Then all at once Betsy glanced at me. It was a glance of alarm, which she controlled as soon as she could, but I read what was in her mind. 'The first bride in every generation,' Felix had told her. But Felix had a sister. Did that not mean the sister, then? And what her look said was: I don't want to give it up; I want it, it's *mine*.

And with that, the little bit of my heart that had gone out to Betsy and been already somewhat rebuffed drew back for good. I decided that she was probably bored to death by *Jedermann* but thought she ought to like it because it was Culture, and my obscure passion for a little English couplet, which was not in her programme, had left her totally at sea. I would have to see more of Betsy before I understood it was more complicated than that, that Betsy's gushy enthusiasms were not simple hypocrisy. In Betsy's circles, paradoxically, 'sincere' was, for character, the adjective of highest praise; but this very sincerity was a hothouse quality, the mark of a democratic elite, a cultivated 'sincerity' which *became* natural as breathing, so that – again paradoxically – even what one deeply felt (if in fact one felt anything deeply) came out with a ring of falsehood. Betsy could weep over a farewell, or a sad event, and two minutes later have dried her eyes and be joking and laughing, if the situation required it. 'I know this kind,' Joshua said to me after he met her later, 'all their emotions are right on tap.' Betsy could *mean* what she thought she should, just as Felix could, just as Felix was quite capable of believing – at the moment – his own wildest lies. What Betsy could not turn off so easily was her greed; and it was the greed that had showed a moment when she thought of my possible claim to the ring.

I said slowly, 'Felix is right that he is giving you that ring, but he has not told you right.' I saw Felix tense and Betsy smile with visible nervousness. 'He should say, it is for the first bride of the first son.' And *I* should of course have said simply 'the bride'. It was only my clumsy English, but as it turned out, 'the first bride' had a touch of prophecy.

Betsy blushed, unable to hide her relief. 'I guess neither of us was talking very straight, we were so – oh, I think you're a wonderful family, and I'm so happy I'm going to be one of you.'

*

119

'So what do you think of my little American?' Felix had tiptoed into my room after everyone else was in bed. I was sitting in my nightgown, brushing my hair. I did not move when he came in, I did not answer, I went on brushing. Felix took hold of my hair and pulled my head back. 'She's right, your hair is beautiful. Amazingly beautiful. It has really grown again, since your accident.'

I reached back and hit his wrist sharply with my hairbrush. Felix said, 'Bitch,' and let go, but he was still smiling, and he did not move away. 'Mitzi, answer me. What do you think?'

'What does it matter? Why do you want to know what I think?'

'Because you are the only person in this house whose opinion I value at all, except of course Grandmama's – if she were not senile. And even senile she can think better than the other three graces.'

'Well, what do you want me to think?'

'Oh, Mitzi, don't be so bloody.' He caught my hair again, and rubbed the ends of it over his mouth. In spite of everything, I felt a sudden keen twinge of desire. I said, as I would have when we were children, 'Let go, or I'll scratch your eyes out. Why don't you ask me what I think of her beautiful engagement ring?'

Felix, his hand still on my hair, said musingly, almost as if I had not spoken, 'It was like Cinderella. It fits her finger perfectly. Thank God, since I don't have the money to have it altered. Or the time.'

I got up and moved away from him. 'How long have you had it, then? Felix, Grandmama is the one person I thought you – tell me, are you never ashamed of the things you do?'

'Mitzi, you *are* a bitch. How do you know she did not give it to me, to give to my future bride? Why do you always assume the worst about everything?'

'If that had been the case, you wouldn't have made so sure that Betsy came in with it when Grandmama was tucked away for the night.'

'You are quite wrong. The senile often give things away and forget, and then get paranoid and tell everyone they've been stolen. I could not risk subjecting Betsy to such a scene. It is all very difficult for her, she's a little girl from the Middle West, suddenly thrown into this crazy decadent family – I

120

don't want things to go wrong from the beginning.' He spoke, with indignant conviction, as though Betsy were a pathetic innocent who needed *his* protection from *us*.

'Oh, Felix, all that drivel is wasted on me, and you know it. How many other things have you taken from Grandmama?' He shook his head and smiled sadly, as if pitying me for my mistrust and cynicism, then he said, 'That question is so vicious I will not even answer it. And there is no need to tell me what you think of Betsy. I'm sorry I asked you. You are cynical and misanthropic and a snob, even more cynical than the rest of them. You cannot appreciate someone fresh and unspoiled. It is not her fault that she is rich and healthy and happy, that she has never gone short of anything, that she has seen nothing of the war –' He stopped abruptly, and reached for my hair again. I pushed his hand away. 'Do you know, Mitzi, it's strange – sometimes you look like Grandmama.'

I said, 'What did you really come in here to ask me?'

He stared at me a few moments. His mouth moved as if to smile, but did not. At last he said huskily, 'How long do you think I will be able to bear it?'

'Betsy, you mean.' And I, then, did smile. 'I don't know. But I fear not long. Not very long at all.' Then I sat down again, turned my back to him and went on brushing. Felix said very softly, 'Let me do it for you, I love your hair so much,' and took the brush out of my hand. He brushed my hair neatly to one side, then I felt his mouth on the back of my neck; but I did not, that time, push him away.

Felix and Betsy were married four months later, in Bellwood, Illinois, the suburb where Betsy's family lived.

We were all, of course, invited, but could hardly afford the fare. Betsy's father did offer to pay my mother's, but what with her and Grandmama's various marriages there was something irregular in my mother's papers and she could not get a visa in time. It was difficult enough to get one for Felix. I think on the whole my mother was relieved. She knew, like me, that the débâcle would come, and she preferred not to see it coming. As long as she was not observing Felix in action, she could retain the hope that this time things would work out.

Felix sent us photographs and newspaper clippings. 'Miss Betsy Coolwell (Felix claimed later this was the Americanization of Kühlbrunnen, and that whatever old settlers her mother might stem from, Betsy's father was the son of an immigrant butcher from the slums of Frankfurt) and Count Felix von Lenauer Bilderheim-Traun were married in St Agatha's Church on Saturday. The bride wore a stunning ankle-length "little Miss Muffet" dress of white organdy with balloon sleeves, a large Peter Pan collar, and a skirt falling in three separate tiers. She carried a bouquet of pink stephanotti and white roses.' Etc. Felix, by announcing that his family was no longer allowed to use their title, had inspired the Bellwood gossip columnist to make him a Count, thus rising far higher than those timid-souled parvenus who, having no claim to any title at all, simply call themselves Baron and are stuck with it.

The Coolwells had been a trifle suspicious, a trifle chagrined, to hear that Betsy had returned William B. Chessington III's Sigma Tau Epsilon fraternity pin. It was not like their Betsy. They had been more suspicious still when Felix took so long to get a visa (with his sojourn in jail and a few other blots on his record, he must have worked wonders to get one at all).

But when Felix arrived, they were all charmed. He had the opportunist's chameleon capacity for fitting in when he tried. And he had the requisite attributes. He could drink like a fish and hold his liquor; he was obviously sporting – though he did not know their games, he could dance and ski and swim and shoot; he was 'lots of fun' and gallant with the ladies, but also displayed a keen and shrewd interest in manly talks about interest rates and the mysterious motions of the market. Felix had always been fond of money.

But there the paths diverged. Felix's hope was to finagle a decent allowance for Betsy, take on some token occupation (it was at this time he began to make faint noises about literary ambitions), possibly handle some of the family investments, and eventually live somewhere more cosmopolitan than Bellwood, Illinois. The old man, however, had other ideas. I always suspected, hearing the story later, that Coolwell was not quite as charmed as Betsy and her mother and sisters; that, since he could not fault Felix's marvellous antecedents, he was waiting for an opportunity to put his intentions to the test.

I must interject here that Coolwell Senior added no little to our own store of family entertainment. For years after the

Betsy episode, Felix would regale us with favourite maxims gleaned in those heart-to-heart, shoulder-to-shoulder, man-to-man talks over bottles of aged Kentucky Bourbon. I still remember a few. 'There's nothing like hunting and fishing, the good sporting life and everything that goes with it.' (Said benevolently to two nephews embarking on a shooting trip, in the course of which one tripped and put a bullet through the other's leg; he bled to death before they could get help.) 'Business is business, Felix, always remember that, but a little pleasure on the side never hurts.' 'A girl's just like a filly, Felix – you want to ride her with a light hand, but you want her to know who's boss.' 'Felix, never hire a man who can't look you straight in the eye.' And, more coarsely, after more Bourbon and having driven a friend of his daughter to the airport, 'Can't say I would mind breaking that little girl's cherry pie.' (This last apparently a Midwestern euphemism for deflora-tion.)

He would also, after more Bourbon, squeeze Felix's shoulder till the bones nearly cracked and say, 'I was pretty browned off when Betsy told me she was bringing home a Kraut to marry. Even though you're a Count, Felix. No one can make my Betsy any more of a Countess than she already is. But I guess you Austrians are different, you're not like the Krauts. They all go for your Viennese charm here. Well, I do too, boy, but just remember, you just go on treating my little girl like a Countess.' Then he would relax his grip and say solemnly, 'It's okay, Felix, I like you.' That particular speech seemed to me to have a distinct note of warning in it.

Felix memorized the maxims, as I have said; they became a high spot of his repertoire. But he did not heed the warning. When the honeymoon in Bermuda was over, it was time, as Coolwell said, for putting his nose to the old grindstone. 'This country's a democracy, Felix, even a Count's gotta learn a business. Starting from the bottom.' And the job his father-in-law selected for him was in (though not quite at the bottom of) the dog-food factory.

If Coolwell had guessed that learning what dog food was made of would show him what Felix was made of, he was certainly right. The dog-food factory was Felix's downfall. He would never talk about the dog-food factory, not to me, not to Joshua, not even to Werner, the writer from Salzburg who became, for a while, Felix's best friend. Whatever he saw in

123

the dog-food factory made him retch, forever after, at the sight of even so innocuous an item of canine consumption as a puppy biscuit.

Meanwhile Betsy was busy fixing up the 'darling apartment' whose rent took so much of his salary. Her father would help them buy a house 'when Felix has really settled down here'. He still gave Betsy an allowance, a fact of which he reminded Felix frequently, but all of that went on clothes and furnishings. Betsy began to nag for more; 'I'd like something to remind us of your old home. Maybe there's something your mother has from the castle, something she doesn't use, candelabra or something, that we could have here?'

Felix, desperate about his job, already bored with Betsy, suggested that maybe they should move back to Austria altogether instead of moving things from Austria to Bellwood. They could live in Salzburg, he could get some kind of job (he did not say so, but Betsy's allowance would almost have kept them), they would be poorer but they would have culture and nature and art.

Betsy dug in her heels. 'I'd have lived anywhere with you but you wanted to live in America. Now I think we should stay here for a while. Unless of course the Russians go and we have to look after your castle. And remember, you've got to get your citizenship.'

'Yes,' said Felix, now out of control, 'I wanted to live in America, but not in a soulless suburb, spending my days overseeing a lot of stinking tripe running through machines.'

It was a serious quarrel, and that night Felix left Betsy weeping into the orange linen cushions on their new studio couch, and went out to a party with some of the 'boys' he had met in Betsy's crowd. He drank rather too much, insulted or was insulted, and ended by pushing someone's head into an aquarium filled with rare and expensive tropical fish. This did not endear him either to the owner of the head or the owners of the aquarium, especially as a good many of the fish spilled out and did not survive. Still, the 'boys' were all heavy drinkers, and Felix had taken the precaution of telling, at his wedding reception, legends of the fabulous tempers of the Bilderheim-Trauns when their noble blood was slighted. With patience and tact, he might have won forgiveness. But Felix had no patience left. And as always when circumstance or his own greedy calculations put him into a situation he then found untenable, the demons took over and brought the whole card house down.

I do not know exactly what Felix did next. Some of this story comes from Joshua, who attended the wedding and whom Felix turned to for help when Betsy's family threatened him later with a criminal charge; some of it from Felix himself. According to Felix, he gave Betsy an ultimatum; he could not stand the factory another day, so either they made a start somewhere else (which her family would have to finance as Felix was still penniless) or he left alone. Then there was a family scene, involving Betsy's parents, in the course of which Felix lost his temper completely. Among other things (Joshua said) he rushed to the kitchen, snatched a plate from Flopsy, the bewildered family spaniel, and flung its contents at a large sombre portrait of Mrs William Harley Dumoulin II, who was Mrs Coolwell's aunt. He then cut a swathe of destruction through the Coolwell mansion on his way out, pursued by the barking spaniel and Betsy's father brandishing a bird-gun. And after that, he took refuge with Joshua.

Felix persuaded Joshua that it was all – well, nearly all – *their* fault. He had been terribly in love, he had not bargained for the family business, the family social life, the cultural wasteland of Bellwood, Illinois. He had visualized an America of grand canyons, giant redwoods, and unlimited dreams, and his vision had ended in the dog-food factory. He was still willing to *take Betsy back* (italics mine) if she would agree to live in Austria or anywhere else that he could bear. For instance, the Bermudas, where they had spent their honeymoon. 'It is the frightful temper of the Bilderheim-Trauns – I know, I should not have given way to it. But I was drunk, I was desperate. And now they want to have my head. I need a lawyer – a very good lawyer. Oh Joshua, can you help me?'

Joshua, dear, reserved, academic Joshua, who had grown up in this same 'cultural wasteland', not a hundred miles from Bellwood, and had hated this wasteland as passionately as he admired European civilization and all it stood for (overlooking, of course, the recent lapse into a Dark Age) – Joshua was a pushover. He had loved all of us at sight. And like many of those good-hearted souls who may cherish dreams of violent action but never indulge them unless truly beside themselves, who while not quite colourless are hardly colourful, who resent authority and convention but seldom really flout them, Joshua would do anything for so flamboyant a friend as my brother. Joshua's family were modest middle-class people who never appeared in the gossip columns. He had been snubbed by girls like Betsy who hardly knew the names of the poets from whom Joshua could recite by heart; he had done menial summer jobs, when a student, for men like her father. He if anyone could appreciate that red face emerging from the tropical fish tank, a strand of algae dangling from one battered ear, and the family portrait splattered with ARF. (He remembered the radio commercials, Joshua said: 'Get your dog ARF and he'll say it. ARF's the best friend for a man's best friend.')

In the end, it was all settled out of court. To save themselves the disgrace of a criminal case and a jailbird son-in-law, the Coolwells would not prosecute Felix if he agreed to a quiet Reno divorce and would then at once leave the country and not show his face in Bellwood, Illinois, ever again. The lawyer Joshua got him advised Felix to accept. Felix wanted a cash settlement. The Coolwells were outraged – the damage to their house, they claimed, totalled hundreds of dollars – these were their final terms and if they were not accepted, Felix would be charged with assault and wilful destruction of property. They did, however, also offer him a plane ticket home. Joshua and the lawyer urged Felix to sign, and this time he did.

A few weeks later, he was back again, sitting in the kitchen gulping down a great slice of Trudi's best marble cake, regaling us with his adventures in America. 'Dear God,' he said at the end of a long recital of his mishaps, 'Why didn't you stop me? You must have known.' With dramatic emphasis, 'How could you consent to let a Count von Lenauer Bilderheim-Traun marry the daughter of a dog-food manufacturer?'

'We did not have very much to say about it,' my mother answered drily, as if he were serious. 'Besides one always hopes against hope that your crazy ideas will work.' She sighed. She was happy to see Felix (as we all were, in spite of ourselves); she would have been much happier still to see him less often but well and wealthily settled in the country of his ambitions. Felix however declared he had given those ambitions up for good.

'I was wrong. Before I went, I saw it all with the eyes of the

little orphan boy standing out in the dark and cold, looking through the lighted window . . .' I observed that it was
hard to imagine him in that role, but he paid no attention.
'. . . the little orphan boy, who has no idea what hard awful
people might live inside the lighted house. You can't imagine it – those endless drunken parties, driving from house to
house until you're too blind to see where the car is going,
women in low dresses spilling whiskey on their breasts, old
men with baby faces telling dirty jokes in corners; not one real
witticism, not one intelligent word . . . and those old baby
faces, brought up on processed pap (Felix really had it in for
the food industry), not even proper mother's milk, are running
the world. It makes me sick to think of it. Oh, I know,
there are others, ones like Joshua – but Joshua too, in the
Middle West, is a lost soul. He's coming soon, did he write
you? He's doing a thesis on Hans Handelbein and I said I
would see if there was anything interesting among Grandmama's papers. He'll stay with us for a while of course, I told
him he must do so. Joshua is an angel, he saved my life . . .'
He cut himself another slice of cake, and went on, a bit wistfully now, 'I do wish I'd seen more of the West Coast. It's
beautiful, the Pacific. Now there maybe I could live . . . But I
think the Coolwells will make it hard for me to go back. No,
it's goodbye America. At least for a while. Well, at least I
have learned something.'

I said quietly, 'I'm sure they have too.'

Felix grinned. 'Darling Mitzi. You always want to wound
me, even when I'm down. Well, maybe I deserve it this time.
You didn't like that goose of a girl, and you were right.'

'So,' said my mother, 'now the great American adventure is
over, what do you intend to do next?'

'I am not sure,' answered Felix musingly. 'But you know, I
have always had a secret wish . . . I think I would like to do
something literary. I talk everything away, that's the trouble
– but maybe I will try, seriously, to write.'

Embarking on this literary life, Felix spent much time in
Salzburg drinking with his friend Werner, and occasionally
Werner came to stay with us. Werner was tall, gangly and
stooped, with shaggy dark hair, steel-rimmed glasses and a
bemused, sleepy face. His hands would have been beautiful,
had the nails not been bitten down to the quick. He was as

shabby and negligent of dress as Felix, within his means, was elegant. Felix said he had nearly starved during the war, and he certainly had the most voracious appetite of anyone I have ever seen. I called him – not to his face of course – the '*Hungerkünstler* in retirement', referring to Kafka's story about a 'Hunger Artist', a man whose circus speciality is fasting unto death. My mother called him 'Felix's genius' and would add sourly, 'I only hope he is a good genius. Of evil genius Felix has enough in himself.'

'No more Salzburg Summer Seminar?' Berti would say to Felix with her weighty jocularity, and Felix would answer, 'Not that. Not ever again.' Then once, to me, 'Oh, Mitzi! If you could meet that little half-French, half-English girl I talked to on the train – now there was someone I could love, and you would too, someone sensitive and artistic, someone with what Grandmama would call an *elegant* soul . . . As soon as I can, I will go to visit her. Or send her the money to come here. If only she doesn't meet someone else.' They were already corresponding. 'I can't do with the girls around here any more, they are almost as stupid as Betsy, nothing in their heads but sports and money, even if they don't have it.' I refrained from commenting that, stupid as they were, they frequently kept him out all night, and Werner, who was there too that time, smiled to himself and said nothing.

It was curious, in fact, how little Werner said, considering that when he was *not* there, Felix was always quoting him or quoting Werner quoting Nietzsche or Goethe or Wittgenstein. 'After America,' Felix would say loftily, 'it is marvellous to be with a truly cultured person.'

I waited, during Werner's visits, for evidence of this supreme *Bildung*. But except for the requisite polite chit-chat with the older ladies of the house, Werner remained veiled in his smiling, ambiguous silence. Sometimes he would pick up a book I was reading, look at the title or even leaf through it, and put it down again without a word.

'Do you know that? And if so, what do you think of it?' I asked irritably, the third time he did this to me.

'Inconsequential.' Werner shook his head, still smiling.

'Why?' I was more irritated still.

Werner shook his head again. 'It is not the book,' he said gravely. 'Women should not read. They are the vessels of intuitive knowledge, the mothers of the earth, the guardians

128

of our racial wisdom.' It was the longest speech I had heard him make.

'If you are serious, Felix must be equally mad – even madder than he usually is – to respect your intelligence. Is that what you learned in school, during the Nazi times?'

Werner looked crestfallen, and became very formal. 'Never, *Gnädiges Fraülein*. I wanted to pay you a compliment, but you have taken offence. Forgive me.'

'I can't forgive the thought, if that's what you really think.'

'It would be equally unforgivable, would it not,' said Werner eagerly, 'to have said it if I did not think it. Because that would imply that you could only be flattered by referring to those qualities which indicate an absence of rational thought. And that in itself would be to accuse you of an even greater inability for rational thinking. So it would come to the same thing, and more. Unless, of course, I were to have said it only to provoke the kind of discussion in which we are now engaged.'

'In which *you* are now engaged, *mein Herr*.'

'Ah yes. But if I said it only for the purpose of provoking this discussion, whether with you or myself, does it change the semantic quality of the statement? It must do. Said as a provocation, the statement implies its opposite. Yet the words are exactly the same. So we have proved that it is only context that determines the ultimate meaning of any statement.'

'No. You are confusing meaning and purpose. The words mean the same, only you do not mean them in the same way.'

'Ah,' said Werner, his face lighting up, 'you have seen that. How marvellous. You are absolutely right, of course.'

'Was it another test then, your saying that?'

'No. Because in fact I must go back a little on that last remark. *Is* there an absolute meaning to any word, a meaning independent of context? Context is use, is it not, and if they are not used, can words exist at all? Unless of course we believe that they are entities in the mind of God.'

This went on for some time. At the end of it Werner seemed exhausted and I was still irritated, and we parted company amicably but no better friends than before. Felix said to me, when we were alone, 'Don't mind Werner. That is his way of flirting. He likes you a lot and he thinks you are extremely clever.'

'Thanks, Felix, but I'm not at all sure I can say the same

129

about him. What does Werner actually write? How does this genius, which you keep talking about, manifest itself?'

'Werner writes everything. Poetry, philosophy, plays – but he has not found his true medium yet. He wants to do something really avant-garde, like the new French writers.'

'Well, I wish him luck. I also wish he could carry on a normal conversation. I mean other than telling Trudi and Berti that it rained this morning, which we all know. (Thinking about it, I wondered if Werner's little weather reports were not also very deliberate and tongue in cheek.) Are you and Werner plotting some kind of masterpiece together?'

'We are thinking about it, in fact. Oh, Mitzi, you are so cynical and so negative! I know it is hard for you, cooped up here with the old women, but . . . when you have a chance to see someone of your own kind, you should not turn away so immediately.'

'You telling me not to be cynical! You sound like Kropetschka telling you to get a job. Or Betsy's father.'

'That is unworthy of you. And not true. I really thought you might like Werner, he is such a gentle person. I have seen him cry over the death of a bird. You will not meet many such people. I worry about you, Mitzi. You should do something to get out of this place.'

'You never worry about anyone except yourself. And what do you suggest I do? I haven't even got my *Matura* yet.' I was going doggedly back to school, and finding the work and the students easier, if hardly enjoyable.

'It's you who are getting like our elders, thinking that idiotic *Matura* will make such a difference in your life. Well, anyway, Joshua is coming in a month. That should open up all sorts of possibilities.'

'What do you mean by that?' I asked suspiciously.

'Well – you know what Werner says about words. I mean only what I have said.' He ran a hand through my hair. 'Not, Mitzi, nasty though you are, that I want you to leave here, as long as I am trapped here myself.'

Grandmama had taken a turn for the worse. She was incontinent now, and no longer even tried to get out of her wheelchair. None of us was good at nursing and Grandmama was even more irritable and impatient then before, as if blaming

130

us for being witness to her humiliation. 'She never liked any of us, except maybe you, Mitzi,' my mother said resignedly. 'She would actually be better with a stranger.'

There was no question of sending Grandmama away; but what we needed now was another Janka, preferably with nursing experience. There were still many Eastern refugees desperate for jobs, and willing to work for a modest salary and their keep. My mother, Trudi and Berti pooled their meagre funds; then several girls came for interviews. 'Real slatternly Slavs,' Felix said disgustedly, having seen one or two scurry out after being grilled by his three graces, who were nothing if not thorough.

I always suspected that Trudi and Berti and my mother picked the ugliest, with an eye to avoiding complications with Felix, who was not above exercising seigneurial rights in a bored moment. She had what we all thought of as a typical Slavic face; long narrow nose, high cheekbones, and that oddly curled mouth that looks bitter even when it is smiling. Small wonder, when century upon century of invaders have ridden over you.

My elders may also have chosen her for her height and sturdy figure; she would be able to lift Grandmama with ease. She claimed to have done some nursing in Yugoslavia during the war, and could cook and sew and iron. And, said my mother with a sigh, falling back immediately into pre-war habits, into the tones which those accustomed to keeping servants always use for discussing them, 'I have made careful inquiries; she has worked in town before, and no one has yet reported that she steals.'

Caring for Grandmama was not a full-time job, so it was clear that Gordana Probitz would be a general factotum, and everyone's lives would be easier. And indeed they were. Gordana was a good housekeeper, although, as Trudi said, 'she has no feeling for the quality of objects. A Meissen vase or a chamberpot, it is all the same to her. A peasant through and through. But I think a decent soul.' And Berti, even more atavistically, 'She can hardly read and write, but that is all to the good.'

True, Gordana had her drawbacks. When she menstruated she lay in bed and groaned agonized groans for three days. We were all quite frightened, the first time it happened. She was fluffing out a pillow on Grandmama's bed when she suddenly collapsed, clutching her stomach, tears and sweat pouring down her face. After that, there was not an articulate sound to be got from her until the doctor came. He gave her some pills, and urged her not to be so hysterical. When she could speak, she told us that during her first period, 'My wicked cousin told my father I had been found with a boy, which was a lie of course, but he tied me to the bedpost and beat me until I screamed for mercy, and I have had these terrible pains every month ever since.' This scene was repeated every month, but as Gordana was so efficient the rest of the time my family put up with it, though Trudi and Berti and my mother all thought she was malingering. 'The Slavs,' Trudi said callously, 'always have fathers who tie them to the bedpost and beat them. How often I have heard this story! It is quite normal.' And Berti would lecture Gordana: 'You cannot be having such cramps, because this is a natural function. No animal has menstrual pains.' Only people as mixed as the Austrians can be so conscious and contemptuous of neighbouring racial stock. It was sometimes all I could do not to recall to my elders Mama's liaison with Kropetschka. Once I did, at very much the wrong moment, and she flared up and did not speak to me for two days – until she realized that, far from being upset, I was basking in the bliss of her silence.

Moreover, Gordana cried very easily and rather loudly. And when anyone would listen, she would tell her wartime horror stories. Gordana's village had been Royalist and *Volksdeutsch*, and her horror stories were not about the SS but about the Partisans. I did listen at first, in sick and horrified sympathy. But there was something about the relish and drama with which Gordana ran through her catalogue of mediaeval atrocities that made me feel she would play them for all she could get, and whereas I knew such things had happened, I doubted she had witnessed them all herself, as she claimed. Now I would perhaps think, why not use them, the girl was poor and unattractive and alone, one uses one's sufferings as one uses one's gifts, it is only human. But at nineteen I was still the absolutist who had jumped off a twenty-foot wall and there was something about Gordana's manner, at once obsequious and familiar, naïve and sly, that made me wary of her. And then again, just because I was wary, I was afraid I had been infected by my family's prejudices and often leaned over backwards to be nice to her.

That too was the puritanism of youth; when and if one becomes mature one accepts or rejects people regardless of whether they fit, probably quite fortuitously, a common stereotype.

VII

That next summer – 'At last, at last!' his letter said – Joshua arrived.

I had forgotten how tall he was, and for such a tall person, how self-effacing. I can still picture him entering our house, as I can picture Betsy; Joshua in a new English tweed suit, bought in London on the way, and with a new bushy beard which he mentioned embarrassedly himself before any of us could; Joshua, his eyes shining, wanting to hug us all but not daring –Americans were much less demonstrative in those days, it was considered unmanly – shaking our hands with both of his until a surge of shyness made him abruptly release them. He kept saying in his now much better but still accented German, his voice hoarse with feeling, 'I am so glad – it has been so long – but how are you – I want to hear about everything, everything . . .' He noticed at once that the piano, which had not been moved back since Felix's rearrangements for Betsy, was now in a different place. He remembered everything about the house, the garden, the town, as if his few weeks with us had been the most beautiful and momentous of his life. Dearest Joshua! I still cannot feel pity for Betsy, nor some other of Felix's willing victims, but Joshua did not deserve us, Joshua at least should have been spared, should not have been allowed to stray, so confused and good and guileless, into that elaborate criss-crossed web.

Later that afternoon, after Joshua had unpacked and given presents all around, he and I walked alone together around the garden. His pace constantly quickened in his excitement at being in 'this magical little garden' again, and then he would remember my leg, and slow himself down, and apologize, until I burst out laughing and said, 'We must make the most ridiculous pair, you starting to run all the time and me limping. Why don't you just go round me in circles – would that be easier?'

It was said without any malice at all, but I saw at once from his expression that I had hurt and humiliated him. Dear God, these Americans; one could not put a foot right – I thought of the English saying, and then laughed again, thinking how apt it was if one took the literal meaning, and then as I had to explain this laughter, in despair told Joshua. He laughed too then, but he was still wary. I looked down at the pansy bed and said, casting about for conversation, 'Isn't it funny – in German we call them stepmothers, and you call them pansies. Ours must be because they have stepmother-like faces, but I've never seen the resemblance. Does the word pansy mean anything?' Joshua said, 'No – nothing that applies . . .' and looked even more embarrassed, more tense than before. What on earth had I done now?

We had both looked forward for years to this meeting. And now we were pacing stupidly around the garden, at a loss for words, already misunderstanding each other. How strange and vulnerable he was, without the uniform in which I had last seen him! Again in despair, I decided to throw my reserve to the winds and break through his, to make up for whatever hurt I had innocently inflicted.

'Joshua – I may have written you something like this, but I want to say it too. Your letters and the books you sent – they were like a light in the darkness. I cannot ever tell you how grateful I am.' He still said nothing. I went on, falteringly, 'Maybe because we have both thought a lot about seeing each other, it's difficult now . . . because of our letters, we expect not to be strangers at all, but of course in some ways we are . . .' This was terrible, this was making it still worse. 'I mean – when you look forward to something for so long, maybe the very anticipation makes barriers which should not be there.' For a moment, I thought of Stefan, of what I would feel were Stefan to appear and walk around this garden with me, even if it were in another five, another ten, another hundred years, and had to stop speaking.

Joshua cleared his throat. 'I know. I am glad you have said

135

it. Oh, Mitzi – I don't know whether to talk to you in English or German – your English is so good now. But I will use English, just for this, though I have promised myself to speak only German here. Dear Mitzi, you've been through so much these last years. I cannot compare my life to yours. When I think of yours I realize that mine has always been easy –'

'You were a soldier,' I said. 'You were in the war.'

Joshua answered, with a curious bitterness, 'Yes, but nothing happened to me. Except that armies are difficult places for sensitive souls. But that kind of problem means nothing when you think of what others have been through.'

'But we were lucky too, during the war. There were no bombs, the Gestapo left us alone, the Russians did not come. And I think suffering is a question of what you as an individual *feel*, not only what happens to you.'

'Yes, I suppose it is. But what I want to say to you is that *your* letters were a light in darkness for *me*, even if I have no right to say that such a darkness was there. And that I have been a comfort of that sort to you – well, that is, I think an even greater light in my darkness.'

'You worry too much, I think, about what rights you have to feel certain things. What you feel is your truth. No one can tell you,' I added with some passion, thinking again of Stefan, 'that your feelings are trivial, that they do not count.'

Joshua said gravely, 'Thank you, Mitzi,' as if I had just given him some kind of absolution. Then, after a brief hesitation, he went on. 'You see, there are places in the world which constitute a kind of darkness in themselves, where people are starved for spiritual sustenance as elsewhere they are starved for bread, only most of them are not aware of the starvation. Did I ever send you that book of Willa Cather's – or Lewis's *Main Street* . . . you have to imagine a life without any kind of grace or polish or elegance, where the only heroes are baseball players . . . it's as hard for you to imagine that as it is for me being really hungry. That is the kind of place I come from. And that of course is not all I'm talking about when I talk of darkness, but a large part of it – a cultural narrowness, a sterile climate where everything individual or eccentric or slightly out of the conventional morality is strangled at birth.'

I could not help saying, 'We didn't have much grace or elegance here, during the war. And all the culture in the world did not stop the Nazis.'

He was immediately apologetic again; but one thing I was to learn about Joshua was that he was never as self-effacing, as deferential, as he first seemed. He would apologize wildly for an idea, but never really let go of it. 'I know, I know. I am talking out of turn again. But you said – didn't you – that we only know our own sufferings, we only know what we feel ourselves.' I wasn't quite sure I had said that exactly, but I let it go. 'And I know that growing up where I did, the way I did, in that desert of respectability where God is a Puritan and Mammon is God – I'm sorry, I'm quoting myself. I'm quoting something I wrote. That's a terrible habit. I must not let myself do it.'

'It's all right. Why not quote yourself? It sounds quite good.'

'Thank you for being so patient. Where was I? Yes. Growing up without the things that you and your kind take for granted – if one is drawn to them as I was – well, I think it is a form of starvation. You are never quite the person you might have been.'

'Joshua, I understand, but I'm afraid some of this is illusion. My schoolmates do not spend their spare time reading Goethe and making chamber music, any more than yours did. If you knew more people here, you might not think what you think now.'

'Mitzi, that doesn't matter – it is all *there*. It's in the very air you breathe. It can never not be. It can never be something foreign and far away and regarded with contempt. None of you I think could ever adjust to living where Felix tried to live. That's why I understood right away when Felix couldn't stand it and went a bit berserk. I was so glad to be able to help Felix, because you all mean so much to me.'

'And we are eternally grateful,' I said somewhat in spite of myself, matching his odd formality. 'But I'm not sure Felix really tried to adjust. Felix – Felix goes berserk quite easily. It wasn't –' I looked at his young serious face. An ascetic's face, I thought, all planes and shadows. It is true what he says about himself, he has the face of someone deprived. Or, more strangely, of someone almost searching for deprivation, someone made to be hurt. How well did he know Felix? He was so starry-eyed about all of us – would it be kind or unkind, wise or unwise, to disillusion him a little? 'It was not the grand passion of Felix's life. It was what I think you call a *mariage de raison*.'

137

'Ah, now *that* is true of girls like Betsy,' Joshua said. 'They usually make what is in fact a *mariage de raison*, whatever romantic hodge-podge they build up around it. The boys I knew at college used to say, when a girl had what they call her "coming-out party", that there was another one up for bids in the marriage market. But about Felix, I think you're wrong. I think Felix, from everything he told me, was really in love, though he may not have begun that way, though he may even have denied it to himself. And that's why he had to break out of the situation with so much violence. I think Felix likes to put up an aggressive and cynical front to hide his own sensitivity.'

Had I, at that time, seen more of the Anglo-Saxon academic world, I would have guessed at once that Joshua had studied not only literature and languages but psychology. Nothing except the social sciences can lead to such blinkered and inverted views of human nature, making it possible to be totally mistaken and delude oneself that one is seeing not only truth but an *inner* truth, the secret hidden behind the façade.

'Is that how it looks to you? I knew myself the marriage wouldn't work, and I am so glad you helped Felix, but I don't believe Felix is quite as you think him.'

'Oh, I know Felix can be very hard at times, but you see, I know – I also understand – what is underneath the hardness. And without Felix the world would be a much more boring place. I am sure you think that too.' I nodded. I could hardly do anything else. 'I feel very close to Felix, Mitzi, as I do to you ... though you and I are much more alike, we are both delicate plants, we draw into ourselves when the world is too much with us, or against us. But I, like Felix, was educated by Jesuits and have learned a certain kind of casuistry ...'

'Felix didn't spend much time with the Jesuits – and I'm not sure what that word means.'

'Oh, Mitzi, I am sorry – your English is so good I keep forgetting that you can't possibly know all the words that I use – and I meant to speak only German! Casuistry is sophistry – but you won't know that either. Ah, I remember now. It's the same word – *Kasuistik*. Dear Mitzi, you said such a lovely thing to me, and I went on from that to talk about myself and the dark patches of my soul and Felix and everything except what I wanted to talk about, which is you.' Thank God, he was being a little lighter now. 'I want to hear everything about the last few years, or at least everything that you can bear to tell me –'

My mother called us in then, and we went back to the house, I a bit puzzled as to what we had, in fact, been saying to each other. And the way the three graces, as Felix referred to them, gazed at us when we came in should have told me at once that a thought which had never occurred to me was already lodged quite firmly in their heads.

This conversation may be a composite of several actual ones, but it does give the flavour of Joshua's talk, that odd combination of obliqueness and passion, humility and intellectual arrogance; *but you see, I know*, was one of his favourite phrases. I want to make it clear that Joshua was not simply a capital example of American innocence faced with European experience, a Jamesian lamb ready for slaughter. He was more complex than that, more self-driven, and the shadows I saw on his face were real. Whatever else, I think he was innocent with regard to *us*, innocent and good. Or was he? Was there not something snobbish and unhealthy in his almost voracious devotion to our culture, our company? This is what I find terrible about getting people down on paper. New doubts spring up everywhere in the process, the firm and cherished outlines blur. No, my fanatical search for what are, after all, only approximations to truth is getting the better of me again. Perhaps the only really innocent friendships are those few where need is entirely absent; which would mean, paradoxically, the friendships based on caprice.

For our first dinner with Joshua, Gordana made a paprika chicken, and served us all like a proper maid, polite and smiling, her cheeks shining like polished apples, a crisp white apron over her plain cotton *Dirndl*, and garnet ear-rings I had not seen before dangling from her prominent ears. She told me later that they were her only good ones, 'and I wanted to put them on because you were all so excited about this visit'. When our plates were full, she sat down and fed Grandmama, who often refused to eat now and had become even thinner; there was something alarmingly fledgling-like about her neck and the way she opened her mouth. Gordana was gentle and patient and efficient, but whenever I watched her ministrations, I felt how terrible it must be for my proud grandmother to be so helpless, and wished for her sake that she could die.

Felix was in Salzburg with Werner that week; he was working intermittently as a courier that summer, and supposedly he and Werner were embarking on their literary project together. Trudi and my mother teased Joshua about being the only man among all these women. 'If you were Paris,' said my mother, with the dreadful middle-aged coyness that always made me cringe, 'to whom would you give the golden apple?'

'To the Countess, of course,' said Joshua smiling awkwardly and carefully not looking in my direction. I thought; he is as embarrassed about all this as I am. I looked at Gordana and Grandmama again, bathed in that La Tour candlelight our six-branched baroque candelabra cast over them, Grandmama dark and gaunt, her eyes half-closed, her mouth opening blindly in that dreadful bird-like way, and Gordana, the light catching her garnets, her deep brown eyes, the silver of the spoon she was holding – in the wrong place, near Grandmama's ear, as the deep brown eyes were riveted on Joshua's face. I said sharply, 'Gordana! Do look at what you're doing!' and then hated myself for it because I sounded like my mother. Gordana started and moved the spoon, which clicked against Grandmama's teeth. Grandmama drew back and said firmly, 'I do not want anything,' then, turning to me, 'Do you remember, Mitzi, when they brought him in? He was wearing a white shirt and there was so much blood.'

'Just a little bit, my darling,' coaxed Gordana, raising the spoon again.

'Don't make her eat, please,' I said as mildly as I could now, 'if she doesn't want to.'

Joshua looked solicitously at the old lady, then said, 'But she still recognizes you. My grandfather, at the end, did not even know where he was. Sometimes he thought he was on the farm where he lived as a boy, and he was afraid the Yankees were coming – that was in the South . . .'

'She only recognizes us sometimes,' I said.

'Does she still talk about her youth? What was it about the shirt and the blood? I seem to remember that story. It was when the Count duelled with the brother of his former fiancée – am I right?'

My mother answered wearily, 'No one is sure. There was also a suicide – more than one. One was on the Riviera –'

Trudi put in, 'No, I thought she went to the Riviera *because* of that scandal. There was a writer who shot himself. I was a child of course and we were in Berlin so I do not remember much of the story.'

'No, you are wrong, Trudi,' from Berti. 'You are thinking of the poet Handelbein. He died of tuberculosis.'

'Perhaps that was why there was so much blood,' Joshua said musingly. 'He might have been haemorrhaging. Oh, I am sorry! What a dreadful conversation for the dinner table!' He turned to me. 'But it is fascinating, isn't it – when someone gives you such glimpses of the past, and you can only try to piece them together. I remember that with my grandfather. What marvellous stories the Countess must have told you when she was younger. Did anyone ever write them down?'

Maria Aurora said suddenly, 'Not Countess. Not any more,' and opened her mouth wide, as if for the spoon, then shut it again.

'She never told any of us very much,' said my mother. 'And I myself lived with her very little when I was a child. She parked me with nurses, and went off somewhere, usually I think with a man. That is what I remember best about my childhood, tall male figures going up and down stairs, chamois gloves and ebony canes in the hallway. Most of what I know is rumour and gossip that came to me from other people. I remember once after she arrived here – I had not seen her for years, I did not expect to see her again – Mitzi or Felix once asked her something and she said, "I don't know any more. If one lives as much as I have, one has very few memories. They crowd each other out."'

'I find all this amazing, *Gnädige Frau*. You never told me before about your own childhood – and your saying you did not expect to see your mother again – well, it's the kind of thing one can hardly believe of a European family. I always thought we Americans take family relationships very casually compared to Europeans.'

'We were hardly a normal family,' my mother said.

I could not resist adding, 'Nor are we now.'

My mother gave me one of her sharp but slightly guilty looks, which I always read as: I know poor Mitzi is crippled, but sometimes she is hard to bear. 'Well, we do our best,' my mother said.

'I think normal or not, you are the most marvellous of families.'

Joshua's effusiveness made me blush, so I turned the conversation back to Grandmama. 'I used to look at some of Grandmama's trinkets and I think she did tell me where they came from, and the stories attached, but I never really listened, I was so fascinated by the things themselves. It's true of course they had histories, and the histories continue. One at least is now in America.' My mother cleared her throat, and this time gave me a distinctly warning glance. I couldn't help myself; Joshua was simply too enraptured with us all. 'Anyway, you see, we hardly know that much about Grandmama ourselves - except maybe Felix. She always liked him best and talked to him most.'

'I shall make a point of asking him,' said Joshua. 'And most especially about Handelbein.' He watched Grandmama to see if the name brought any response. Grandmama, who was folding and unfolding the napkin in her lap and humming to herself, turned suddenly to my mother and said, indicating Trudi and Berti, 'But who are they, Anna? You never tell me who they are.' Then to Gordana, 'Janka, I want my shawl now. No, I know you are not Janka, nor are you Paula whom I had when I was young. But you will have to do. We all have to sacrifice something. But for what? That is what I would like to know.'

'Well,' said my mother, 'that is more than she has talked in days. Gordana, I think she has finished eating, and you can take her upstairs.'

Joshua, a little tipsy by now, raised his glass. 'I drink to the Countess, and to you all. You will never know what it means to me to be here. Ah, there – I have not even looked at the bottle, and I knew at once it was a *Grüner Veltliner*. You see, there are so many things that I remember. That, like this evening, I will remember all my life.'

In the days that followed, Joshua and I spent a great deal of time together. We walked in the woods and the hills behind the town – I could do that now, if I went slowly. We sat or strolled in the garden, and spent rainy days by the kitchen fire, while the living room was occupied by my mother and her pupils. We talked easily now and endlessly, discussing ideas, politics, the war, the past and the future, the books we had read and the books we wanted to read. I gave up trying to hint that my beautiful home, my Imperial resort on a glacier-fed river, might be in its own very different way as spiritually arid as Joshua's despised Middle West. Some instinct told me it would be cruel, as well as probably futile, to challenge Joshua's cherished illusions; and besides, it might never be arid for him. Joshua was quite capable of going to a local *Weinstube*, hearing a group of old Nazis singing a war song together, and coming back full of enthusiasm for our marvellous jocular folk music. He had been inoculated with the idea many of my countrymen have ardently promulgated, that it was basically all the Prussians anyway and the music-loving, humane, artistic Austrians only had the New Order imposed upon them by force of arms.

I broached the subject of my going to America to study. 'In university, there couldn't be the cultural wasteland you talk about.'

'But it's an island,' Joshua said, 'completely out of the mainstream –'

'We're hardly in the mainstream here. And I would love that feeling of freedom and space and – *possibilities*. It is there. Even Felix said so. And whatever American education is, the universities must be more exciting than here. I know that from what you sent me. And after all, most of our best minds – Freud, Einstein, Thomas Mann, for instance – have gone to the English-speaking world.'

Joshua answered seriously, 'Yes, Mitzi, I think you're right. I think you should go. And maybe we could even get something more done for your leg. You could get a Fulbright scholarship, maybe, or . . .' He coloured and did not go on. Then after a pause, 'You know, we are so funny, we two, we are like the Jewish joke about the two old friends who cross the Atlantic right after the end of the war, one emigrating to America, the other going back home, and as the two ocean liners pass, they just have time to yell, both of them, at the top of their voices, *"Bist du meshugge?"* (Are you out of your mind?)'

Then Felix returned from Salzburg with Werner and I was, at least temporarily, eclipsed in Joshua's eyes.

Not that I minded. It was great entertainment, watching the three of them. Werner and Joshua took to each other at once. Joshua had the patience for Werner's philosophical and semantic peregrinations. ('Tell me, Joshua, if a myth is a collective dream, and I am sure you will not deny that, is an

143

individual dream an individual myth?' And similar questions, ad infinitum.) And Werner, who in his desultory fashion was also working on a doctorate, proved an inexhaustible source of knowledge about the vanished intellectual Vienna Joshua loved and was writing about. Felix, like me, mostly sat back and smiled during their ardent discussions, but there was something in *his* smile I did not entirely like or understand.

But whatever the undertones, we had a glorious time together. We meandered for hours along the river banks, past the ornate villas asleep in their tangled gardens. We fed the swans, and Joshua treated us all to *Eiskaffee* on the promenade, where the *Conditorei* now had tables outside with white wrought-iron chairs and orange umbrellas. On our third day together, we walked up the *Calvarienberg*, the Hill of Calvary so common on the outskirts of Austrian towns. Our particular one had grisly late baroque Stations of the Cross, which I had always hated. I had not been here since my accident, and I shuddered, just as I had when a child, at the painted peeling body of Christ lying in Mary's lap, with its deep crimson tracks of blood running from under the thorny crown across the death-contorted face. Joshua said gravely, 'It reminds me of my Catholic education, that terrible sense of sin and atonement, that paying for everything with innocent blood.'

'They are nothing but local kitsch, these statues,' Felix said contemptuously, 'they are not good enough to evoke anything. It just makes the local proletariat feel virtuous to walk up here on Sunday with their snotty kids.'

'You are quite wrong.' Werner's voice was as serious as Joshua's. 'It is not proletarian kitsch, it is true peasant Expressionism. The very soul of our country people lies in these disgusting statues.'

'But it was not peasants who carved them,' Joshua said, and they were off again. I limped behind, enjoying the sunshine, the green of the leaves, the peaceful glimpses of town and hills and river at every gap in the trees. I was closer to happiness than I had been in what seemed a very long time. Except for my days at school, I had become almost a recluse since my accident, and except for my abortive meetings with Helene and her friends before I knew Stefan, I had never been out with a group of young people. And I must admit I was not sorry to be the only woman among them. After years of girls' schools, and my lonely life in a mostly female household,

144

with Joshua as my long-distance intellectual companion and no one I could talk to as I could write to him . . . well, perhaps I was a bit like Joshua, perhaps I had been as starved for outings in male company as he felt starved for Gothic churches and chamber music and parks with Classical fauns (yes, I know why I have chosen that last, and that it reflects not Joshua's hunger, but mine).

With Joshua and Gordana both in the house, Trudi and Berti had to share a room again, as in the time of the Schweissers, while Felix and Werner slept on the glassed-in veranda that was the one twentieth-century addition to our house, uncomfortably surrounded by Berti's potted greenery. As the days went by, Joshua began to worry that he was overstaying his welcome. 'Are you certain you are not too crowded? I could go to Salzburg earlier.' He had been planning to stay for a month.

'No, no,' my mother answered. 'Felix and Werner are only going to be here another day or two. Please, you have been so good to us. Don't worry about it.'

I realized, although she did not, that this was the wrong answer if she really wanted him to stay. Joshua was much too sensitive and insecure to remain with us if he thought our hospitality inspired by a sense of obligation. When two more days went by and Felix and Werner were still there and showed no intention of going, Joshua insisted again that he was imposing and should leave. He said this at dinner, looking briefly at my mother, then alternately at his plate and at me.

I found this curious, as I had hardly talked to him alone since Werner's and Felix's arrival. Everyone chorused that he must stay. My own invitation was as warm as I could make it, and I did want him to stay, of course; but I liked it best when Felix and Werner were there too. Joshua's intensity, when I had to cope with it alone, had begun to make me uncomfortable. It was as if he had really been starved for culture, as he said, just as Werner had been starved for food; and the rapacity of the appetite, in both cases, made one shrink a little.

Joshua said, his voice almost breaking with emotion, 'Well, then, I will stay,' and we all cheered and raised our glasses.

Werner and Felix stayed too, and we continued to explore the countryside together. Felix took us to places even I had never seen before. Felix knew everything; the obscure inn on the branch-line railway which had a thousand-year-old tree in its garden, with a hollow trunk and a table inside, where all four of us could sit and drink beer. The tiny village church ten miles away that boasted a twelfth-century black Madonna. An equally obscure little museum which had the largest piece of mountain crystal in the world. Another country inn which made, he said, the best *Palatschinken* (rolled jam-filled pancakes) to be found anywhere. And he knew the most beautiful views, and the nicest picnic places, even a beach on the nearest lake one could reach by rowboat, and where one could bathe in total seclusion if one didn't mind the leeches. I asked him once, 'You've been away so much, Felix – how do you know all this?' Felix grinned. 'One has to find somewhere interesting to stage the seductions. So I do. And even when I forget the girls, I never forget the places I have taken them.'

Joshua was enchanted, and they all insisted that I come along on every excursion. They adapted their pace, with great patience, to mine; they helped me over the rough places, sometimes they even carried me for short stretches. 'You must never give up, Mitzi, trying to lead a completely normal life,' Joshua said once to me, with his usual gravity. 'That's one thing where we are far in advance of Europe, we do give many more chances to handicapped people. Ever since Roosevelt, who made us aware what a handicapped person can do.'

'Yes,' I said obediently, 'I will try,' though I did not feel that my handicap was bad enough to require such homilies. Everywhere there were war amputees, there were people scarred or damaged beyond repair, who would never lead normal lives, and Joshua's exhortations seemed a bit out of place; but I took them in good part. And it was true, these excursions made me more limber, more eager and able to start going out on my own. I would come back from them walking almost quickly, my hair tangled, my face flushed with sun and wind, we would all come back, even Werner, laughing and glowing and garrulous, full of our sights and adventures.

Then my mother would almost spoil it all by saying, 'Mitzi, how red your cheeks are, how wonderful to see you smile like that again.' Once she added, 'It is all your doing, Joshua. You are working wonders with our Mitzi.' Joshua blushed, and I remember thinking how tactless it was for her to call attention to the fact that it was Joshua (for of course it was Joshua) who, on these outings, paid the transport and all the bills.

'Kitty Kleinholz is coming to tea, with her daughter. I think it must be because all the town is so interested in Joshua. She has not called on us in years, not since Felix . . .' My mother stopped, and coughed. I knew the story; Felix had gone off skiing with the Kleinholz daughter when she was sixteen, and they had not come back from their skiing until seven the next morning. My mother went hastily on, 'Yes, I am sure it is only so they can have a better look at our young American. They are gossiping all over town, Mitzi. They are all green with envy, because –' both Felix and I looked at her hard, and she caught herself again – 'because they see you out walking with two handsome young men.'

'Three,' said Felix softly.

'Oh, of course,' said my mother. 'But they know you are her brother so you do not count.'

'You see, Joshua,' Trudi explained, 'there is such a shortage of young men here, because of the war, and there being so few jobs in the country – well, when we have a new young man here, an American especially, all the girls, and their mothers, want to have a good look at him.'

Felix, who was slightly drunk that evening, said loudly, 'It's a bit like the story of the Russian peasant family who were so poor they only had one piece of sugar, and they put it on a plate and stared at it every time they all drank their tea. Some of the young ladies of our *Prominenz* may seem content just to stare. But with a little encouragement, they easily do more.'

'Enough,' said my mother to Felix, in an undertone.

'Do you remember,' Berti asked my mother, 'how Kitty came around the first time Joshua sent us a package? We had to collect it from the post office, so the whole town knew.'

'That was before I went skiing with Brigitte,' Felix said.

Joshua smiled embarrassedly at his plate. 'It makes me quite shy, to be such an object of curiosity. I'm surprised, though – there have been so many Americans here.'

'Yes,' said Felix, 'but they were soldiers, and most of them did not make a highly educated impression. An American *scholar* is something no one in this little provincial town has seen before. I know you think we are very cultured, but we have not had many intellectual lights. When Schubert sat down for five minutes on a bench by the river, someone immediately put a plaque on it. I am surprised they have not put plaques on the toilets in the *Weinstube*; there must have been some famous person who once –'

'Felix,' interrupted my mother, 'let us have this conversation after dinner. And I do not think you should have any more wine.'

Joshua sighed. 'How long have I been here – my God, it's already three weeks! I can hardly believe that in another week I will be going to Salzburg, then Heidelberg –'

'Maybe you won't have to go,' said Felix. 'Maybe you will find enough material about Hans Handelbein to occupy you here for a while longer. Don't forget Grandmama – our beloved Countess – knew him better than anyone.'

'But I do not think she can speak about it. Not any more. God, what a pity that is. If only I could have known her sooner!'

'She hasn't been very good lately, but she does still speak quite coherently sometimes. And I remember a few of her stories – I've promised to tell you, haven't I – and maybe with patience we can get still more.'

'I'm afraid it will not make a doctoral thesis,' Joshua said sadly.

'Well no, maybe not. But there are also letters. Grandmama brought a trunk full of correspondence with her. Werner and I could have a look and see what we find.'

'You never wrote me letters, child,' said Grandmama to Gordana, who was feeding her. 'Poor Janka. You cannot even read.'

'I don't remember a trunk full of letters,' said my mother, looking a trifle worried.

'Of course you don't. You never knew what was in half the boxes she brought. But I saw they were there, and after her accident I put them away safely. I was afraid some of you fanatical housewives might be inspired to throw them out, or use them for kindling when we were so cold. I wanted to go through them, but never got round to it, and these old handwritings are hard to decipher. In fact, I took some of them to Salzburg just recently, so Werner could help me. He is much better than I am at reading the old Gothic script.

'I would love to see those letters,' Joshua exclaimed. 'Do you think you can show me some before I go?'

'Of course. But we'll need a couple of days to sort them out. And tomorrow afternoon you are going to be occupied with entertaining Kitty Kleinholz.'

'Kitty Kleinholz,' said Grandmama suddenly. 'I remember her when she was a young girl, the most witless creature who ever walked. If you must entertain the locals, Anni, why not the mayor, who might be of some use?'

'You don't know,' Kitty Kleinholz exclaimed, 'what it means to us to see whipped cream again, and real coffee. We are a nation of coffee addicts. Yes, please, Anni, a little more. My dear Mr Prescott, I cannot tell you how impressed I am by your German. Very few of your countrymen bothered to learn even one word of our language. And when they did I can tell you it was not the nicest words that they learned. So it is such a pleasure to meet you, a truly educated American. After what we have had here, one began to think they do not exist. But I suppose it is always the worst elements that make up armies of occupation. Yes, dear Anni, I will have another slice of *Linzertorte*. It is not bad at all – who makes it – the Yugoslav girl? You are so lucky to have someone competent again. We had a refugee girl too, for a while, but she was hopeless, she lied, she stole . . . it's the same as always, if they come from the East you have to be twice as careful. One would think they would be grateful just to have a roof over their heads and enough to eat three times a day. But no. Has Mitzi done her *Matura* yet? Oh, it's next year – yes, of course, I remember now, she was ill for so long.' She and her daughter exchanged brief but obvious glances. 'How is your leg now, Mitzi?'

'Much better, thank you. I have been for some real walks this week.'

'Ah, I am glad to hear that.' She did not sound so at all. 'One must never give up, isn't that the secret?'

'Something of the sort,' I answered. She peered at me a little suspiciously with her obviously near-sighted but unbespectacled eyes – alas for Kitty, the lorgnette was no longer in vogue – and turned to Joshua again.

'I understand that in your country, Mr Prescott, the young women are very free, that some of them do not even want to get married, they all want to have professions, independent

149

lives. To our generation it seems strange but maybe it is a good thing. What do you think, Brigitte?'

'Oh, Mama, please,' Brigitte said wearily.

'What does that mean, Oh, Mama, please? The young are so critical of their elders nowadays, one is always saying the wrong thing, one hardly dares to open one's mouth. Is Mitzi like that with you, Anni? I am sure Mitzi is more sensible. She does not go out so much, she is not exposed to so many contemporary influences. I think there was a great deal to be said for educating children at home with governesses, as we used to do, I mean of course those who could afford it. Yes please, Anni, just a little more, it is so good. You can't think what it means to us, Mr Prescott, to have these good things again. Not that we get them very often yet. It must have been marvellous for these dear friends of yours, having you sending packages so regularly. But we are lucky too sometimes. Brigitte has just been sent two pairs of beautiful new nylons – hold your foot up, Brigitte, so Anni and Mitzi can see.'

'Mama, for the love of heaven,' Brigitte said.

'There you are, I have done it again. Perhaps you and I should take a turn in the garden, Anni, and leave the young people to themselves, since we embarrass them so.'

'You don't embarrass me at all,' I said. 'I enjoy your conversation. It is quite amazing to see someone so animated and never at a loss for words.'

'You are being kind, my dear, but I talk too much, I know, it has always been my great fault.' This time it was Brigitte who looked at me suspiciously, but Kitty sailed on. 'Hugo used to say – my husband Hugo, Mr Prescott, was a flier, and he was killed over Eng – he was killed quite early in the war – Hugo used to say, when we went sailing together on the Schmarnsee, this boat could go right over a waterfall and you would still be talking.'

She laughed, then looked grave. 'Actually, that did happen to the boat of some friends of mine. A very beautiful little boat. The Americans quartered in their house took it and let it go over the falls, just for the fun of seeing it smash on the rocks. It was a lovely boat, they had it built specially, and it was named Margaretha after their daughter, and poor little Margaretha cried for days. I cannot understand such wanton destruction of property. I know a great many things were said about our soldiers – I mean about the Germans, of course, the

150

Prussians have always been militaristic, we Austrians are an easy-going people, it is actually quite hard to get us to fight anyone – and no doubt some of the things were true – but our armies were more correct about some things, there were never these cases of wilful damage. I suppose it is being brought up in your free and easy way. One hears that American children are much less disciplined.' She drew breath a moment, and I stared at Joshua, waiting for him to say something; but Joshua was sitting bent forward, his arms on his knees, his head bowed, in a posture I knew Kitty would take as evidence of sloppy American manners, and I realized, with fury, that he was not going to say anything at all.

'That is true,' my mother said. 'I knew an American family who came here and it was quite amazing what the children were allowed to get away with. Not that the kind of case you have spoken about, Kitty, was usual here.'

'I only meant that it shows a certain difference in attitude. I suppose that it is just that in a country where everything is so big and so rich and so new it may be hard for these young men to realize what something like a boat or a painting can mean to somebody in Europe. A lot of our best art works, you see, Mr Prescott, have found their way to America. One can only hope that they will have a civilizing influence.'

If Joshua wouldn't after this last, I would. 'I suppose, Frau Kleinholz, you would rather have had the SS than these undisciplined American troops. If the little girl the boat was named after had been Jewish, they might have machine-gunned her, but I am sure they would have left the boat alone.'

There was a very loud silence. I thought, well, now we shall get rid of Kitty and her daughter and I hope that will please Mama too. But my mother did not look pleased and Kitty made no move to go. She said, with surprising smoothness, 'Forgive me, Mr Prescott, if I have spoken out of turn, as Mitzi seems to think I have. We have been so long occupied, you see, first by the Germans, then by the Russians and the Americans, and we were once a great empire and now we are just a little spot on the map, not even so big as one of your States – isn't it that Texas is as big as the whole of Europe, Mr Prescott? I suppose sometimes we feel a little resentful. And I have only told what I know to be true. I hope you did not take my remarks personally. They were certainly not meant personally in any way. In fact I really want to say

151

what a pleasure it is to meet an American who seems so European in so many ways.'

'He is European,' Trudi said proudly. 'He became so Europeanized already in the few weeks he was here, six years ago. He is the best of both worlds.'

Joshua, at last, spoke. To Trudi he said, 'Thank you.' And to Kitty, 'It's quite all right. I am not offended. I am sure it is profitable for me to hear another side of things.' Then, to us all, 'And now, if you will excuse me, I think *I* will take a turn in the garden. The *Linzertorte* is delicious but it is very heavy. I think I need to stretch my legs for a few minutes.'

'I think I must do the same. Please excuse me as well.' I got up and followed Joshua. Oh, how difficult it is to make a good exit with a dragging leg! Kitty murmured to my mother, 'But she is walking almost normally now,' just as I escaped. I was tempted to say something more, but I controlled myself. Perhaps I would get in a last riposte before she left – as if anything would penetrate that elephant hide.

Once we were safely outside, I said to Joshua, my voice still shaking, 'Now do you see why I want to leave here? That woman Kitty – she's even Baroness Kleinholz, or was – is one of the bright social lights of our town. Lots of people dislike her, but no one refuses her invitations, and she runs half the things that go on. You know, Joshua, these last weeks I've had such a lovely time I've been in a kind of dream, I've begun to see it all with your eyes – the little churches, the thousand-year-old tree, the river, the mountains – yes, all that is here, but Kitty Kleinholz is here too, and she is the kind of person you have to live with. And did you see my mother? I think my mother is actually pleased that Kitty has come to visit us again. They all snubbed us for a while, because Felix has offended nearly everyone, and because my mother went out with Kropetschka the ironmonger who can hardly talk proper German, and also because of me. Except when times were really bad – then they came around because you were sending CARE packages. And even my mother – she doesn't tell Kitty to shut up – she almost agrees! You want me to read books like *Main Street* – what about this Main Street, this provincialism! At least on Main Street they were not Nazis. Oh it is beautiful here, but human beings didn't make the beauty – and when they did it was probably slave labour – those churches you love, how do you think the people lived

152

who built them, why do you think it is not possible to build such churches now? Not only because our faith is gone - but because you cannot get someone to carve stones all day for a single crust of bread –'

'Mitzi,' said Joshua, 'Mitzi, Mitzi!' He took me by the shoulders.

'And you – you said nothing, you didn't defend your country, you didn't defend yourself –'

'Mitzi, oh, Mitzi! I didn't know you could be so vehement.' His eyes were searching my face, his hands still gripping my shoulders. I said irritably, 'Joshua, let go, you're hurting. I don't want to hear about my vehemence. I want to know why you didn't say anything.'

Joshua sighed and released me. 'I'm sorry, it's just – you were getting so angry. Do you know, in ways you're like Felix. I said nothing because it would only have made more bad feeling and she would not have understood. You cannot argue with people unless you have some basis of agreement to argue from. It is just a waste of energy. And I meant it, it probably does me good to hear the other side. I know, you think I'm reasoning like a coward. I can tell it from your face.'

'No, I don't think that. I just think you make too many excuses for everything here. There are not two sides to everything, Joshua. There are different sides to different things, but that's not the same.'

'Maybe I do make excuses,' said Joshua. 'Maybe I forgive a great deal in your vicinity, simply because – because *you* are there.'

'I don't see –' I began, then I broke off, realizing what he had said. I did not know how to answer, so I answered nothing. He waited; then he shrugged, smiled and said, 'Before you came in, Brigitte invited me to play tennis with her. Or rather, her mother invited me to play tennis with Brigitte. They said we should all come for tea, and Brigitte and I could move on to the tennis court. Do you think we should go?'

'You can. I won't.'

'I'm afraid your mother has already accepted, for all of us. Not of course Felix, who wasn't there and still seems to be in disgrace with that family.'

'She can't accept for me. I wouldn't set foot in Kitty's house.'

'If you don't go, I won't,' Joshua said.

153

'There's no need for that. If you'd like to play tennis – I mean, you know I can't – and Felix is barred from the court because –' I broke off again. He was looking at me in that same ardent, searching way. I said uncomfortably, 'Let's go back inside. Maybe they're leaving now.'

We did, but they were not. Kitty Kleinholz was still going full speed ahead with what was evidently a favourite topic. 'And a maid!' Kitty exclaimed. 'In no time at all, a cook and a maid, even some clown or other dressed up to wait at table when they had dinner parties. Because they discovered, of course, that servants are cheap – no wonder, after the war, when everyone was starving. I mean, people were happy to get food and a roof over their heads. She knew nothing, that poor woman from – how do you pronounce it, Eye-oh-wah? It was like those awful stories Oscar used to tell when he was drunk about the Poles when they get rich. She had probably been a maid not long ago herself. It was all so ridiculous – I tried to be polite, but there were times when I could hardly keep a straight face.'

Trudi and Berti and my mother were all nodding, and my mother put in a contribution. 'It's true – there was a colonel billeted on a friend of mine, and the canned meat he used to feed his dogs – when we never saw meat from one week to the next –'

My mother was sitting with her back to the door and had not seen our entry. Kitty flashed us her vulpine smile. 'There you are – how is it in the garden?'

'More pleasant than inside,' I said sweetly.

'Well,' said Kitty, 'that is usually the case with gardens. Though I have always found this a charming house. Small, but comfortable, kept so entirely in the old style. When you go back to America, Mr Prescott, perhaps you will furnish your house too in *Bauernrustik*. That would be something new. I am sure they would put pictures in all the magazines.'

'It will be some time,' Joshua said, 'before I go back to America.'

'Ah. That is good to hear. Then you must most definitely play tennis with Brigitte. I am sure you are an excellent player, you have just the build for it. We will have a friendly battle, America against Unter-Kaltbach. And you must all come for tea.'

*

154

In the two – almost three now – years following my accident I had achieved a kind of numb calm, broken by fresh surges of misery, as when I first went back to school, but on the whole a bearable state. I should have known that I was too young, and had too much of the family temperament, for this to last very long. In that week of outings with Felix and Werner and Joshua, I had been wrested from my plodding studies and premature retreat, not by misery but by joy; for the first time since losing Stefan, I had felt honestly glad to be alive. Kitty Kleinholz's visit was the first sour note, Kitty and my family's unprotesting acceptance of her, as if to slide back into the old attitudes, the old bigotries, they only needed someone else to voice them, even in front of Joshua.

But the sour note was more than that. In the moment Joshua held me, I was suddenly forced to acknowledge a possible new element in our relationship; or perhaps it had been there all along, only I had not seen it, because I did not want it to be. And in the hours following that episode in the garden, I became painfully aware where before I had been blind, blind to the beaming smiles, the little innuendos, our elders lavished upon us, blind to my mother's regular manoeuvring to place Joshua next to me at table, blind to the determined way they kept coaxing him to stay on. It was so logical, so obvious – why had I not realized it? The problem son had not managed to settle himself in the land of milk and honey (and it was that to them, however they sneered) but the problem daughter might. What could be better – a Catholic-educated academic, a thoroughly *decent young man*, shy and deferential enough that he might not mind my handicap nor my early escapade? I understood all at once something I had overheard Trudi saying to Berti, 'No, no, he would never let anyone down, he would always do the proper thing, he is such a decent young man. With him one would have no worries.' They had not solved the problem of Felix, but they would get rid of sharp-tongued troublesome Mitzi; my mother would be spared the double shame of a feckless rogue son and a disgraced, handicapped spinster daughter. And they had simply assumed that nothing would make me happier, that Stefan was a fleeting adolescent infatuation, that I *must* want Joshua because he was already my friend, he was young and eligible and presentable, he was *there*, and he was also a passport to America. They had assumed that I could not be so stubborn, so

155

impractical, so unreasonable, as not to turn away, at the first good opportunity, from the lost love for which I had been ready to die.

Well, I would put a stop to it, then and there. I would put a quick end to their little machinations. I would tell them what I thought of their cheap intrigues, I would tell them that though Joshua might be my dearest friend, I could never love him, nor marry him, nor sleep with him, and if that was why they wanted him to stay, they had better tell him to go to Salzburg at once.

For there was something else that had happened when Joshua touched me. Just as it flashed into my mind that he might want me – a thought that had truly, naïve though it seems, not occurred to me before – I had known that I would never want him. It was not only that I still loved Stefan. The chemistry between us, as one says now, was simply wrong. Or perhaps for me it would be wrong with anyone. *Anyone? Then why not Felix?*

No, I said to myself with the vehemence poor Joshua had admired, *no*, you will not think about that. You were sick and crazy and desperate when it happened, you were not yourself, you reached like one drowning for the person nearest you. But the other times, Mitzi, the times after that, the time that Betsy was in the house, the time –

And then with a tremendous effort of will I shut my mind on what had happened and might happen again. Amazingly, I still did not feel guilty; my reason told me I should feel guilty, that all my upbringing, my religious childhood, my own personal sense of honesty and fairness which Felix's actions – those that had nothing to do with me – constantly outraged, destined me to feel guilty, but the guilt was simply not there. But I knew that what had so miraculously hardly touched my mind as an act would, as an obsession, destroy me. So, to escape the hint of that obsession, I worked myself up into an even fiercer romantic rage and went to confront my family.

As fate would have it, however, the first person I met after my long black brooding was Joshua himself. Joshua had seen Felix, who had accompanied Werner back to Salzburg and stayed a day, returning that afternoon. He had discreetly absented himself during Kitty's visit, but had dropped off a packet of letters for Joshua to peruse.

Joshua was in a state bordering on delirium. He waved the packet of yellowed paper, he laughed and spluttered and stuttered. I had to submit to his hard grip on my shoulders again, and not only that, he hugged me, and broke away, blushing, just as my mother came into the room. She said at once, 'Oh, pardon!' and smiled with iron benevolence on us both.

'Mama!' I shouted, wanting to set her straight, but she paid no attention, and went quickly out; she was determined to leave us alone to finish our tender scene. 'Mama,' I shouted again, and started after her.

'Mitzi – Mitzi – don't go – you can find her later – Mitzi! You must listen! If these letters are – what what what I think (he really was terribly excited – he had stuttered before sometimes, when he was shy or tense, but never like this) – if these letters – I can't go to Salzburg – not yet – and there are dozens of letters from Hans Handelbein – and Felix says there may be still more. There are letters from Stammlos, and Kafka and Freud, and Adlerhorst – oh, Mitzi, you of all people must see how exciting this is. Here, read this one – it's a letter from Handelbein – and tell me what you think.'

He handed me a piece of tattered paper, scrawled upon in faded brown ink.

And that was the beginning.

My beloved Countess,

Joy needs more bravery and a more profound surrender than pain. When we give ourselves to joy, we challenge the lurking unknowable darkness. Forgive me then for last night. It was my lack of courage, my fear of the darkness, that spoke, not my braver and truer voice, not my better self. To be with you, to know you, to penetrate the magical depths of so elusive and glorious and unique a being, is to dare the anger of the Gods. When I said to you earlier, 'I could die now', it was almost the expression of a wish; for if the immortals suffer a mortal to experience such bliss and remain alive, it can only be that in their jealous rage they are preparing a more lingering and dreadful death, a death commensurate with his ecstasy – but a death commensurate with that ecstasy would be so terrible I think even the envious Gods would show mercy and mitigate it a little.

And still, you see, it is morning, and I am alive and well and have drunk my coffee and eaten my Kipferl with jam and find it harder now, as one does in the morning, to take so seriously the forces of Olympian

157

darkness. So forgive me, Countess, for my brusqueness, for a moment's cowardice. There will not be another. I will dare the Gods as often as you wish; I will rise in you like a rocket to the undiscovered, most distant stars . . .

    Tuesday at seven then, as we arranged.

      I love you.

        Hans

Our late-nineteenth-century *haute bourgeoisie* put art on the thrones of both Kaiser and God. It was in those days that the up-and-coming, enlightened middle class, denied the power and prestige that would, in a less atrophied system, have been their due, began to worship Goethe and Beethoven, and, barred from the Almanach de Gotha, cultivated nobility of soul. Even though it might be bruited about that 'every water-closet manufacturer is now made a Baron' and the old Kaiser was sometimes, with a touch of *lèse-majesté*, referred to as an '*Unterschriftsmaschine*', a machine for signatures, not least of patents of nobility, the aristocracy kept their inner circles, the exclusiveness that often hardens just before power fades. *They* knew the difference between a water-closet manufacturer and an offspring, however illegitimate, of blue and venerable blood. Occasionally, of course, the parvenus did climb up and the titles down, and was any banker who patronized arts ever more indulgent and long-suffering than, even longer ago, some of Beethoven's titled remittance-givers? And one of those who climbed down was Maria Aurora, the young widowed Countess of Bilderheim-Traun.

The Countess must have been an extraordinary phenomenon; a woman of great elegance, arrogance, irony and verve, shining at social functions while simultaneously demolishing them with what someone called her 'silver dagger of a tongue', a woman whose sarcasm was feared as much as her beauty was adored – and who suddenly turned from her frivolous, bored pursuits to a spiritual and sensual (rather more of the latter) devotion to talent, originality, Mind. A later debunker has viciously said that since my Grand-mama could not in truth join the aristocracy of the spirit, she slept with them instead; but most of those who have read and commented on her letters and diary jottings feel that she was a worthy member of any aesthetic circle she chose to grace.

At all events, this is the elegant muse who emerged from the packets of yellowed paper, from those long walks Felix and Joshua took under the linden trees. What Joshua *knew* was a broken old lady in a wheelchair, who hardly spoke any more except to demand necessities or ask sharply who some one of us was. When she did say something else, when there was even so much as a phrase from those few rambling, disjointed stories of the past – which as I remember them were hardly artistic or literary – Felix would pounce on it and elaborate for Joshua's benefit. 'The fishes, Grandmama? The goldfishes? Do you know, I think I remember this, Joshua. That very suggestive painting by Klimt of *Goldfishes* or *Fish Blood*, I'm not sure which, maybe there were two – I believe she said once she posed for one of those. It would have been a great scandal, of course, and she was already a little confused when she told me that, so it might not have been true ... but if it were it would certainly have been kept a secret from everyone. And what a fuss there would have been if it were known! Klimt, whose murals for the University had all the old professors hopping with rage and signing petitions against him – Klimt, painting a member of the aristocracy as an erotic nude – what an idea! Of course we will never know.'

And Joshua, carried away by these tantalizing possibilities, would sometimes, in spite of Felix's remonstrances – 'It's no use, Josh, she can't even hear you' – attempt the gentlest of probes, his gangly figure bent low over the little crumpled one of the old lady, his dark beard almost brushing her thin crown of white hair. 'Countess – dear Countess – Excellency – do you remember the Secession? The paintings, Countess, of Gustav Klimt?'

With all this attention and Gordana's careful tending and primping, my Grandmama, though no more communicative or coherent - it was too late for any change in that – did achieve a sort of last blossoming. Or maybe it was simply all the fresh air; no one had ever wheeled her around the garden so endlessly before. Felix wheeled, Felix talked, Joshua, when the sun was too hot, held up an ivory-handled parasol of ruffled ecru silk that must have belonged to a very young Maria Aurora, and juggled it awkwardly when he scribbled a note. A normal umbrella, Felix observed to me one evening, would have been more practical but detracted from the *fin de siècle* atmosphere.

Whatever it was, Grandmama had never, since her accident, looked so well. Gordana took particular care and pride in dressing her. The remaining treasures had been sorted and catalogued by my mother; there were to be no more unexpected engagement rings for Felix's next Betsy. But Gordana saw to it that they were used, that the old lady had a brooch at her throat and a lace handkerchief up her sleeve, however impractical this might be. In fact, she changed the few remaining pieces of jewellery with a frequency and regularity which seemed to proclaim that there was certainly no need for suspicion or inspection with her, Gordana, in charge. One could almost be certain that it would be amber on Tuesday, that is, if Grandmama was in black moiré; if Gordana put her in dove-grey silk, it would be garnets and crystal, or seed pearls and jade.

So Gordana mixed and matched, mended and washed and pressed. She stitched fine old collars onto Grandmama's faded dresses; she even for Sunday, a day that Grandmama, when in possession of her faculties, had not bothered to observe, put silk shoes on the old lady's feet. Nor did she ever neglect the more crudely physical side of her *tableau vivant*. She saw to it that the old lady's nails were manicured, her face powdered, that she smelled becomingly of lavender water. Once in a while her efforts to capture an aura of bygone elegance bordered on the grotesque; when Grandmama appeared for her wheeled walk in a mauve straw picture hat at a slightly crooked angle with chiffon veiling tied under her chin, Felix commanded Gordana to remove it. 'She will choke in that get-up.'

'I thought it would be good against the sun,' mumbled Gordana, crestfallen and as usual ready to cry. Grandmama herself commented with rare lucidity as the hat was lifted from her head, 'I told you, Janka, only the grisettes wear such things to the Prater.'

There was also the heavy watch on a gold chain necklace that Gordana liked to hang around Grandmama's neck. The watch was missing a hand and had probably stopped decades ago. Its blank, motionless face, dangling under Grandmama's, always made me uncomfortable and would, had she been capable of it, have led me to suspect Gordana of a crude and cruel symbolism. And there was the tortoiseshell lorgnette, which opened at a touch. This was also hung on Grandmama,

160

though quite useless to her; it snapped open at supper and flew into Grandmama's soup, which made my mother scold, Gordana weep and Felix choke behind his napkin. Only Grandmama said with dignity, 'There is something in the soup. But what else can you expect, in wartime? Last week a piece of the ceiling came down. When Papa plays Tarok, he always loses. Please –' here a note of anxiety came into her voice – 'please tell Fritz to take the soup away.'

But on the whole Gordana succeeded, and we all praised her handiwork, especially as it seemed good for Grandmama's morale. So the two images flourished side by side, the anachronistic fashion plate Gordana created from her researches in the trunks, dressing up Grandmama like a limp withered doll, and the passionate, eloquent *femme fatale* that Felix and Joshua unearthed from theirs. There was no contradiction then in anyone's mind between Gordana's mannequin and the literary lioness who was Joshua's great trophy for the academic world. Perhaps senile old age, like infancy, is a *tabula rasa* upon which all in charge of it can write what they please. Joshua and Werner, I seem to remember, had one of their abstruse discussions on this topic, Werner saying that those without memory are indeed like infants, ready for anyone's shaping, only what one could shape was not the future but the past.

At all events, if we see Maria Aurora in the tradition of those well-dressed French ladies whose courtly life only stimulated the flow of their pens, there *is* no contradiction. The strange thing is that her literary outpourings seem to have begun almost on the day that she forsook frivolity for culture, and that this day was a milestone in her life, a conversion as sudden and shattering as the conversion of Paul. It is recorded in full, in the letter called by Joshua himself and most of the commentators who followed him, The Letter of Awakening. This letter is one of the few addressed to a woman, and like most of the other letters, it was returned to the sender, or else never sent. There are three other letters to the person called Alix, all written at critical stages in the writer's life, but no one has been able to discover who Alix was. There is a theory that these letters are merely disguised pieces of interior monologue, that 'Alix', the abbreviation for one of her other middle names, refers to Maria Aurora Alexandra herself.

*

161

Dearest Alix,

Yesterday I went to Pupsi's to hear chamber music. (I should note here that the aristocratic habit of referring to people only by nicknames has made it impossible to identify many of the characters named in Grandmama's correspondence and notebooks, and her maddening way of almost never dating anything is another great difficulty for researchers. Pupsi, for instance, could be anyone named anything, male or female; it was quite possible to find men nicknamed Dolly and women called Freddie.)

In morning-blue silk I went, very low cut, determined to épater *the serious wagging heads that are usually at these things and be, myself, bored to death. Oh, not that I do not like music, but I like it at my choice, at my command. When Papa had musicians at Hundertlinden, before he gambled so much away . . .*

They are already wary when I come through the door. When the footman announces my name, it is as if he had said The Scandalous *as a preface, a little additional title. And that is precisely why I am always invited. The very best people are waiting to see and hear what I will do next, they come to see me as much as to hear the music. There is never a failed, a boring, a provincial evening if I am there. Only I am bored. Sometimes I feel it as a great burden, as if it were only Mitzi's bad behaviour and wicked tongue that keeps all these doddering scarecrows amused, awake, alive. Ridiculous, Alix, is it not?*

So there I sat, Alix, in my blue silk with my chin on my gloved hand, listening to a young man with a head like a haystack (I suppose since Beethoven and Schubert looked like Struwelpeter, all serious young musicians feel they must do the same) play – yes, of course – Schubert. And I thought with weariness of the next day's engagements and the drive along the Ring and the flirtation and the clandestine rendezvous, and how sometimes I would like to give up all appearances and gamble away what little money Papa did not and Robi did not squander and become a mere grisette so life would take me seriously – I know it makes no sense but that was how I thought it. What things these hypnotists must unearth if they can make one say all one's thoughts! And then, all at once, it was as if this music, this Schubert sonata, which I was hardly listening to –

But no, I cannot describe it. It was one of those experiences for which words give only a poor and feeble approximation. But suddenly it was as if every nerve in my body vibrated like the strings of the piano young Carlowitz was hammering so passionately. I thought, this is Schubert and yet it is not Schubert, it is like no music I have ever heard

162

before. The sensation was almost too great. I wanted to escape, but I could not move – the music filled me completely, overwhelmed me, ravished me – and then a hot, hoarse voice whispered into my ear, 'Countess, do not move, but lift your chin just a little more.'

And as the music faded, came to its end, the despicable creature who had shattered my ecstasy continued to hiss shamelessly into my ear. 'Countess, Excellency – oh, thou most heavenly of all earthly beings – you see, I know how far away you have been in the last ten minutes – but it will remain a secret between us forever. An eternal secret. For I, dear Countess, humble being though I am, have made it eternal. Condemn me, Countess, now if you will, but first, look at how I have captured you. Captured you so that you can never escape me again.'

I turned full of rage to confront this impudence. But we were seated a little apart from the others; I had been so rapt I had not even noticed him as he crept up behind my chaise-longue – and before I could rise, he thrust a sketch-book into my lap, and in spite of myself I looked down, and the angry words stuck in my throat.

Dearest Alix, dare I write even you, how upon that evening I was ravished twice – once by the music of Schubert, and once by my own beauty? Or should I say, more justly, that it was his beauty, the beauty of my face made by his hands, seen through his eyes?

I gazed at this picture like Narcissus trapped by his pool. How often our French governess told us that story, attempting to cure in us the youthful stirrings of vanity. But like so many stories told for the sake of a moral lesson, it had an opposite effect. I fell in love with the story of the boy Narcissus and his watery mirror, it seemed to me an admirable way to spend one's time.

They were still all applauding, or talking again – whatever, for some amazing reason, no one was paying attention to me, nor to the big dark shaggy man who hovered over me, and then suddenly tugged at his rough pencil sketch with even more rudeness than he had shown in thrusting it, and himself, upon me. 'Forgive me, Countess, but there is something I must correct.'

I answered, 'There is nothing to correct. You have taken my likeness without my permission, and made the graver error of letting me know. Now, since this is my face, and back in my hands, I see no reason why I should not keep it.'

By now our tête-à-tête was beginning to attract attention. But my gypsy bear of a genius was oblivious to that. He dropped noisily upon his knees and seized my free hand, the one not holding his sketch, in both of his. His coarse red lips burned a moment against my fingers. Then he raised his head, his face full of the wildest longing, the lights of Pupsi's tasteless chandeliers flashing from his spectacles. He stumbled to his feet. 'Keep it then,' he said, 'but promise me, promise me, to come to the atelier, so I can do a better.' Then he rushed out.

Pupsi came waddling toward me, stupidly anxious as always, wanting to know was anything wrong and had I enjoyed the Schubert? To which I answered, 'Pupsi, who is that very peculiar man who has just drawn me, and where does he live?'

Dearest Alix, that was seven days ago.

I have spent my time since then – the part of it I have spent alone – making poor Amelia throw out much of the debris of my past, letters, souvenirs – not so much from aversion to it but because I suddenly feel that my life and my rooms have been full of clutter, that I want a sort of physical and spiritual spring cleaning – and perhaps it is that, the spring, that makes me so restless now.

Dearest Alix, what is happening to me?

I wake in the morning – whenever, wherever I awake – with the sun like a mantle on my bare shoulders, and the motes, the little drifting hairs and specks of dust, dance in the beams (there is so much dust – it is a good thing I have never had housewifely instincts) like golden snow, like the magic snow in the paperweight Papa gave me when I was a child. I lie with my hands on my cold bruised arms and look at these motes and think there is nothing more beautiful. I wake, knowing for the first time in years, that my day will be both a defeat and a triumph; and a day worth a thousand others.

I have seen no one, gone nowhere, done nothing. For the first time in my life I am faced with a will as unbending and capricious as my own.

I can say no more. My heart is too full. Adieu, dearest Alix, and may Heaven guard you until I can return to you again.

> *Always your*
> *Mitzi*

This letter was another of the first that Joshua saw, and showed to me. My reaction, though I tried to hide it, was puzzled and a bit sceptical. The beginning seemed in character, as far as it went, but there was a slight air of contrivance, more distinct when it came to the Schubert *Schwärmerei*. But I somehow could not imagine Grandmama lying naked in a scruffy artist's studio (this no doubt being the intended inference) watching dust in sunbeams. It seemed to me that if Grandmama had slept with this scruffy artist she would have been matter of fact about it, and she probably would have felt no need to write dear Alix letters about it at all. (The theory advanced by Dr Theo Goldfarb, that not only is 'Alix' Maria Aurora Alexandra herself, but that these particular letters are an expression of growing schizophrenia, the record of and apology for things Maria Aurora did when she was 'out of herself', and that the phrase 'May Heaven guard you until I can return to you again' is particularly significant in this connection, I have always regarded as absolute nonsense.)

But then, of course, none of us had known her at the time. In fact we had all, even my mother, scarcely known her before she was old. The other letters Joshua had then – it seems they were in total disorder, she had probably packed hastily once and never sorted things out again – were mostly from and to Hans Handelbein. He was even more enthusiastic about these. And there were many more letters, and Felix and Werner were working on them (I must admit that even then that phrase had for me an ambiguous ring), sorting them out and getting them in sequence, as far as it was possible. Joshua would write to the university, try to get his grant extended – he could get a room in town if we wished but there was now no question of his leaving. And, oh, Mitzi, are you not happy for me?

It was not a question to which one could answer no. And in truth I was. Of course I was. It is also true that my happiness was tinged with unease that these letters should be so opportunely discovered, and that it was Felix who had discovered them, Felix and Werner who had *ipso facto* charge of the whole collection. But it would have been pointless and cruel to say this, then, to Joshua.

Then came the second question, the still more difficult one. 'Oh, Mitzi, are you happy for yourself? I mean, are you glad that I am staying?'

I said again that of course I was, that he must know he was my best friend, so how could I not be happy? I said this very carefully, watching his eyes. And to soften it I added that now he would be here longer and I was walking so much better there would be many things we could do together. We would walk up the hills again and go by train to the lakes for boat trips, I would teach him about mushrooms and we would go mushroom-picking, and there was a castle I had not been to since childhood where I wanted to go, with him . . . but Joshua was too sensitive to be put off with that. He knew that I knew what his question had meant, and what I had answered. He said abruptly that he hoped we would have time for some of those things, but really, he was now going to be absolutely buried in work. But wait. What did I think of these? And to cover his embarrassment he put more tattered pieces of paper with spidery writing into my hands.

Beloved Mitzi,

Oh my angel, my radiant light, how much longer must I vegetate here without you? I am already so tired of the southern spring with its effortlessness, its cheap easy colours, not a season but an exhibition of spring. I expect at any moment to see signs declaring 'Spring' sprouting from the trees. To make it worse, my refuge is now infested with Germans. You know the German sensibility faced with a southern land-scape, it begins soaking and softening like a white roll in water, and watching the Germans watching the beauty I came for, I lose my per-spective, my appetite, my temper – ah, but Mitzi, if you were here, a million riveted German eyes could not dim your lustre for me, nor my appetite for you . . .

I have been running a slight fever almost ever since I have been here. This does not worry me; on the contrary. We are so eager to possess things, so overjoyed at any fidelity, that we can appreciate even a steadily recurring rise in temperature. This fever at least is mine, and no one else longs for it, as they do for the source of that other fever to which this one is but a candle to a burst of flame . . . (The rest is lost.)

My dearest Hansi,

I do not like the fever. Please see someone, please look after yourself. Ah, Hansi, I can imagine it so well, you raging amidst the good burgers taking their innocent holiday, quite unconscious that a bête fauve *skulks among them. And how right you are about the German soul. Germans are so proud of the depths within them when all their soulfulness is merely a lack of style, a formlessness, as if nature had intended us to appear without skins, all viscera and vertebrae . . .*

While you have been away, Waldmann has been plaguing me. His German soul will not let him believe in my lack of interest. Yesterday he made a dreadful scene in the street, following me out of Demel's. You have never yet recognized my presence, he said, and there is noth-ing I want more in the world than to know you, to have you know

*me. I asked him not to speak to me as if I were someone he had just
picked up in the dining car of the Paris Express, but even this did
not subdue him. How terribly inelegant these philosophers are! I fear
it will end badly. He is quite close to madness, Waldmann. I think
his preoccupation with* Being and Being There (*and Not Being
There at All Anymore*) *is affecting his brain, which was never very
clear to begin with. The Germans should leave philosophy alone. Perhaps the Austrians should as well; fortunately most of us are too frivolous to engage in it and prefer aphorisms which, even if they are
false, clear the mind where philosophy befuddles. I am tempted to say
that since the ancient Greeks no one has really been able to think
who looks upon thinking as a profession. I have asked Lolo to persuade Waldmann to see Dr Freud, who does wonders with such
people. I fear Waldmann will challenge you to a duel when you
return, and as you know, I am very nervous about duels.*

*Otherwise without you everything is dull. Why do I say otherwise?
I suppose it shows the extent of my dullness that even Waldmann can
provide some kind of distraction. It is as if I must have something to
grate on the nerves which your absence leaves raw. Remember it was
your wish to go away. You could not bear Vienna another minute,
and my presence was too distracting for your work. Now you cannot
bear Ascona; and does not my absence distract you more? I know
what your absence does to me, the absence of your eyes, your hands,
your mouth . . . and now you wish me to join you in your exile and
parade me among the landscape-worshippers, your own secret discovered country. Hansi, how well I understand you, how like myself
you are, at once so direct and so devious in your gratifications, sometimes almost longing for that exacerbation of loneliness which is found
only in crowds, or for that drumming on the nerves which makes
escape into a private world the sweetest of necessities, just as music
can be at its most uncannily beautiful heard over a background of
vulgar everyday noise. I remember the night in Venice when you insisted on throwing our windows wide open; the disturbance, you said,
only makes my sensations still more exquisite. Or is it that the sensation is too much, that one must have a disturbance so as not to
drown altogether?*

*I am relieved to hear you have not tired of me. I will come to Ascona
in a fortnight's time.*

   Your Mitzi

My dearest Mitzi,

   I am not sure about aphorisms. If you shake an aphorism, a lie falls out and a banality is left. Still, as you say, they clear the mind in some way. A thing which your letter has not done for mine. I no longer take my temperature, because my brain is an inferno that no thermometer could register. Send a telegram; I will be at the station, hours in advance. Do not worry about Waldmann challenging me. Waldmann is so large and cumbrous even I could not fail to hit him, even at a hundred paces.

Tire of you, Mitzi? You mock me, as always, you are only under-lining your power. When a man tires of his mistress, it is never his—that flags but his imagination; and you feed imagination as the sun feeds the earth, Zeus himself could not tire of you. And your own imagination will give you an idea how much is in mine. I cannot even write that I love you; I am in that state where desire is so agonized it drives out love; one hates its object for not being immediately present to assuage the pain. Oh, Mitzi, do not come in a fortnight, come at once, come even sooner. If you feel a tenth of what I do, there is no need for me to ask this, for you must already be on your way.

    Hans

'It was the great passion of Handelbein's life,' said Joshua when I finished reading. 'Yes,' I murmured, 'it certainly seems to have been. And they are certainly unusual letters.' Unusual, yet, here and there, there was something that seemed familiar, and my secret suspicions were hardly allayed.

'Well,' said Felix, 'the old one is really pleased that Joshua is staying.'

'Which old one, Mama or Grandmama?'

'Malicious as always. Mama, of course. You know I would never call Grandmama old. Anyway, at the moment she doesn't know Joshua is there. She thinks he is her father's footman Hummelpein and keeps telling him to go out and call for the carriage. Well, as I said, Mama is pleased and I hope you are too. She has been racking her brains for a way to get Joshua to stay longer. It's a good thing I found those letters.'

'Found them? You said you'd had them for ages. I wonder why you never mentioned them before.'

'Well, it was Werner who really got me interested in de-ciphering them. You know I am not exactly a scholar,' Felix said smoothly.

'Yes, I know. It is wonderful though how things sometimes

168

turn up at just the right moment. But why,' I added in a tone of complete innocence, 'is Mama so anxious to have Joshua stay?'

'You of all people must know that.' He came closer to me and looked hard into my eyes. His face was serious and concerned. 'You know, it would not be a bad idea. He is a good man, Joshua, intelligent, cultured, kind, not at all bad looking . . .'

'He is all those things, yes. But I could never think of him as anything but a friend.'

'Even with time? He is so fond of you, Mitzi – one has only to see the way he gazes at you . . . do you think it impossible then, for love to breed love?'

'When you are pompous, Felix, you are simply disgusting. And you who said – well, never mind. Love to breed love! It hardly worked with you and Betsy, did it, Felix?'

'Betsy? That little sow? It was her airy castle that she loved. If you could think for a minute that I –' I burst out laughing at his indignation.

'All right then, Mitzi. I do try sometimes, you know, to play the conventional big brotherly role, good advice and all that, and I do, really, have your best interests at heart. You ought to get out of here, as I intend to. But if it won't work, it won't. I only hope that it is not because of me.'

'Because of you? What could it have to do with you?' Then I felt my cheeks burning. I had thought there was a tacit understanding of no mention, no reference, ever, and now Felix had broken it, as lightly as he broke everything. I went on, trying in vain to keep my voice casual and mocking, 'You know, you really are the most colossal egotist in the world.'

Felix smiled. 'No, Mitzi. I am a realist, that's all.'

'I think that is one thing you are not.'

'I am. And you, hopeless romantic that you are, would be incapable of telling if I wasn't. Well, then. If it's like that. I thought, really, you know, it might be doing you a favour to get Joshua to stay. You have always been such marvellous friends. Anyway, perhaps you should disabuse *die Alte* and the two Amazons. They are already planning the trousseau. Or no, better yet, don't for a while. They are so happy in their ignorance, and Joshua is so happy with his letters. Poor Joshua. What magic is it, Mitzi, that he does not have?' His voice made my blood run cold. The only failures or disappointments that Felix could ever regard without mockery were his own.

'It's not him, it's me. *He* is worth a hundred of you.'

'That may be. But if there were a hundred of *him*, most women would still rather have one Felix. So would you.'

At that moment Trudi came in, and knowing I would now have to keep back my rage, he added, as if it were the end of a normal conversation about something quite else, 'In that case, Mitzi, I would suggest leaving the bedroom door just a little open. It may be the only way,' he continued, smiling benevolently at Trudi, 'in the height of summer, to get enough air.'

'Felix, I don't want to do this, ever again.'

'That seems a great pity, when you do it so well. What is it then? Are the conventions getting to you, after all? How curious, do you know, it is the first time we have actually talked about what we are doing. I suppose therefore it must be the beginning of the end. But why, precisely?'

'You know all the reasons.'

'If anything ever happens, I can get it seen to. I have always promised you that.'

'No. It's all the other reasons. Felix, I like you less and less. I hate what you are doing to Joshua, I hate your arrogance, I hate –'

'Later, Mitzi. I am going to France soon to find my ballerina and then you will be rid of me. But please do not lecture me this evening. Since it is the last time let us not spoil it.'

'Felix, just get out, just please go.'

'You don't mean that,' said Felix, and in fact I did not. Oh, but dear God, I wanted to mean it. And I did mean what I said I hated. But all this seemed to have nothing to do with Felix's physical presence, which like Grandmama's when she was young, set its own rules – and in spite of my strongest effort of mind and will, was becoming indistinguishable from my memory of Stefan, so I had to bite Felix's shoulder not to cry out Stefan's name.

'Ah, Mitzi,' said Felix, 'what nonsense you talk, what nonsense you try to convince yourself of, just like all the others. Because you do want to, Mitzi. Mitzi, my darling; oh, Mitzi. Don't ever say you don't want to. Because you do. *Because you are.*'

*

170

'Well,' said Trudi cynically, 'they used to come around, I think, for Joshua's CARE packages, now they come for Joshua. All the *Prominenz*. Who could blame them, we were all so hungry. And now they all seem to have eligible daughters, and I suppose they hope . . . not even Felix's reputation keeps them away.'

'But after all, we *are* the *Prominenz*,' Felix observed lazily, from behind Joshua's American paper.

'There speaks the Count again,' said my mother. 'Not enough to make up for all your offences. Do you want me to enumerate them?'

'You would have to, if you want me to remember. But it is all so boring. It is all far more important to them than it is to me. I think they have formed a tennis club now only so that they can put me on the blacklist.'

'Anyway,' said Trudi, 'in spite of Felix, they are coming back like the swallows. I do not know when we have had so many invitations to tea.'

'And the way they look at Mitzi when Joshua is with her,' said Berti. 'It must amuse you a little, Mitzi, to make them so jealous. When we walked into Puffingers the other day, the way they looked at you! Dear God, it seems only yesterday you were the little thing we were pulling on the sled. And now you are –'

Trudi nudged her. Felix yawned and pushed back his chair. 'I had better go up and help Joshua.'

'We hardly see Joshua these days,' said my mother, as Felix went out. 'It is a pity, this beautiful weather, and all these invitations for you both, and he is buried in those letters. There seem to be more and more. How extraordinary of Felix to have rescued them. And he is not a scholar. I don't know why it isn't you who is helping Joshua.'

'Let her be,' said Berti, 'she will have enough hard studying to do this year. It is better if she keeps Joshua company on his time off.'

'But surely you would be much more help to him, wouldn't you, Mitzi?'

'I don't think I would. Felix and Werner seem much better able to decipher the handwritings.'

'Anyway, he is staying,' said Berti. 'That is the most important thing. A sweet young man, so courtly, so kind, so completely unlike one's idea of the Americans. Perhaps a little slow in making decisions'

Now it was I who got up. 'Perhaps he is not slow at all. Perhaps other people imagine decisions when there are none to be made.' Then I too went out, hearing behind me the beginning buzz of Trudi and my mother upbraiding Berti for her tactlessness.

VIII

In the autumn, I went back to school, Werner went back to university, and Joshua and Felix stayed on. Joshua had written to the university authorities and hoped in due time to get a larger grant to pursue his researches into my Grandmama's literary love life. On the strength of this hope, he was borrowing from his parents and paying Felix for his help in deciphering the letters and interpreting them in the light of whatever Felix could remember of Grandmama's anecdotes. Felix was free to devote himself to this. His courier's job would have ended with the summer season, and being Felix, he had left it before.

Joshua, for all the good Austrian food with which we regaled him, grew thinner, more nervous, more intense. Grandmama's correspondence was eating him alive. We saw him mostly at meals, when he was polite but distraught. He hardly took me out any more. Since he had first given me one of the precious letters to read and asked if I was glad he was staying, and I had, with clumsy pointedness, called him my best friend, a coldness, an awkwardness, had grown between us, though I had tried to go on as before. When we were alone together, he talked feverishly about the letters, about Handelbein and Kafka and Freud and Schnitzler and Tollmutter and the mad playwright Adlerhorst, and Stammlos, the 'gypsy bear' who had drawn Maria Aurora while she listened to Schubert, and whose correspondence was chiefly remarkable for its succinctness:

My dear precious Countess,

I hate Paris. There is too much painting going on.

You know that writing letters makes me feel seasick and since there is so little space on the paper and so much in the bed that is where I will go and think of you being there with me.

Always your Rudi (Stammlos)

It was also Stammlos – or was it Klimt? – who said of one of his models, 'That little girl has a rear which is more beautiful and intelligent than most people's faces.' But no, I am digressing.

It seems that Maria Aurora had kept everything, even the ravings of the doomed philosopher Waldmann when he finally understood that she was not to be detached (by him at any rate) from the poet Hans Handelbein, and that she had been the mistress of the crude lowborn genius Stammlos, a fact long known to the whole artistic and aristocratic world of Central Europe but apparently not to Waldmann, lost in his wrestling with The Being that May not Be There (*Das Dasein das nicht da sein darf*). 'There are no words,' Waldmann wrote, 'to express my disgust at the slime through which you have waded, through which I have been made to wade by my devotion to you, I who am now compelled to think of you sullied by the weight of that unwashed ape, you who were my evening star, my Venus in darkness, my clear pure spring.' Maria Aurora had written in the margin, perhaps with the intention of sending the letter, for his amusement, to Handelbein, 'Compared to Waldmann, Stammlos in fact smells like an angel!'

(Joshua's theory, elaborated at length in his book, was that to preserve his pride Waldmann had to pretend it was because of Maria Aurora's past affair with Stammlos that he was breaking off their entirely one-sided relations, since he did not dare challenge, with weapon or word, her present lover; nor could he bear to admit defeat. It was following this episode that Waldmann spent some time in an old-fashioned mental clinic. He was unfortunately too suspicious and stubborn to consult Freud, whom both my grandmother and Handelbein, who was really quite a kind and generous man, recommended. Not long after, he committed suicide – not however in Maria Aurora's presence. That one was probably the obscure

174

Magyar poet Koloman Ragy, though even Joshua was never sure.)

Joshua seemed particularly fascinated by some of the later correspondence, particularly that of the neurotic playwright Adlerhorst, who poured out hypochondria as Handelbein had poured out passion.

My dearest dearest Mitzi,

Oh, my Countess, my Queen, I should like to garland you with all the flowers of fairy tales – but from what miraculous month of spring could I pluck them, what season could bring forth anything fine enough to enhance your unsurpassable grace? And my heart burns before this grace like the candle before the holy portrait of Maria, burns and gutters a little, as you are not there to animate the portrait with your living breath to fan the flame. (Adlerhorst, who wrote plays with care but letters in a hurry, was somewhat given to mixing his metaphors.) *Yet for all its guttering it is a brave and determined little flame and even the tempests of illness, disappointment and the world's growing evil will not put it out.*

Today it was the hand of my hairdresser that set off the migraine. This terrible perfumed hand, washed, manicured, scoured and scented; all at once I could not bear it waving in my face, jutting from its white cuff like a fearful flabby odiferous spider – my eyes and nostrils burned, my head ached to bursting. I pushed off the terrible hand, threw down my towel and rushed out of the shop. If I had stayed another second I should have seized his razor and murdered him. Poor little man, he is a good hairdresser, he means well – ah, dearest Mitzi, what is to become of me?

The headache lasted all day. Also there is a new pain in my back. Also there was a fly in my coffee this afternoon. The flabby spider, then the fly. These images can only mean evil. Oh, Mitzi, I cannot bear it. If only you were here, I would lay my head on your knees and sink my soul into yours as the battered ship, after its long long voyage, lowers its anchor into the long-ago harbour that is its home . . .

Dear Friedl,

Forgive me, but I am still young enough to need a lover and not old enough to be content with a patient. I do not want a head on my knees. I am bad enough with real children, I cannot possibly be any man's mother. I will help you all I can to escape your world of threats and symbols, but I cannot be what you ask, I can only be what I am.

175

(Friedl, undaunted, or perhaps she did not send her letter, wrote back in the same vein.)

Darling Mitzi,

Oh, my dearest, how much I miss you, my clear mountain spring – no, spring in the desert, source of the oasis, the blessed shade-giving trees where the weary nomad tethers his camel and pitches his tent forevermore!

Yesterday I was brushing my teeth when that mysterious sensation I have written you about came over me again. Sometimes even the slightest muscular activity seems to bring it on. It is as if all the muscles I have just used go into extreme mental *tension, a kind of cramp of the nerve impulses, if you can imagine that, as if though I can still use my hand, the* volition *to use it is being overstrained, and I have a sudden fear that the hand holding the toothbrush will not be able to cease or let go, and I shall stand forever with a fear-contorted open mouth in front of the mirror brushing and brushing and brushing my teeth until my gums are streaming with blood. And how all this terrible anxiety interferes with my work! I begin to understand the lust for agony of the ancient martyrs. It is a kind of impatience, a longing, to experience the worst that one's nerves can do so as to be free of their continued interruptions and intrusions and devastations . . . but why do I pour out my trivial miseries to you, oh, most beautiful Countess, except that to tell them, to* you, *is already half healing, a kind of white magic, as if they lost some of their evil force over me only by being put down for the cool perusal of your violet eyes.*

I am sending you the first act of Offene Verborgenheit. *It is dedicated to you. Let me hear what you think.*

        Always your Friedl

Dear Friedl,

Calm yourself. The play is marvellous. I can hardly wait for the next two acts. Your bewildering symptoms may be only a reaction to the expenditure of so much creative energy. If they do not pass you should see Dr Freud, who is excellent.

Dear Friedl, please do not tell me again that I am a pure clear mountain spring, an inexhaustible source, etcetera. I have been presented so often with this metaphor that I feel I must soon go about with a label, like a bottle of mineral water. I am not trying to be unkind; your fertile mind will certainly devise other and more original forms of flattery. In any event I am no longer a young woman and at my age the miraculous source begins to be troubled, though thank God I still feel as

healthy as my last coachman kept my horses. In what curious contexts do
we remember things!

I hope fervently that the mysterious 'cramps of volition' have not
affected you more generally. If they have, I foresee difficulties. Perhaps
you really should see Dr Freud.
                    Always your Mitzi

It was at this stage that at last I did what I should have done
earlier. I determined to find a handwriting expert and get
him to look at a couple of the letters – one from Handelbein, I
decided, and one from Adlerhorst. It took some time for me to
track down an expert, and when I did, I planned a secret trip
to Salzburg to confront Werner (I had better sense than to
confront Felix) with what I had done.

Meanwhile Joshua went on with his obsessive work. Even
when Felix was not there he accompanied Gordana and
Grandmama on their outings, he made suggestions to Gordana
about Grandmama's dress, he pored over Grandmama's
photographs and tried in vain to elicit some recognition of
them from the old lady's weak vague eyes. He no longer
asked my opinion of the letters; it was as if he sensed my
suspicion and was afraid of facing it. And some of the letters
he was working on now, he explained, blushing furiously,
were extremely intimate ones, were really quite embarrassing
to read.

But once, I remember, Joshua did talk about something other
than his work. He talked about Gordana.

She had been regaling him, it seems, with what my elders
called her *Schaudergeschichten*, her horror stories, and he was
quite shaken. 'But Werner gave me a book about that part of
the war. It is all true. They took young boys and pulled out
their tongues, and made them stand back to back and drove
spikes through them with their mothers watching. And then
Gordana says the Gestapo – the Gestapo! – rescued her family.
Oh, I know, I know, there were atrocities on the anti-German
side – and the Balkans are known for their cruelty – but such
atrocities – sometimes it makes one wonder what it was all
for.' He was already manifesting that crisis of political conscience that was to grow and grow in the Anglo-Saxon
countries. Political conscience, like many other good things, is
seldom found among those who could use it most.

177

'What happened in Yugoslavia was also a civil war. And you cannot be responsible for everyone who fights under the same banner. You are only responsible if you encourage those horrors instead of trying to stop them. Where would we all be now, if the Allies had not won?'

Joshua said huskily, 'Thank you, Mitzi.' I realized that, young as I was, he persisted in regarding me as a fount of moral wisdom as well as culture, because I had lived through the Nazi occupation, because I had suffered and nearly died, because I was European. There were times when this blind earnest trust, as with the letters, not only worried but annoyed me. To cover my annoyance, I went on about Gordana herself.

'Berti said the other day Gordana is getting weepier, and also beginning to put on airs. To which my mother said that she needs a man. My mother would think of that, because that's what she usually needs herself.' Joshua blushed furiously. I had done it again; he must be deeply shocked that I was being so disrespectful about my mother. I was, of course; but having been open with him about so many things, I tended to forget it was not only me he idealized, that he still bore flawless images of us all engraved upon his honest American heart. To relieve his embarrassment, I rushed on. 'I do wish for Gordana's sake we could find her some nice young farmer, so she could marry and settle down and not have the worry of being a D.P. But they only want local girls, most of them, they're still terribly provincial and prejudiced. And she doesn't want to marry a fellow countryman. She says she doesn't want someone who will beat her the way her father did. The men in her village, she says, were just like wild animals. If we could only get her to wash her hair more often! You know the way she wears it – in a coil – well, I've seen it down once when she was sick and it's five feet long, and it could be so beautiful – but she only washes it twice a year. I've tried to tell her but she can't be bothered. Joshua! Is anything wrong?'

'No – no, of course not. I'm sorry, I'm really so absorbed these days. I can't really discuss anything, I suppose, Mitzi, except the letters. I suppose I had better get back to work.'

'You look charming, Mitzi,' Werner said.

I made a face at him. I neither looked nor felt charming,

178

after having limped up four flights of stairs to his shabby Salzburg eyrie.

'But' – Werner took my hand and kissed it with teasing formality – 'although I am flattered, I am also puzzled. You have surely not come all the way to Salzburg only to inspect my humble premises.' He waited. I said nothing. I was inspecting his books. Freud, Rilke, Kafka, Nietzsche, Handelbein, Schnitzler, Kraus . . . At last I said, 'You have an amazing library. There was so much that needed to be reprinted, even rediscovered, after the war – and so much of it is here.'

Werner grinned. 'You forget I am a scholar as well as a writer and that all this is my bread and butter. It was an incredible period, well, actually two incredible periods, *fin de siècle* Vienna, Vienna between the wars. The beautiful rotting fruit, the blossom with a worm in its heart, the girls of Schiele with their tender breasts and tubercular ribs and death-filled eyes, a society so brilliant, so febrile, so sick and yet so creative that it haemorrhages art and glitter like a consumptive coughing blood. Oh, Mitzi.' With sudden wistfulness. 'We had a lovely time this summer, the four of us.'

'Yes, we did. And yes, it was a brilliant period, and Grandmama spanned the whole of it. I would never have known so much about it myself if it had not been for Joshua sending me books, and telling me to get others. He knew much more about it than I did. So many of the refugees from that world went to teach in America . . .' I was still looking at his library, when something caught my eye; a little book about the painters of the Secession, printed in New York, which I had got from Joshua. I pulled it out and looked at the fly-leaf: to Mitzi from Joshua with love, April 1950. I handed the book to Werner and said, 'Felix could at least have asked.'

Werner smiled apologetically. 'You know Felix.'

'Did Felix get you a lot of these books, then?'

'Only some. Is that what you've come to talk about?'

'Not directly.'

'I'm sorry, I have been neglecting my duty as host. I was so overwhelmed by your wanting to visit me, you the most distant person in the world. Can I make you a coffee, or get you a glass of wine?'

'Maybe you had better wait until you hear what I have done, which is also what I came here to tell you about. I've sent two of Grandmama's letters from famous men to a handwriting expert. I should have his opinion in a week or two.'

Werner stared at me, then blinked and looked down. He was still holding my book; he put it absently back on the shelf now, his big hand trembling a little. At last he said, 'Mitzi, why?'

'I find it very curious that these letters turned up just when Felix was at loose ends and everyone – whatever their reasons – was trying to get Joshua to stay. I also find it curious that Grandmama should have asked for, and got, so many of her own letters back. I know how vain she was, but still . . . And that Felix and you have made yourselves custodians of them, and are still 'deciphering' more to pass on to Joshua. These letters have now become Joshua's thesis, and in a way, his whole life. If it should turn out that they are forgeries, his whole career, everything, would be in ruins. I don't know what it would do to him. He trusts these letters, he trusts us, and he thinks, God help us, that he has made one of the great literary discoveries of the decade. I cannot let him go on believing that if this is some kind of elaborate hoax. The kind of hoax you know, and I know, Felix is perfectly capable of.'

Werner said slowly, 'Neither Felix nor I can do forgeries, Mitzi.'

'No. But Felix would know somebody who can. Somebody who might even owe him something. How do you think he got himself clean papers to go to America with Betsy? You are a writer and a scholar and Felix has ideas about being a writer too. You are an expert on this period. You could provide the background and both of you the text, and Felix could find the forger. If this is a monstrous and groundless suspicion, forgive me. I pray that I am wrong. I pray that the letters are genuine. Because if they are not, I really don't know what we are going to do.'

Werner reached for a cigarette and then thought better of it, apparently still unable to control the trembling of his hands. Then he said, almost in a whisper, 'Why have you come to tell me this?'

'Because I thought it was the only fair thing to do. If the letters are forgeries, I would rather hear it first from you. You could tell me now, and we could discuss how to get Joshua out of this. Look, if they are forgeries, you know it will come

180

out sooner or later. And please, I am not really accusing you of – I mean one can start these things as a joke and then get drawn in too far to go back. I know that Felix can make one do almost anything.'

Werner swallowed, then burst out, 'But is it *not* monstrous – to use your own word – monstrous and crazy and paranoid – for you to think that Felix and I would do this complicated thing, just to keep Joshua here? For what reason? What reason can there be? The hope that he will marry you?'

I answered, my voice cold and surprisingly calm, 'That was not worthy of you. And you know there are better motives. Grandmama did have an affair with Handelbein, probably with some other famous writers and artists. Her letters might be valuable one day. And for Felix at the moment it's a job. Anyway, it is the sort of game that amuses Felix, just as it amused him to invent that ancestral castle for Betsy and see how far he could go. And maybe he really wanted to write, and this might be his big literary success. And you, with your abstractions, would never be strong enough to stand against him.' I was paying him back for what he had said, but I looked at his blank stricken face, his nervous fingers, and knew I had been more cruel than he, because I had been right. 'I'd better go now, Werner. You see, I didn't think you'd want to give me a coffee. Please don't be stupid and tell Felix that I have been here or what I have done. We can worry about Felix when the report comes.'

Werner stammered, 'Forgive me, Mitzi, for what I said. And of course I will not tell Felix. I would not dream of exposing you to his temper, neither you nor myself. I am a pacifist, Mitzi, by conviction and inclination, though I know pacifism never works, not in this world. No, here, please, please, don't go. Let me get you some wine.' Now he was all solicitude and feverish attention, and kept insisting that whatever happened, we must always continue to be friends.

So, feeling guilty about his obvious anxiety and pain – I did know, after all, how bitterly hard Felix was to resist – I stayed, and we both drank a good deal of wine, and talked ardently about other things, in Werner's usual abstractions. But not only. At one point he took my hand and asked if he had understood me rightly, if I was really not thinking of marrying Joshua.

181

'Dear God,' I exclaimed, 'you are as bad as all the old hens. Joshua has never proposed to me, and if he did I would say no. Why does everyone think because we are good friends that we must automatically fall in love?'

Werner looked very serious, as if this question were not rhetorical but one deserving all the concentration of his ponderous brain. 'I think because it is so logical and reasonable and to them all, desirable. You do not tire of each other's conversation, you are moved by the same things, he is shy and you seem cold and you are both more warm and animated in each other's company. The whole basis of a relationship is there. I think the human mind – even mine (I could not help smiling at this) – is always taking events to their conventional outcomes and looks at every situation in terms of its convention before it looks at the particular. And all these conventions are of course made only to keep the social fabric together –' He was off again, and I wondered if his steady stream of words was partly an attempt to ward off speculation about the answer from the handwriting expert, which we seemed to have tacitly agreed to wait for before Werner said anything more. But he finished, surprisingly, 'So – but then – you really have not thought of – my God, you must be the only girl in Rehbruck who has not. But it would be such an escape for you – your life would be so much easier. We have so little here, and it will never be what it was, the world your grandmother –' He stopped. We were back on dangerous ground.

'That world has been dead for some time now.'

'Yes. But not so deeply interred. Well, whatever – I would not hold it against you, Mitzi, we all make arrangements, we all compromise –'

'Yes. And I with my leg will not have so many opportunities. Is this what you want to say?'

He seemed genuinely shocked. 'No. Dear God, no. I think it's just that I feel your refusal to compromise as a reproach. Because I am weaker. I do compromise. You know that I compromise. But I also feel it as an inspiration. And, Mitzi –' He swallowed again. 'I wanted to be sure. Because – because I am glad. That you will not. Marry Joshua, I mean. Oh, Mitzi, you are so confusing. In spite of the way I talk about women as vessels of intuition and all that nonsense you see how helpless and confused I am. Here, please, you cannot go yet, please have some more wine.'

182

At the end of it all Werner saw me to the station and kissed me goodbye as if we were lovers; and to my surprise, drunk as I was, I kissed him back. And later, sobering up on the train, I realized how little right I of all people had to lecture Werner about his weakness – then thought, *No*. What I do after all can hurt no one except myself. But I am hardly in the impeccable moral position he thinks me. And what, after all, did I accomplish with this visit – except to create perhaps still another confusion, another situation from which I will have to disentangle myself?

A week later, Werner phoned to ask if I had heard from my graphologist. I had. There was a silence, then Werner said hoarsely, 'And – and what? Please tell me.'

'Well, you can sleep soundly tonight. It's all right. He says it is difficult with such scruffy material' – I had to be careful, Joshua and Gordana were in the room – 'but he thinks yes, genuine.'

There was another silence, then Werner asked, 'Will you try again? Or do you believe him?'

'It doesn't matter what I believe. I may be entirely wrong. And as long as an official opinion backs it up, I have decided there is no reason to cause pain and disappointment. It's all, as I said, so far along . . . I only did not want things to proceed if there was no chance of success.'

'Ah,' said Werner. Then, 'Curious, isn't it? I do not know if I am glad or sorry. Goodbye now, Mitzi. But please come and see me again.'

And that was as close to an admission as I, or anyone, was ever to get.

Joshua stayed eight months. Not all the time, of course; he came and went, to Salzburg, Vienna, Heidelberg, France. All worked out according to his highest hopes. His new subject was accepted, his grant extended. Felix, who managed to siphon off even more money from Joshua than the 'salary' Joshua paid him, inventing research trips, hunting for obscure relatives who might have more letters or information, wangled a sudden journey to Paris to see the dancer called Juliette with whom he had been corresponding ever since their meeting on the Arlberg Express.

Not that Felix had been faithful, of course, to this distant star. If I have not said more about Felix's girls it is because there were so many, and most of them we never met. We were more likely to meet their irate swains. Another reason Felix left precipitately was because the husband of a young Viennese socialite who had summered in Rehbruck was threatening to shoot him, and actually appeared one day with a revolver. Fortunately, Felix was out, and Joshua and Gordana were out also, taking Grandmama for a taxi ride. (Felix had hinted to Joshua that occasional changes of scene might stir the old lady's memories. I think he was indebted to that particular taxi driver, who was a friend of sorts and had rescued Felix from several unpleasant situations. Getting Peter to pay Paul was another of Felix's talents, and like the girls, I have not elaborated on it because Felix's network of contacts and debtors, some of which went back to his school and black-market days, was out of our ken and would, to be properly dealt with, need a book to itself and far more research than even poor Joshua devoted to Grandmama.) Trudi and Berti, 'the faithful Valkyries', Felix said afterwards, wrested the gun away from the husband and sent him packing; he was not heard from again.

With Joshua so absorbed in his work and I in my studies, and all the remarks I had made to disabuse my elders of their hopes, I thought the subject of my great romance with Joshua was closed. But a day after Felix left, my mother, prompted perhaps by worry about the son to make a last attempt at inspiring reason in the daughter, took me aside.

'Do you know, Mitzi, Joshua has been here almost a year. And he is such a wonderful young man. I must say, I had hoped – he has told me on many occasions how fond he is of you. But you seem completely indifferent, and I must say –'

'There is nothing you must say,' I interrupted rudely. Hearing her talk like this brought all my old rage back. But she went on, oblivious. 'Please let me finish, Mitzi. I must say I do not understand your attitude. It seems to me that far from making any kind of effort – when he has invitations from Kitty and the others, you encourage him to go without you. They are all wondering, gossiping – such a handsome young man, they all say, and so well educated – and I am sure he is still fond of you – would still be – I must say, I do not under-stand what you want out of life.'

I got up. I had to hold on to the table, my legs were shaking so. 'You do not understand what I want out of life. I want all sorts of things, but what I wanted most was Stefan. And you destroyed that. And now as then you think only of appearances, you are upset because Kitty Kleinholz might have a little triumph over you, when your concern for appearances has already cost me my leg and very nearly my life. And in a way it has, it has cost my life. I thought I had stopped hating you but I have not. I will never forgive you as long as I live.'

There was a knock on the door and Gordana entered, her face very blank, as it often was. She said softly that she had come in to get Grandmama's shawl, and that Joshua was taking the afternoon off and since it was sunny and the snow almost gone, would like to walk with me up the *Calvarienberg*.

'It seems a long time, Mitzi, since we have been out together like this. But the paths are still wet – does it bother you?'

'Not at all. Look, I'm walking as fast as you. I will never ski, I know, but my leg seems so much stronger this year I thought I might try Trudi and Berti's old sled. You should ski. I know Kitty has asked you to go up to their little chalet with her and Brigitte.' My rage at my mother was making me malicious. 'Why don't you go? I am sure they think you are safer than Felix.'

'Yes, much safer,' Joshua said with such acrimony I could have bitten my tongue. We walked on in silence for a bit. The sun shimmered on the still, frosty pines; then the mist rose again, and the little town below became a sepia print, a gentle gradation of browns and whites in which now, at siesta time, only the river moved. In the spring thaw, the caged statuary looked even deathlier, and I shivered as we passed the limp wooden Christ with his bright blood and painted peeling limbs. 'I will always hate that statue. It makes me think of the convent where I jumped off the wall. It makes me think of Janka, and the prisoners in the woods. Why, when there is so much suffering, do we worship it, and do so little to make it stop?'

'I'm sorry, Mitzi. We should have gone somewhere else. But the days are so short, and we are both so busy – Oh, Mitzi! It is redemption, that suffering. Once I believed in that and you did too. If one believes in the redemption, the atone-ment, it does not seem morbid, it is a token of how much one is loved by a supreme power. But I have not brought you here to talk about suffering and religion. Mitzi, you said I was your best friend. I am going to tell you something only a best friend should be the first to hear – something that will surprise you; and I only hope that it will not make you angry, that it will not make you think differently of me. No, I hope – I hope against hope, I suppose, that in the end we will only be closer because of it.'

My first thought was, my God, he still has not caught on, he is going to propose after all. Then I thought no, it doesn't sound like that. Is it the letters? Is it possible he too has begun to suspect?

Joshua was mumbling, 'I only hope your mother won't be too upset, and of course I realize we will have to move at once – I only thought, until we find somebody to look after the Countess – I realize of course that that should be our re-sponsibility –'

'Joshua, what is it, what in heaven are you talking about?'

Joshua took my hand and held it tightly in both of his. 'Mitzi,' he said. 'You are the first one to hear, and for the sake of our friendship, you must help me, Mitzi. My mind is made up. I am absolutely certain that for me it is the right and only thing. But I know they will be shocked, we shall have to prepare them. You say I have helped you, Mitzi. Well, I need your help with this, I need your help now, as never before.'

'Joshua, for God's sake –'

'Mitzi,' Joshua said again. His eyes were the eyes of a stricken deer, the eyes of the Christ under the crown of thorns. 'Mitzi, I am going to marry Gordana.'

I looked away for a moment, trying to master my shock. Joshua let go of my hand, seized it again, then once more, let it go. 'Mitzi, please – I know it must come as a total surprise. There was a time when I thought that you and I might become something more than friends – but I felt you did not want that, and – I suppose I have realized all along that I could never be happy with an intellectual wife, such a one and I would soon be throwing plates at each other, it wouldn't work, it's never worked with anyone like that up till now. I need someone old-fashioned and warm, and well, I suppose

186

you could say, a salt of the earth person, like Gordana. Oh, I know she is totally uneducated but she is not insensitive at all, you can tell it by the way she cares for the Countess, the way she dresses her, and by many other things – and she is really interested in my work, and there is something so fresh and good and simple about the way she looks at life. I think we can be happy together.' How desperately, I thought, he is trying to convince himself. 'But I know your family will be upset and I want you to help me tell them.'

'Well,' I said, having managed to collect myself during his long frantic speech, 'I won't say it's not a shock, but if it's what you want, it must be right, and I hope you will be happy.' I thought of the face the three graces would make and could hardly keep from smiling.

'And you're not angry – you didn't think you and I –' In his clumsy compulsive way, he had to spell it all out. 'Your mother was always hinting – I think she would have liked –'

'*No*,' I said, very firmly. 'I have never thought of you except as a friend, you know that; and you are still my friend, just as before.'

It was some time later, when we were walking down the twilit hill, I remembered my mother remarking that Gordana must be getting over her monthly troubles, as it was now ten weeks since her last collapse.

'I know I should have phoned,' said Kitty Kleinholz. 'It might not be the most opportune moment to call. But they are all talking in town. I could not believe it, but today I saw them together. It still doesn't seem possible. That nice, well-educated young man – he is really going to marry a Croatian servant?'

'He is not going to,' said my mother shortly. 'He has. They did not even put up banns. They were married very quietly in Salzburg yesterday morning and they are living at an inn until they can find some rooms. At least he was discreet enough to leave with her as soon as he told us. She offered to stay until they found someone else for the old Countess, but of course we refused.'

'Of course,' said Kitty with heavy sarcasm, 'of course. You cannot tell the wife of a future professor to empty chamberpots! Do you know, the last time I was here, I had the impression she was putting on airs already. How she must be laughing at all of us. And here we all thought – we thought he and Mitzi – oh, Mitzi,' turning to see I was there, 'I'm sorry, I didn't realize –'

'It's quite all right,' said my mother, looking daggers at me in case I denied this. 'Mitzi rejected him.'

'What a sensible girl you are, Mitzi,' Kitty cried. 'Everyone was so enchanted with this young man, but you must have sensed that he was not quite normal, that somewhere he had this mad streak, this *Drang nach unten*. Imagine if you had married him and he had begun carrying on with your servants in America. Or perhaps it was your rejection that deranged him. If so you must feel quite a *femme fatale*, quite like the old Countess.'

'Actually,' I said, 'it was a mutual rejection, so I am quite sure he was not deranged by it. Joshua and I have never been anything but good friends. It is the incurable romanticism of the middle-aged that reads love into every relationship between the young. Or perhaps one should say, especially in this case, the incurable practicality.'

My mother cleared her throat. Fortunately Brigitte, who was there too, came to her rescue. 'Mitzi was right, Mama; he looks attractive but he would never have appealed to me either. And you kept trying to arrange those tennis games.'

'I? Arrange tennis games? My dear child, I only did it because *you* were so eager. *I* too sensed all along that he was a most peculiar young man. But of course he seemed so charming and so polite one tended not to believe one's instincts. Tell me, how long do you think, Anni, all this had been going on? What an incredibly sly creature she is, to have kept it so hidden, to wait until she was certain of him and then fling it into all your poor faces! But of course no one is more devious than these Yugoslavs, except the – ach, I forget, that is something one is not supposed to say any more, and anyway, they are all gone – poor souls,' she added, with quick perfunctory piety. 'Which is more than you can say of the Yugoslavs, who are multiplying like rabbits. Soon there will not be a German name left in the town. But tell me, *how* long was it? And none of you ever suspected *anything*? But tell me, is she – ah, is *that* why it is?'

My mother nodded.

'Do you mean,' gasped Kitty, 'that it is already visible?'

'No, no,' my mother said. 'But we are fairly certain.'

'So that was it! She has trapped the poor man, this poor naïve stupid young American. Poor man? Oh, Kitty, what are you saying!' she chided herself breathlessly. 'He is not a poor man at all, he is a scoundrel. To carry on like that under your roof – to abuse your hospitality in such a disgusting manner – I cannot find words for it.'

'I doubt that,' I murmured, 'you seem to be doing quite well.' Kitty glanced at me sharply and then away again.

'Well,' said Trudi, 'he will have his reward. A professor, saddled with a wife who can neither read nor write –'

'Oh, come. We have all seen her read the newspaper,' I said. Now all of them looked askance at me, greatly annoyed by these little dampers on their righteous indignation. Except Brigitte, who was gazing furtively at a photo of Felix.

Then Kitty smiled. 'My dear, it is noble of you to defend your friend, if you can still think of him as that, but you must realize what an outrage he has committed. Still, as Trudi says, he will pay for it bitterly.'

'I suppose it was his American puritanism,' Trudi said, 'that made him feel he had to marry her. But a woman so much his social inferior . . . something could have been arranged. If he had only come to us and confessed – we were all so fond of him . . .'

'Yes. There are so many poor refugees, I am sure that for quite a modest sum of money a young man from her own country might have been found – but it is true, these things are not so easy to deal with as in the old days. I am older than all of you, I know that much went on in my childhood that no one talked about, but there were always ways around. But then, how do we know she is so much his social inferior? In America it is what they call the great melting pot, isn't it, you do not know anyone's background – and university, that does not mean so much there either. Why I have been told that in America even Negroes go to university. Perhaps he is really just finding his own level. No man with any kind of fine feeling would do such a thing. Under the roof of his best friends! Even the worst Austrian rakes I have known –' Kitty looked at Brigitte, and stopped.

'If she were beautiful,' my mother said, 'maybe one could understand it.'

'Yes,' agreed Trudi, 'but a girl who looks like a horse –'

'And a carthorse, too. No thoroughbred,' Berti added, and

189

they all laughed. Then Kitty cried, 'But no, it is not beauty, it is pure animal sexuality that often traps such intellectual men. Just because they are buried in their books and know so little about life, they have no resistance. They cannot resist these dark Slavic women with their strange wayward eyes. And of course these women will stop at nothing to get the man they want. Especially one they think superior, who will put them on a higher rung. That way they are like the J—' She caught herself again, smiled nervously and went on. 'My mother had a maid once from Transylvania and she even made witch's potions to catch the groom, and do you know, it worked?'

'Oh, Mama,' Brigitte said.

'There you are, the young will never believe anything they do not find in their scientific textbooks. But I tell you, although all that is supposed to be discredited, there is a great deal to be said for folk wisdom. These primitive people would never get so far without it. But no, I still think his marrying her is the craziest thing I have ever heard. Can you imagine that woman presiding when he is entertaining the other professors –and I understand his research, those old letters he has found in your house, are quite important, so he may become important, too.'

'It will ruin his career,' Berti said sadly.

'Well,' Kitty remarked, 'that would only serve him right.'

But Berti shook her head. 'No, no, I do not wish him evil. He was very good to us all.'

'I admire your spirit of forgiveness,' said Kitty stiffly, 'but I know how I would feel if this had happened in my house. Or do you think he is planning – what is that play, Brigitte had to read it in her English course –'

'*Pygmalion*,' Brigitte said, yawning.

'Yes. Do you think he is planning a miraculous transformation, to awaken the sleeping mind of this *Dornröschen* (Rose of Thorns, or the Sleeping Beauty)? Though I would say it is not sleeping at all but very wakeful to its own interests.'

'I do not think,' said my mother, 'that she is really *Pygmalion* material.'

'No, I fear she is not. Though of course the Americans think anyone can become anything. Again, it would be some excuse, if there had been any hope of that, any sign. After all,' Kitty smiled and folded her hands on her bony knees, 'there is a bar sinister in many of the best families. If we knew our entire family trees . . . but one hopes at least a fall from grace has something to commend it, that it is an injection of vigorous fresh Aryan blood which our effete old stock sometimes needs. But of course one does not wish to see the injection again at the breakfast table. And in this case it does not apply, because the heredity of poor Gordana is, I am sure, not something any of us would wish to see grafted onto the family tree. But how is the old Countess taking it? And have you found someone for her?'

'Yes, we have,' answered my mother, 'but not anyone very good. And the Countess is so confused, poor soul, she knows nothing about Joshua of course, and she thinks Gordana is Janka, who – a servant she once had, who died. And you do not know the worst. Gordana told her she was getting married and she took off one of her brooches and said, "Here, dear little Janka, this is for your trousseau. You must promise to sell it, it will buy you sheets and cooking pots."' My mother did not quote the other thing Grandmama, who just then had had one of her rare talkative days, had said: I am glad you are going to America, little Janka, because there the Gestapo cannot find you. 'And the shameless creature accepted it! When I, who was there, pointed out that the brooch was not meant for her but for Janka, who was dead, and that it was not decent to accept such a valuable thing from a senile person who does not know what she is giving or to whom, do you know what that creature said? She said,' my mother's voice was shaking with rage, 'She said, "She has often called me Janka so how do you know she does not mean me? And after the salary you paid me and what I have done, three of those brooches would not be too many. Sometimes those who wipe other people's –" my mother stopped, almost in tears, shook her head, and finished, "are entitled to something out of life too."'

'She said *that* to you?' My mother nodded, and for a moment even Kitty was speechless. Then she launched into a delighted tirade about both Americans and Yugoslavs, which threatened to go on until dinner-time. I decided we had had more than enough of Kitty, so when she interrupted herself to say, 'My dear children, I have been talking too much as usual, I am quite thirsty. Do you not think we should fortify ourselves with a rum tea after this dreadful news?' I answered quickly before anyone else could. 'Yes, I'll put tea on. Felix will want

191

some when he comes and he's due from the station any minute.'

'Felix?' asked Berti, who was always slowest on the uptake. 'I thought Felix was not due until –'

'No, today,' Trudi exclaimed. 'Yes, Mitzi, please do go and put on the tea.'

They were glad I had done it, but they would not have done it themselves. Kitty paralyzed them, somehow, and in spite of everything, she was one of their set. At any rate, it worked; Kitty remembered an appointment, made her excuses, and hurried out. She and Brigitte were talking in low tones as they passed the kitchen window on their way through the garden. On impulse, I turned off the water and listened.

'But, Mama, do you really think she rejected him?' Brigitte was asking in her bored plaintive voice. Kitty answered, 'No. Men are physical, after all. He might marry a peasant, even one who looks like a carthorse, but he would not marry a cripple.'

At this I opened the window wide and shouted at the top of my voice, 'But sooner a carthorse or a cripple than a vicious cow for a mother-in-law.' They fled, and I slammed the window shut, feeling quite cheerful.

My mother came in then, having heard me shout. 'Mitzi, what is it?'

'Nothing, nothing. But I think I have just got rid of Kitty Kleinholz for good and all.'

'You have? What did you say?' I told her, and why. 'Oh, Mitzi, how awful for you to hear that. I suppose we are well rid of her. Still, as she is an influential woman, it was perhaps not wise to call her a cow . . .' Then, to my surprise, she sat down and began to cry. 'Still, there you are, she is crowing over us, that fearful woman, we are the laughing stock of the whole town. What have I done that for my children everything must always go wrong?'

'Oh, Mama, what nonsense. You talk as if Joshua jilted me for Gordana, when I never dreamt of him except as a friend.'

'Is it so abnormal,' my mother said operatically between sobs, 'to want to see one's children settled and secure? After all we have been through these last years? I wanted to see you both living a safer and happier life than I have lived. Do you think it was easy – the war, your grandmother, Janka, the man I loved killed on the Russian front?' This last was news to me, as I had not been aware that my mother loved her Wehrmacht officer much more than she had loved Kropetschka. The old anger came back, and I found myself saying, 'If you knew what that word means, you could not have done what you did to me.'

'Mitzi, you were too young, I had to protect you. I could only do what I thought was right.' She raised her face; it was blotched and puffy, the china-blue eyes swimming with tears. For a moment I wanted to say, 'I forgive you, I love you', but the words would not come. They would have been meaningless, they were not true. I could not really love her any more than she could love Grandmama, or Grandmama had loved her. But I would be dutiful to her, as she was to Grandmama, bound by something as strong, as lasting, as love.

Before either of us could say more, the door opened and the new general factotum, a local girl from a remote hamlet in the hills, wheeled Grandmama into the kitchen. The girl had a badly repaired harelip – 'But after Gordana, who can be sure what appeals to men,' Trudi had said grimly, 'who knows, perhaps this one will marry Werner.' She was gentle and hard-working, but she addressed Grandmama, and also spoke of her, with the awful nurse's *We*. She had done some nursing, and probably picked up this habit from a matron. 'We ate quite well today,' she simpered. 'And now I thought we would just come in and greet the family, and then I hope we will do our big number and then we will have our rest.'

My mother wiped her eyes and Grandmama smiled and said formally, 'Good evening. Although I am not certain where we met. Was it last year in Ischl? They tell me Janka has married. She was much too young. I do not like this one' – indicating Hannah – 'her face is wrong, her hands are so red, and she snivels.'

Gone were the brooches; my mother had taken them all, not wanting to risk any more gift-giving. Gone were the lavender shawls and lavender water, the elaborate coiffures. My Grandmama was a straggle-haired old lady dressed in black cotton and smelling of carbolic soap. Suddenly unable to bear it all, I brushed past the simpering Hannah and went out. I thought, I must get away from here. *Soon.* If only I get a scholarship. If only I can go.

*

Joshua had finished his work on the letters, and was due at last in Salzburg. Before leaving, he came to say a formal goodbye to us all. We had thought he would come alone, but probably Gordana had insisted on accompanying him. It was she who rang the bell, and stepped ahead of Joshua into the sombre wooden darkness of our hallway. Gordana greeted everyone coolly, with a calm smile on her face. After her scene with my mother, neither my mother nor Trudi wanted to ask them into the living room. But Berti relented, and when they were seated, my mother offered them a glass of *Schnapps*, as that was quicker than tea. Joshua nervously drained his in a couple of gulps, and Gordana reprimanded him.

A few frozen civilities were exchanged between the women, while Joshua sat looking down at his shoes, a cigarette burning unheeded between his fingers. 'Watch your ash, Joshua,' Gordana said. She was wearing a neat tailored suit with padded shoulders, and her hair, probably washed now as it was all one colour, was done in a new way, a sleek braid on top of her head. 'I wanted to cut my hair,' she said to me, leaning forward confidentially, 'but he likes it so much, he has forbidden me.' Then she turned to my mother. 'I hope the old lady is satisfied with your new help. You must tell the new girl to oil the wheelchair. And polish the hall table better. This furniture could do with some polish as well.'

'Do you want to see the Countess?' Joshua asked anxiously.

'No, no,' his wife answered. 'She will only remember that I am gone and be upset again.'

At last Gordana finished her *Schnapps* and as no one offered more, Joshua got up, thanked us brokenly for everything, and steered Gordana out. We were left alone in the hall; my elders shook hands briefly and vanished, saying I would see the two visitors out. Joshua realized how much of an insult this was, and I was moved by the pain in his face. At the door he turned and took me by the shoulders, as he had that night in the garden, and we kissed formally on both cheeks, in polite European fashion. He whispered, 'If you still want to come to America, Mitzi, I will do what I can to help you.' I nodded; I was close to tears. Gordana watched us narrowly, sucking in a corner of her mouth. I knew from her expression that, what-ever Joshua did to help me, she would do what *she* could to see I did not land under their roof. She, like everyone else, had thought I wanted Joshua; and she feared I might still try to get him if I could.

'Goodbye, dearest Mitzi,' said Joshua, still holding me. I was filled with a grief that seemed out of proportion to the parting, that made me wonder if I had not loved him a little, after all. Now I wonder if it was because I sensed that this parting was final, because I thought, for no reason I could name, of the Christ on the *Calvarienberg* and the way Joshua's face sometimes resembled his.

Gordana said sharply that she had forgotten her gloves in the salon, and asked Joshua to go back for them. Joshua let me go, and went. Gordana leaned toward me confidentially again and said, in a very low voice, 'Always remember, Mitzi, a man is like a fish. You let him out a little, then you pull him in.' It was the kind of dictum that might have come from Betsy's father; and it made me ponder the strange similarities in the workings of very distant minds.

IX

The next few years, nothing unexpected happened. I finally passed my *Matura* and began university, which was only slightly less stultifying than school had been. But with a bad leg and no skills or talents except for calling spades, a talent which did not endear me to anyone, I still saw the academic world as my only avenue of escape. I was not going to marry; but neither was I going to sit at home and get old with my mother and Trudi and Berti.

During the first of my university years, in a vague and tentative way, Werner paid court to me. I accepted Werner, with some misgivings, as a friend (he was too much a side-kick of Felix, the weak man who puts his greater intellect to the service of a stronger person). But as a lover, let alone – there was even an oblique hint of that – as a husband, he was out of the question, even if I had not been bound to my memories. Quite aside from his weakness and the wearing quality of his conversation (Felix once said that if it were possible to imagine Karl Kraus without humour, to imagine an animated negation of Karl Kraus, the result would be Werner), he simply did not attract me physically. But for some time, I let it be thought by others that he did. It saved me from speculation and pity, of which I had had more than my fill.

Werner and I talked about many things, but never, by common tacit consent, the letters. I knew he would not tell me more than he had, and whatever he had done was past undoing. For Joshua's sake, I could only hope that it had

196

been done truly well. The next year, Werner moved to a teaching post in Innsbruck and we drifted apart.

As for Felix, he married his dancer, Juliette; and Juliette surprisingly became, now Joshua was gone, my best friend.

My mother took up with a manufacturer of hunting hats for the tourist trade, somewhat younger than herself, and just the degree of parvenu to be inspired by her *von*. She discovered a sort of second life to her voice, and now sang frequently in the church. Felix claimed that the bones of saintly Father Ignatius, down in the crypt, trembled audibly at her vibrato. Trudi and Berti also took up their old interests, coaching skiers on the nursery slope that was gouged into one of our peaceful wooded hills in hopes of winter tourist business.

So everyone grew a little fatter, a little richer. Except Grandmama, who in spite of Hannah's determined ministrations, died of pneumonia that next winter.

By then, there was so little left of the proud elegant old lady of my childhood memory that I fervently wished for the pneumonia to end her helpless, ignominious existence. But Hannah, wanting to keep her job, forced tisanes into Grandmama's blue lips, chafed her wrists, surrounded her with hot-water bottles, urged her to cough into basins, saying, 'Come, my darling, we must spit,' or 'Come, my darling, we must drink,' until I exploded. 'For God's sake, Hannah, it is no use. Leave the poor woman in peace.' At this Hannah put Grandmama's head back on the pillow and began to cry. I thought, this is what happens when you get too old, she was first a doll for Gordana to dress, now she is a doll for Hannah to nurse, she who was so proud, so independent of everyone, so overbearing, so beautiful. I must never let myself get this old, never, never. My mother, who was watching by the bedside and waiting for the doctor to come, asked me sharply to leave the room. Once again, I flared up. 'You have never cared for her, and you know it can only be a mercy,' I said, and ran out.

The doctor came, for the third time that day; but there was nothing he could do, and being more sensible and disinterested than Hannah, he did not much try. Grandmama died a few hours later. She had not spoken in days, but just before her breathing stopped she opened her eyes and said loudly, 'I cannot go on the bicycle with Hansi, it is too far. I want to go

197

in the carriage, Papa, with you.' And that, like most of what she had said since her accident, was a confused riddle not even Joshua would try to solve.

Joshua and I still wrote to each other, though not as often as before. He did not say much about his wife or his new son, but always closed formally with 'love and best wishes from both of us'.

He should have been walking on air, Joshua. His thesis was accepted and published, and not long after that, his more 'popular' biography of my Grandmama. It was an astounding success. All those nostalgic for the wit and glitter, the creativity, the sensual decadence of a vanished Vienna – and there were many more than I would have dreamt – devoured Joshua's *Maria Aurora*. So did all those who liked a bit of scholarly salacious reading; for as my quotes have indicated, the letters hinted, with an ambiguousness and discretion unthinkable now in the literary climate of Perdita Blank and her ilk, at things which in the 'fifties one was still not encouraged to spell out. And there were the famous erotic poems of Hans Handelbein, poems reputedly inspired by the water nymphs of Gustav Klimt but also by my arrogant grandmother:

I come after long journeys to slake my thirst at this fountain
To feel the crystal gush in my throat, and the laughter
Of the finned beings who slide between my limbs
    and my fingers,
Laughter like light, the light in the crystal water,
I drink the light and my body shines with their alien scales.

This is a poem particularly impossible to translate, because of its complicated allusions and repetitions, but one can see what fun the new crop of amateur Freudians must have had with it. There were more such. The treasure Felix had unearthed for Joshua was not infinite but, with judicious research and a bit of stretching, there was enough for another book or two. Later there were to be novels and later still, a film. Not that Joshua had any say in that, or any profit; nor did we, except for Felix, who managed at one stage to get a sort of consultant's job, as he had done with Joshua, but far better paid. These productions were all, of course, dreadful. One cannot, unfortunately, copyright a life, which seems to me a gross in-

198

equity, especially with the present media madness of using lives still being lived.

This growing interest, however, kept the scholastic pot on the boil. Joshua's reputation, and his professorship, were now assured; and if anyone else ever had the letters examined for forgery, they must have passed, as I have not read of their being doubted again. One literary critic did remark that it was extraordinary the Countess should always have asked for, and got, her letters back, that almost none of them were found in the possession of her correspondents. Joshua explained this by her vanity, and her knowledge of her own mercurial temperament. When she went on to the next lover, she did not want anything out of her hands that might be used against her by her last. In fact, one of the dear Alix letters even said something to this effect.

But now I am going ahead a bit too far. At all events, Joshua's career was already then off to a flying start; but there was little enthusiasm in *his* letters, and little joy. Reading between the lines, I could tell that something was gravely wrong. I wondered if it was his marriage; or if he had begun to suspect what I was still almost certain of, that the letters were fake.

In my last year of university, I wrote to Joshua that I was applying for a Fulbright scholarship; would he give me a reference, and if I did not get the Fulbright, could he suggest anything else? Joshua sent back a strange, stiff answer. He hoped I would get the Fulbright, but he really thought that England would be a much better place for me to study. The universities had a much higher standard, the intellectual temperament of the country would be more congenial to me. Last but not least, I would be so much closer to home. As if the distance from home were not part of what I longed for! He offered to put in a word with a colleague in England, and give any references I wanted, as glowing as he could make them.

The message was clear. Joshua would help me get to England, but not America. Whatever his reasons – Gordana's jealousy, or some quirk or resentment of his own, Joshua wanted to keep me as far from him as he could.

I did not get the Fulbright, and I swallowed my pride and asked Joshua for his recommendations and British contacts. This time I got the scholarship I applied for. And in England

I made friends with Juliette's family, a friendship that out-lasted her marriage to my brother, and was in fact my mainstay until her mother died.

Juliette's background was almost as odd as our own. Her parents had been divorced since she was a young child. Her English father led a Bohemian life in Provence with his new French wife. Oddly, *he* was the practising Catholic parent, and Juliette was quite devout as well. Her French mother had a new English husband, a historian who lived and taught in London. I got to know them all, but it was the London family, the Greers, who took me into their house and their lives with a warmth and ease that belied everything I had ever heard about the reserved haughty English and the cold calculating French. I was to meet such stereotypes too, of course; but never at the Greers'. They introduced me to a whole new world, where my sharp tongue, my iconoclasm, were not shunned but welcomed, where ideas were taken seriously but also played with, with a lightness and dexterity Werner and Joshua had never shown. For once in my life, without fol-lowing any of my family's cynical worldly advice, I had landed right. As in the early, idyllic days of Joshua's visit, I was very close to happiness, and in the end I stayed. It was on one of my rare visits home that the next act in the family drama was played to its denouement.

Juliette's was a beauty very different from Grandmama's and Felix's, diffident rather than proud, fragile, vulnerable. Unlike Grandmama, she looked as small as she was. The Dresden fairy, Werner called her. She was so exquisite that almost anyone else seemed coarse and clumsy beside her; poor Trudi and Berti, who adored her, like ogresses in the company of an elf. The amazing thing about Juliette was that she was not only beautiful but exceptionally nice, with none of the vanity that could have corroded such beauty. She seemed unaware, even uncertain, of her looks. She worried that her pale blonde hair was too thin and her ankles getting too thick, she examined herself compulsively for flaws and signs of decline. Perhaps this almost pathological concern *was* her form of vanity; in any case, it was the only thing in her I found dis-turbing. She was shy but responsive; she truly listened when one talked to her, and her expressions of delight or dismay at some happy or unhappy confidence were so immediate and warm one felt there was no one in the world to whom one would rather have made it. She seemed to have not a trace of the *Schadenfreude* that is stored like a dram of poison in the depths of so many outwardly benevolent people I know. Not only that – she was sensitive, cultured, intelligent and apparently a talented dancer. Though we could not imagine Felix really settling down, he seemed so in love and with such good reason that we all hoped, and began to believe, that it would work.

Except Werner. Werner, who still, on the rare occasions we met, said things to me I knew he would say to no one else, had his own theory about Julie. 'Seldom do you ever find so perfect an *ingénue*. And such a born victim. Juliette is so beautiful it wrings one's heart, but it is an unhealthy beauty, it is in fact the masochistic element, which is so strong in so many women, that both makes her beauty and blights it. One can hardly imagine that perfect swan's neck except with a knife poised above it. And Felix of course *is* the knife. Just as Julie was born to be hurt, Felix was born to inflict pain.'

'You never change, Werner. Leave aside Julie as an archetype and Julie as a hypothesis and tell me what you think of Julie as a person.'

'I have just told you. Julie is much too beautiful to be anything but an archetype. As a person someone so beautiful can hardly exist.'

'Absolute drivel. Grandmama managed very well.'

'Ah, the Countess. But she was a victimizer, not a' victim; that is where Felix inherits it from. Wait and see,' said Werner lugubriously. 'She may need you, Mitzi. She may even need me.'

Juliette had given up her *corps de ballet* job to marry Felix. 'I'm not that good anyway,' she said to me cheerfully when explaining this, 'and I can't do something that means travelling all the time. I'll try to find a studio where I can keep in shape and maybe later I can teach. Or dance in local things.' She laughed. 'I don't know what local things, but something will work out. He jokes about being a German beast, trying to keep me to *Kinder, Küche, Kirche*. Actually, I know it worries him, my leaving the company, but I wanted to, I did it of my own accord. He never asked me. And now he's so sweet and solicitous about it – well, he needn't worry. After all *I* don't want to be away from *him*.'

Werner had a theory about this too, a theory which tallied, this time, with my own ideas. Just as Felix's schemes and lying were a substitute for real creativity, he had a secret respect for, a secret envy of, talent, and in his ambivalence was torn between wanting to build it up and pull it down. In this respect his relationship with the world of the arts was something like the picture certain critics have of Grandmama's. One side of Felix probably wanted Juliette to have her career, another to destroy it.

As it was, they began their married life in an idyllic village close enough to Salzburg that Felix could work there. Felix got a job as a car salesman – all he could find – and almost immediately things began to go wrong. He hated his job, as he hated most jobs; Juliette found she hated her life in the village, its provincialism, its rudeness, the hostility she felt from the villagers, not used to foreigners actually living among them; and many still had enough Nazi sentiments to regard anyone French or English as part of the enemy. Julie's letters told me a little of this, and her family told me more. Her letters still said not a word against Felix. There were only things like: 'Felix comes home very late sometimes, and I get really depressed in this tiny dead place on my own.' Or, 'Felix says I exaggerate, but I know the people here hate me just because I'm English. Or French, it doesn't matter. They push ahead of me in the shop, they say things, the sour old women mutter when they see me out in shorts in the garden. Yesterday one complained because I hung my laundry out on a Sunday! I know it's hard to find a good flat and Felix wanted country life, I did too – but I didn't know it would be like this.' Then, a few letters later, 'Mitzi, you will laugh at me, but I go out shopping after dark, just before the shops close, because there's so much hostility here that sometimes I can't face it. I want to move to Salzburg but Felix doesn't. He has this *idée fixe* about a country idyll . . . I suppose I did too, I suppose it's really my fault, I wanted a garden and animals, I pictured something like Daddy's place in Provence, only Alpine. Well, it's not like that! Oh God, how naive I was. And Felix is so busy at work, and I am so much alone.' Still later, she wrote: 'Werner was here to stay a few days, but there has been a bitter row between him and Felix – I won't go into the gory details. I suppose there is always right and wrong on both sides but I am really sorry because it looks as though we won't see Werner again.' Then for a while there were no letters at all, and it was almost a year before I myself saw Juliette again – the following Christmas, which we had all agreed to spend at my mother's house.

But it was not the same Juliette. Gone was the springy dancer's walk, the English Rose complexion, the quick shy smile whose brightness always touched and surprised one. Julie's movements were weary, her hair darkened and lifeless, her face blotchy, her eyes bright not with animation but with fear. 'Oh, Mitzi,' she said breathlessly, 'how glad I am that you're here,' and her haunted eyes searched my face in an anxious, obsessive way that worried me still more. Nonetheless, I tried to hide my shock at her appearance. Not so my mother, who trumpeted, as soon as greetings and kisses were over, 'Julie, child, you look ill. Is it the 'flu again, Felix?'

'Yes, Felix, I warned you last time. Has she not been looking after herself?' This from Trudi. They had a way of treating Julie like a child, asking Felix questions about her as though she were incapable of answering them herself.

'It's just the excitement of the drive, I hope,' Felix answered with forced heartiness. 'She doesn't like speed, my beautiful child, and I wanted to see what the Mercedes would do. After all, the only perk of selling these damned cars is that you get something good to drive. It's true though that the child has not been well lately. I've tried to persuade her to see a doctor but she won't go.'

'Juliette,' said my mother, 'what is this? Of course you must go to a doctor. She could see old von Grillkäfer.'

'Yes,' Trudi agreed, 'he is a bit shaky but still quite sound. But why didn't you go to someone in Salzburg? The people at the hospital are quite good.'

Julie said, 'Oh, please – I've been telling Felix – I would much rather just go home for a little while, and see my doctor there. I used to be ill a lot as a child, and he knows me so well . . .'

'But Julie!' Berti exclaimed. 'If you are ill, you cannot make such a long journey.'

Felix said, with a nasty smile, the joviality cracking, 'The truth is, my dear wife thinks all Austrian doctors are butchers who performed experiments on howling victims, and she does not want to put her body in their evil Nazi hands.'

'Oh, Felix,' Julie said desperately, 'Don't. Please don't start again.'

'It's you who start, by saying you will not see anyone but your doctor in England. You see, as we all know, Julie's step-mother was in the Resistance and her stepfather in War Archives and she feels she has to keep up the heroic family tradition by boycotting Austrian medicine.'

'It's all lies, what you're saying about me,' Julie burst out. 'I did go to a doctor, and Felix knows what happened.'

'No, I don't. At least, I don't at all understand what you were so hysterical about.'

Julie seemed to shrink into herself. She sat down, as if she could no longer stand, and murmured to my mother, 'Please, Anna, could I go upstairs and lie down?'

'Of course you can, poor child,' said my mother. 'I will go up with you.'

'No, please. Please, I'll be all right. It's just my head – and that I'm so tired. If I could just sleep a little while –'

I said quickly, 'I can get you an aspirin.' To which Juliette answered at once, 'Oh yes, please. If you could bring it to me upstairs –' making it clear that, while she did not want my mother to accompany her, she did want me.

Felix said, 'You know, Juliette, you have aspirin in your handbag.'

'I've already taken those.'

'Have you? All of them? No wonder you feel ill. It is probably a case of acute aspirin poisoning.'

'Felix,' said Trudi, 'Leave the child in peace.'

Julie said nothing, and I followed her up the stairs. I gave her a few minutes to collect herself while I pretended to look for aspirin, and then knocked on the closed door of her room. Juliette's voice said anxiously, 'Mitzi, is it you?'

'Yes. And I've got the aspirin.'

'Oh, Mitzi, please come in.' She sat up as I entered. Her face was flushed, her hair tangled, her cheeks streaked with crying. 'I don't really want an aspirin, Mitzi.'

'I know.'

'I wanted – I have to talk to someone, and the way I feel now, there is only you in this whole country I can talk to. It's not that I'm ill, although it's that too, it's that I want to go home – I *have* to go home – and Felix doesn't want me to go. He's afraid, you see, that I won't come back.' Then she shook her head, as if she had said too much, and went on with a sudden air of defiance, as if expecting me to doubt her. 'It's true that I'm ill, and I do want to see a doctor, my own doctor. I suppose that's really it – only Felix doesn't understand –'

I said, 'Julie, listen. I want to help you. If you want to go back to England, I will try to help you to do that. I won't ask any questions. But if you want to tell me what is really wrong, please don't be afraid. I will never say a word to anyone. And it might be easier for me to help you if I knew.'

Juliette shook her head again, and said, more firmly, '*No*. I'm sorry, Mitzi, I shouldn't have broken down like that. Just let me rest a few minutes and then I'll come downstairs.'

During dinner, Felix continued his nasty bantering. About Julie's dislike of the Austrian villagers, about her piety. 'In one respect my wife has really gone native. She is attending not only Mass faithfully every Sunday, but even goes to Vespers. Church seems to be the only place where her neighbours do not scare her to death.' About her longing for her own country. 'Countries, I should say. She will go miles to see another Englishwoman. And even more to see a French man.' In between the jibes, he was suddenly solicitous and affectionate, and, as he had more of the good *Kalterer* my mother had brought up from the cellar to celebrate our homecoming, the swings of his mood and conversation became wilder and wilder. Trudi and Berti and my mother tried in vain to calm him, to gloss things over. It ended with Julie fleeing upstairs again, this time openly in tears, and Felix throwing his wineglass across the room and declaring he had had enough of hysterical women and was going out for a drink in town.

I ran after him, and stopped him at the door. If Julie would not talk, perhaps Felix would. 'Felix, you can't dash off like this. You're being cruel and vicious, and I don't see how Julie stands it. She is the dearest person I know, and I can't bear to see what you're doing to her. Why are you doing it? Do you want her to leave you – do you want to drive her away?'

Felix stared at me, then snapped, 'She *is* going to leave me.

That's why I'm being the way I am,' and tried to push me aside.

'No. Felix, that's too easy. If you want to keep her, you couldn't do what you're doing. Not if you cared about her at all. You've done something to make her feel like this, or she's found something out . . .' I stopped, remembering her story of a quarrel with Werner, wondering if one of the things she had found out, or suspected, concerned the letters of my Grandmama.

'Dear God, Mitzi,' Felix's voice was almost breaking. 'I haven't done anything – oh, I haven't been faithful, but that means nothing – she must know that – I love her – I would give her the world –'

'Maybe she doesn't want the world. Maybe she only wants you to act like a decent human being.'

Felix grinned suddenly, his nastiest grin. 'Ah, Mitzi, what a marvellous trite remark. You are becoming like the three graces, Mitzi. Decency, respectability. How soon you will be old. If you want to know, my darling pious sister, one of her reasons for wanting to leave is that she found out about you.'

'I'm not making it much of a Christmas, am I?' Juliette was standing at the window in her faded, childish bathrobe, chipping at the frost-flowers on the pane. The weather had turned bitterly cold, and Julie had come down with a real 'flu. She had spent three days in her room, subjected to my mother's teas and broths but only a modicum of questioning.

'It doesn't matter, Julie. You can't help that.'

'I'm so sorry to be such a burden on everyone. And I may be even more of a burden. I thought Felix would come back that night, but I'm glad he didn't. I've had three days alone to think and now I'm much better, I'm not so afraid. You see, Mitzi, I've somehow just realized – I could just get on a train and go.'

'Go where, Juliette?'

'Go where? For God's sake, home! Either home, if it comes to that. By tomorrow I'll be strong enough. Mitzi, can you lend me some money? I haven't got quite enough for the fare. And can you cover for me – say you don't know where I went – or that it was to the home I decide not to go to – oh, Mitzi, please, will you help me?'

'Of course I will, if that's what you want, if you're really

206

well enough to travel. I wish you had seen a doctor, Julie. By the way, Mama has been trying to ring Felix, but there's no answer. I really wonder where he is. Day after tomorrow he's supposed to be back at work.'

Juliette smiled. 'Is that what he told you? He lost that job two weeks ago. The beat-up Mercedes is his severance pay. We can't even pay the electricity bill. He told me not to say anything about it, and he won't tell me what he's going to do now. Or what he's doing. You needn't wonder where he is, he's probably with one of his girls . . .' She turned back to the window.

'Is it the girls – is that why you want to leave?'

Julie spun around. 'That? That's maybe the least of it. Don't you *know* Felix, Mitzi? You can't have lived with Felix all those years and not know him. Or maybe you can. Maybe no one knows him. I don't, but I thought I did, I thought I knew him, I thought I loved him. I thought, like all of you, that his escapades made a nice family joke –' I wanted to interrupt, but she held her hand up to stop me – 'Betsy, and whatever he did on those crazy trips, the Princess who kept him, the jealous husband who came with a gun – oh, I heard all that and I thought it was funny too, or maybe I thought I had to learn to think it was funny, to become cynical and sophisticated, like the rest of you, pretending no one ever really got hurt, no one who didn't deserve it. And I told myself that anyway all the stories were exaggerated, he wasn't really like that – and if he had been he was changing, that everything was possible because we were so much in love. Have you ever understood, any of you, that Felix is not a joke, that he will walk over anything and anyone to get what he wants – and when he has it he doesn't want it, when he has it he only wants to see it destroyed?'

I said nothing, and waited, my heart beating, wondering if this outburst, the longest and most vehement I had ever heard Julie make, was only about Felix, if some of it was a veiled attack on myself. Not, of course, that a word of it was untrue. And Julie, her eyes feverish, her voice shaking, drew breath and went on again, as if now she could not stop.

'I wrote you once that he had a quarrel with Werner. Werner was staying with us then, and they were still very close. They need each other, there is too much between them, and Felix fascinates Werner, in spite of himself. Felix is always the serpent in Eden. It began because Felix and I had a fight and Felix went roaring off in his car, and Werner got drunk with me and said, I can't bear it, his treating you like this. You are the only good thing in his life, you are the crystal fountain in the desert. (I could not help smiling; this was Adlerhorst's line to Maria Aurora.) And all sorts of mystical nonsense about women and me in particular. Then he told me a few things I had begun to suspect, but didn't know. For my protection, he said, because his fear for me was greater than any loyalty he might still have for Felix. But he said Felix would kill him if he ever found out. And Felix, when he came in again, as if he *sensed* what Werner had been saying, told him to get out, right then and there, in the middle of the night, and never come back.'

'I don't think Felix would really –' I began, but she stopped me again.

'Mitzi, he would. Felix could do anything.'

'Maybe he could. You're right, Julie, maybe we have taken it all too lightly. And I, who am the one who should know better, am guiltiest of all.'

Juliette shook her head; the fire was gone now, there were tears in her eyes. 'No, no. It's I who am wrong, and unfair. How can I accuse the rest of you? You're tied to him by blood. But I – I fell in love with him. I *chose* him.'

'But you didn't know. And do you think I can't understand your choosing?' I saw her eyes, and added quickly, 'When so many others have made the same choice?'

Juliette shrugged, and began to pace the room, then said, now as if to herself, 'And the worst of it is, he can make me in love with him again. There's something in me that *is* still in love with him, even though I know if I stay with him, I'm lost. That's what Werner understood, better than anyone, because he's what I am – something for Felix to use up and throw away. Only Werner, now at last, I think, has the strength to say no. And I'm not sure that I do – that's why I have to go before Felix comes back. If I don't he may talk me into staying.'

'That is certainly not how he's been talking. He acts as if he *wants* to drive you away.'

'Oh, Felix is just as mixed up. He hates me because he loves me, and because he loves me, though he's not faithful, he's no longer free. It's like those crazy complicated Handelbein let-

ters, and he blames me because our country idyll didn't work.'
She took a deep breath. 'Oh, Mitzi, I'm so glad I'm telling
you this, that everything is coming out at last. You don't know
how long I've bottled all this up, how it's been eating at me
inside. I've prayed and prayed for guidance, I've lit so many
candles . . . Felix laughs at me. He laughs at my faith, as he
laughs at everything. And then, if all that weren't enough –
there's something else. Something I wasn't ever going to tell
you.'

'That's up to you, of course. I honestly can't think of anything you *couldn't* tell me,' I said, keeping level my lying
voice.

'It's – very strange.' Julie began, of course, to tell it after all.
'Felix sometimes says names when he's sleeping. And the one
he says most often is yours.'

'Because of childhood, of course. Mine is probably the first
girl's name he knew. And it's also Grandmama's.'

'Of course! I didn't think of that. But I mentioned it to
him, and he always just smiled and said, well he was very
fond of you, you'd been so close as children. Then one day,
when he was very drunk – he drinks more and more, it's because he hated this job so much, and because he can't really
bear to be responsible, to be settled down – and we had a row
about something, I forget even what, and I said, to hurt him I
suppose, that I didn't understand how he could be so vile,
when he had someone like you as a sister. And he said, "She is
no different from all the others, she –"' Julie's voice broke.

I said, with a calm that almost startled me, 'Well, whatever
it was, it is not true. One thing I do know about Felix, and
you must know by now, is that he is the greatest liar in the
world.'

Juliette wiped her eyes. 'Oh, I know. He was jealous, of
course. He couldn't bear my looking up to you. And I didn't
for a moment believe him. He's jealous of you too because
you're stronger, because you don't compromise. Werner said
that once; Mitzi is the strongest of us all. But it was so dreadful,
what he said, so poisonous, he makes one begin to doubt
everything. If I stay with him in the end I will doubt God.
Oh, Mitzi, you will help me to get away?'

'Of course I will help you.' And I thought, with a sharp
twinge of that irony that never seems to leave me, the poor
marvellous girl, she really cares about me, as I care about her,

209

and it is only her peace of mind I am saving with my lies. Juliette, like Joshua, has to be spared the truth. She could not bear to think of me in a state of mortal sin. Oh, but Mitzi, you should feel guilty at presenting so perfectly false an image, an image worthy of Felix himself. But what I felt was not guilt. What I felt was a small, secret, bitter joy, that Felix, whom by now I hated – whom by now I should have hated – of all the names he might have said in his dreams, said one name. Said mine.

Felix telephoned the day after Julie left. We never knew what mysterious errand or passion had taken him away, but he must have truly thought she would not go then; or he must, with all his ambivalence, have somehow wanted her to. It was my mother who talked to him. He asked her if Julie had said anything to me, had left any message. He knew better, after what had passed, than to ask to speak to me. My mother reported his final words: 'I'll find her, I'll get her back. But if she has gone to Werner, I'll kill them both.'

No, it was not much of a Christmas. My mother and Trudi and Berti and I sat glumly around the carefully trimmed tree with its now burnt-out candles and ate up Christmas leftovers, and they exchanged their local gossip for my news about life in England, but there was no heart in what any of us said. When I was packing to leave, my mother came in for one of those rare heart-to-heart talks whose uselessness she had still, after all these years, not entirely grasped. Perhaps it is simply a compulsion of mothers. Never having been one, I cannot say.

'Sometimes I think, Mitzi, that this family is cursed. Was she really so unhappy with Felix? You were her best friend, Mitzi, she always said so. You must know. Did she have to leave?'

'I think yes. I think she did the best thing.'

'Nothing works out for Felix, does it? And he was so much in love with her. He still is. If you had heard him on the telephone –'

'It doesn't work out because he destroys it.'

'But do you think it was entirely his fault?'

'If it were someone else, I might wonder. Since it's Felix, I'm afraid I would say unequivocally that it was.'

'I always thought you were fond of your brother, Mitzi.'

'My fondness has nothing to do with what I know Felix to be. And I don't know that I am fond of him. No. Not any more.'

'You mean because of what he did to Juliette?'

'I mean because of what he has done all his life. I suppose I have just begun to see it a little through Juliette's eyes. We all treat Felix as the prodigal son, but the prodigal son did not come back just to stock up for the next bout of sinning.'

My mother sighed, 'You were such good friends when you were little,' in the way of mothers; and that also had not been quite true.

'We have actually been better friends,' I said, with that irony I can never resist, even when it is quite lost on my audience, 'since I grew up.'

'But you think that Felix is getting worse?'

'Yes, I do. I think he did love Julie, as much as he could, and to have wrecked that will really cut him adrift.'

My mother, not really following this, sighed again. 'Then you do not think she will come back to him. We all tried so hard to be kind to her ... if she had only confided in me! Perhaps I could have talked to him. In a way, you know, I think she has not given him enough of a chance. He was working very hard at that job; I don't think she realized how difficult it was for him to settle down ...'

'Mama, you heard how he treated her. She gave him every chance she could.'

'Yes, but that was because he was so upset at the idea of her leaving.'

'Then why make it unbearable for her to stay? And why disappear for three whole days?'

'Ah,' said my mother triumphantly, 'he explained that. Just because he was being so awful, he wanted to give her a rest from him.'

'Is that what he told you?' I laughed. 'It certainly was not clear to her that that's what he was doing. Nor to me.'

'You would take her side of course, Mitzi. Her side entirely. I am not at all sure she did give him every chance. I think her hatred of living here was pathological; but you would understand that, you look down on us all too. You are so much happier, aren't you, in your England? I hope it for you. I hope you will always be happy there, and that you will find a wonderful Englishman who will make you happier still ...'

It was her acute worry about Felix, I knew, that was making her attack me, but I had no patience for it. 'You sound like Kitty Kleinholz,' I said. 'Please get out of my room.'

211

X

That Christmas was the last. I did not go home again for more than a year. Then a letter came from my mother saying she had to sell the hunting lodge, and wanted me to 'pay a last visit to the dear old house with all its memories, happy and unhappy, but all precious', a letter like the legend on a cheap greeting card, that made me wonder what they were brewing up now. I went, although I did not want to, and I went for a surprising reason. The idea of losing the house was absurdly painful to me. I had never thought of living there again but I realized that, in spite of everything, the *possibility* was one I did not want to disappear. It was my only hold on a still-beloved landscape, and if I was to lose it, I would have preferred not to see it again, to have it gone before I knew it would go, as one prefers a death to be sudden. But knowing, I could not stay away.

'But why, Mama? Where will you all go, what will you do?'

'Trudi and Berti are going to take an apartment in the Pilzfest villa, which is being converted. And I – I wanted you to be here when I told you.' She smiled nervously, and I saw she was twisting a new ring on her finger. 'Of course it is ridiculous at my age, but I am getting married.'

'Oh? Well then, congratulations.' I realized the flatness of my voice would annoy her, but she knew how well I knew her. She could hardly have expected me to display either enthusiasm or surprise. She must have known, also, that I would guess what manner of man she was marrying, and my

212

guess would probably be right. 'Who is the fortunate gentleman?'

'Oh, my dear Mitzi! Can you never unbend, can you never share anyone's happiness? No queen – not even your Grandmama – ever had such an air of looking down on the rest of the human race. The way you said that, I really don't know if I even want to tell you.'

'Well, there is no hurry,' I answered cheerfully. 'I will find it out in due course.'

'Anni, don't be childish,' said Trudi, as years ago she might have said it to me. 'Tell her.' The tone of Trudi's voice confirmed that my mother's choice lay at the lower end of the possible spectrum, and it was better to get the announcement over with.

'Well.' My mother cleared her throat violently, as when she was about to sing. 'It is Gustav Krammel. I do not know if you remember him. He has a factory now, making sausages. They are very successful.'

'The Krammels or the sausages?' I couldn't help this, but went quickly on before she could start raging at me. 'No, I don't know them, but I hope for your sake, dear Mama, that this alliance will work out better than Felix's brief foray into what we might call the intestine world. What is it, I wonder, that my family sees in tripe? Do you think Baroness Kleinholz will approve?'

Trudi and Berti were trying to look shocked, and sympathetic to my mother, but I could see they were amused, and suddenly my mother herself began to laugh. Whether it was from nerves or because she really saw the joke of the whole thing, I never knew, but it was the moment I might have forgiven her for Stefan. But she stopped herself too soon. And the moment, passing and denied, my mockery, her brief acceptance of it, then her denial, her renewed hypocrisy, rankled in us both and laid the ground for a new and bitter quarrel, the quarrel that was to be our last.

'Oh, but Herr Krammel,' said Trudi, 'moves in the best circles. He is also an expert in *Jugendstil* furniture, as was his father before him. They did some trading, you see, after the war . . . and that is how it all began.'

'Well, that sounds very interesting. I shall look forward to meeting Herr Krammel. Is that why you are selling the house then, Mama? Couldn't you keep it and Trudi and Berti stay on here?'

'No,' said my mother. 'No, it is simply not convenient. But never mind that now. Mine is not the only wedding we have to announce. There is to be a still more surprising wedding, now she has her divorce – though after the episode of Joshua and his Cinderella I suppose nothing should surprise us very much. Felix tells me that Werner and Juliette are going to get married and are already living together in Ireland. It was to Werner she went when she left here. Or did you perhaps know?'

'No, I didn't,' I lied. 'I haven't seen Julie in months, nor the Greers. But really, in a way, that one is not surprising. Not to me.' I thought of Juliette saying, he's what I am, something Felix can use up and throw away, he is the only person who understands. And Werner saying, Juliette is a born victim. Their marriage was logical: it was both an escape from Felix's power and a confirmation of it, for Felix was and would always be what they most had in common; and perhaps he had never been closer to anyone than the two of them. Anyone, that is, outside the family. But I could hardly explain any of that to my elders, and Felix himself would never see it that way.

'There you are, that is our Mitzi. So cynical she is not surprised by anything any more, but only expects the most incongruous to happen.'

I let this pass, and asked, 'But how did Felix know? There's certainly been no contact between them since the divorce.'

'You know how Felix is,' said my mother. 'He has his ways of finding everything out. He came here, he was absolutely wild, I have never seen him as wild as that. He said he would go to Ireland and murder them. It took us a day to calm him down. Poor Felix, he did love Juliette so much, and he has been out of work again . . .' She caught herself, but not in time. I said, almost without thinking, 'So that's why you are selling the house.'

'No, Mitzi. It is not that at all. It's because I am getting married.'

'And so you would turn out Trudi and Berti, who more than anyone kept us going for so many years?'

'It can't be helped,' said Trudi quickly. 'It does not matter, the house is too big for us alone. We did not want to go through the business of letting rooms again –'

214

'The house is too big? Oh, come. It was never before big enough.'

'No, we do not need all these rooms, small though they are. Of course, if you, Mitzi, had had an interest – but we never thought you would want to come back –' Berti put in. My mother was silent. They were covering for her, they were in it as much as she. Any of them would have given the shirt off her back to rescue Felix yet one more time.

'Oh,' I said, 'I wasn't thinking of myself. I couldn't live here again. But it is a wrench. You have all been in this house so long now – I can't think of anyone else here, or you anywhere else. Then it really is not because of Felix?'

'No. It really is not.'

I wanted so much to believe them that for once I let it go. 'And it isn't really my business anyway, I suppose. Let's talk about something else. Let's talk about Herr Krammel.'

'There is no need to talk about him,' my mother said. 'He is coming for tea this afternoon.'

Krammel was dressed in a *Tracht*, our national costume, the grey suit with green piping, chamois-brush hat, and green wool cable-knit stockings which did not become his somewhat fleshy legs. He was a small man with a large genial head, and he was at least fifteen years younger than my mother. Which still made him, I thought, old enough to know better. Or perhaps he did know better. After all he was getting himself a place, however dubious, in Society.

Krammel was very deferential to us all. He called Trudi and Berti not by their first names, as he might well have done by now, but *Gnädige Frau*, as if they were many years older than my mother. Perhaps she had told him they were. Me he called *Gnädiges Fräulein*. It reminded me of the days when Kropetschka was coming around. Only now there were good cakes and good tea and the Meissen was back on the table, and all the rustic oak was polished and gleaming with what was to me a sinister shine, because I knew it was to impress prospective house-buyers.

Krammel talked at length about a visit he had paid recently to a certain Countess in Vienna who wanted to sell him a few items of *Jugendstil* glassware. 'Really such a simple woman, so charming – and from her youth she remembered (to my mother) your mother very well.'

215

'Hohenbreiten? A Countess Hohenbreiten? I don't recall the name,' said Trudi a little testily. My mother and Krammel exchanged sympathetic looks, and Krammel changed topics. He began to talk about improvements to the town, a new roundabout, a big modern bridge, all of them sad but necessary because of the increasing traffic. 'No one loves the old more than I do, *Gnädiges Fräulein*, but we cannot have the twentieth century leave us behind.'

I said I did not see why. Considering some of what had gone on in the twentieth century, it might be quite good to be left behind by it. Krammel answered with what I thought quite ingenuous incomprehension that he could see I was inclined to the traditional; small wonder, with my famous grandmother, who must have been a great influence in my life.

The conversation went on in fits and starts until Krammel, inhibited at first by my presence and Trudi and Berti's not quite hidden feelings of his inferiority, gained courage and began to talk with much flourish about his latest coup in the antique trade. 'Her chest was in terrible condition but I knew at once it was Biedermaier.' I smiled, thinking how in English this would be a *double entendre*, and Krammel stopped at once, his little pudgy hands fluttering nervously, and asked me, '*Gnädiges Fräulein*, have I said something that was amusing to you?'

After that I simply nodded every now and then and let my mind wander, trying to take in every detail of the room, to engrave it on my memory: the Bosnian rugs, the family portraits crowded between stags' heads as there was no other space for them, the bulky oak table, the faded green velvet curtains, the conservatory with Trudi's jungle of plants and a little chaise longue and a view over apple trees and the misty blue slopes of the hills. I had looked at it for years and not really registered anything. I had thought it a fusty boring tasteless room, crowded with mementoes of hunting and Empire, neither of which meant anything to me. I had been free to think that way about it because it was always there, I had felt free to leave it but also free to come back; and I understood suddenly how much easier that second freedom had made my leaving. At last I said I wanted to go out for a little walk before it grew colder. Krammel, to my surprise, jumped up and asked if he might accompany me.

We turned down the lane, past the big gates of the Holderland place. I wondered how I could, politely, shake off Krammel.

'*Gnädiges Fräulein*, it must be sad for you, to think that the house is to be sold,' Krammel said.

'Well,' I answered stiffly, 'I never intended to live here again, and I can understand that you might not want to.'

'Oh, but I did,' said Krammel quickly. 'I love this house. These little hunting lodges. So perfect, such fine taste. Just the right blend of Biedermaier and *Bauernrustik*, though I would have loved to put it all back into its proper style . . . a little restoration . . . but your Frau Mama would have none of it. She needed the money, she says, she has a debt to pay. I said I would help her but she said she could not allow that, it is too much, she insists on selling. If I did not think the town would laugh at me, do you know what, *Gnädiges Fräulein*? I would buy it myself.'

When I said nothing, Krammel went on. 'Do you think – may I perhaps call you Maria, or Mitzi, since after all I am soon to be your stepfather? I hope you will not mind.' His eyes moved nervously; they were milky-blue, lifeless, eyes like clouded marbles. 'Do you think perhaps you could persuade your mother to keep the house? Do you know what this debt is that she needs so much money for? Between you and me, *Gnädiges Fräulein* – or Mitzi if indeed I may – I suspect it has something to do with that rascal of a brother of yours. Yes, I am sorry, but rascal is the only word for him.'

'I'm afraid I can't do anything, Herr Krammel. I would if I could. But thank you for telling me all this.'

'Please call me Heinz, *Gnädiges Fräulein*. After all we are soon to be related.'

'Goodbye then, Heinz. I'm sorry, but I really want to think things over now, I want to go on alone.'

'*Gnädiges* – Mitzi – I hope you are not angry with me.'

'On the contrary. The thank you was meant. I am deeply grateful to you for telling me the truth.'

'I hope,' said Krammel, his voice very nervous now, 'I hope I have not made a mistake in talking to you so openly. I hope you are not going to upset Anna – your Frau Mama –'

'I shall certainly not upset her, Herr Krammel, through any fault of yours. You have only confirmed what I would

217

have learned anyhow. And the person who will upset her is of course herself.'

I have said it was the last quarrel, but in truth it was hardly a quarrel at all. I told my mother coldly and calmly that I knew she was lying, that Krammel wanted her to keep the house, that she could only be selling it for Felix. There were immediate, profuse protestations. After all, I was settled in England and making a good academic career, I did not want to live in the house, nor did I need money from her – and how did I know it was Felix, it might be anything else, I knew nothing about her life, nothing about the debts she might have incurred when I was studying . . . I cut all this short and said, with the same calm, that if Felix was in need it was his fault. There was not only need in the world, but also need for justice. I had never had justice from her, never, and if she sold the house now for Felix, against Krammel's wishes and mine, I did not know if I ever wanted to see her again. My mother wept copiously but did not budge an inch, as I had expected, and nor, as I had expected, did I.

By now I was almost detached. There was a hollow feeling, a waiting pain, somewhere inside me, but it was only the echo of a much older pain. I knew then how imperfectly I had ever recovered, how deeply, after Stefan, the iron had entered my soul. And I was aware that we were playing a much older scene, a variation of her battle of wills with my grandmother, which Grandmama, when she bothered to do so, had always won. But now there were no winners, there was only this sterile deadlock. My mother, the unloved child, would squander the last of her love and her means for a selfishness and arrogance even greater than the one that had left *her* so deprived. And I, deprived in turn, could understand; but even remembering my own weakness, could feel no forgiveness and no pity. And suddenly I did not want to stay another day in the house. I wanted to impress nothing on my memory, where it would only, after all, confound and hurt me. I did not want, ever again, to see the old silver on the table, or the apple trees flowering in the garden, I wanted to flee what was there now only to be lost.

I left the next morning. My mother by then had done a turn-about too; she was collected and almost cheerful. She kissed me goodbye and said, 'One day you will understand,

Mitzi. I cannot tell you everything now, but please believe it is for the best. And you will come back to us. I know you will.'

I said, 'Think so, if it pleases you', and kissed her in turn; I kissed them all, and left.

She was wrong, of course. I did not come back for five years. I wrote, but I did not come. And when her marriage to Krammel ended, like the others, in divorce, and I had begun to think myself dramatic and foolish and wondered if I should not relent, if she might not need me, it was too late. The next news that came was a telegram from Trudi saying she was dead.

She survived Joshua by two years. The news about his suicide came two winters before. Joshua had stopped writing to me, and it was only academic gossip that supplemented the terse black-edged card with Gordana's name and the name of her boy; Joshua Felix Maria, as in the Catholic countries where they still sometimes give Maria to boys as a middle name.

The academic gossip, quite reliable gossip in this case, was that Joshua had hanged himself, 'something of a feat,' said my informant, 'in a modern, one-storey, ranch-style house.' His marriage, it was rumoured, had been unhappy for some time and on the verge of divorce. There was also talk that he was depressed because someone had discovered, in Maria Aurora's correspondence, echoes of Rilke and Schnitzler and von Hoffmansthal; not in letters of their own. But with a film being made that year, the legend was too big to deflate easily, and anyone trying to deflate it was suspected of jealousy or spite. Also, as someone else pointed out, how did we know, among contemporaries, who said what first, who plagiarized whom?

So it might have been anything that led to Joshua's final suicidal depression. Perhaps the very size of the legend and its growing vulgarity, the travesty of his scholarship, the muse made movie material. Or a sudden realization of the untruth that had made his reputation and his career. And then again it might have been Gordana. Easily Gordana. My informant said that she made his life hell. He left no note, so we would never know. So much naive aestheticism, so much enthusiastic pedantry, was bound to fall foul of the world. Joshua, if anyone, was a born victim, and that might have been why his face always reminded me of the ghastly wooden Jesus on the *Calvarienberg*.

But I was startled and shaken by how greatly this death affected me, after all that distance, estrangement, time. I felt a grief all the keener for its ingredient of guilt, guilt for not knowing, not caring, enough. I thought, over and over, of how close we had once been, how readily I would still have welcomed, at any point, his turning to me as an old friend, his saying there was something I could do that would help. Then I thought how absurd that was, because the one thing he had perhaps needed from me most was the thing I could not give. But one always feels like that about suicides, in what is actually a surge of wounded egotism; why, why did you not call *me* before you knotted the rope?

Still, I should have kept up, I should have written, I should have made more effort to see him, even if he did not seem to want me to. Dear Joshua, how much he had done for me, what love and kindness he had shown to us all, how terribly we had repaid him! At the beginning of his involvement, I should at least have somehow warned him. About Felix. About Werner. About myself.

I am lost in all this when the telephone rings.

'Is that Dr Stone? Hello, this is Dr Crump. Dr Stone, I'm phoning from London. I've just come back to continue my research here. In the British Library. Later I'll be going on to Vienna. I must say I am sorry to have had so little co-operation from you, and even sorrier to have been sent on a wild goose chase. I suppose you did not know that your brother's ex-wife Betsy is in a clinic for the mentally ill. Has been for some years. She's completely incapable of remembering if there were any unpublished letters – if she ever knew. It seems she and your brother were divorced before the first letters were even deciphered.'

'In a clinic? No, I didn't know, I had no idea at all. Really, I am sorry. And sorry you went to all the trouble of tracking her down for nothing.'

'You're sorry, Dr Stone? That's nothing to what I am.'

'Dr Crump, I did warn you I hadn't been in touch with Betsy for years.'

'You didn't warn me that no member of her family had

ever been in touch with yours since the divorce. Nor did you tell me how long ago that divorce had been.'

'Nor, as you may remember, did I ever suggest you track Betsy down.'

'No, but you most certainly implied – well, never mind. No doubt, Dr Stone, you had your reasons. Anyway, I've had quite an eye-opener. I did talk to Betsy's brother, who remembers your brother very well. It's a shame that such a brilliant and essentially radical woman as Maria Aurora should have had such a perfect example of what I can only call the most bestial sort of male chauvinist as a grandson.'

'Well, perhaps that was why women, including my grandmother, adored him so. Dr Crump, if that's really all you have to say –'

It isn't. She goes on for ten minutes, getting more and more irate, until I hang up. My little joke has gone sour. The proof that those who are too serious, too reflective, like me, should never try the sort of game that to Felix was as natural as breathing. I was prepared to enjoy a mental picture of Dr Crump quizzing Betsy, but Betsy gone mad is no longer a subject for irony. How quickly, how superficially perhaps, I judged her. Or was I only prey to another romantic illusion, that mental illness implies some vulnerability, some sensitivity that the truly shallow do not have? Or was the very shallowness, the bright chatter, the effervescence and *sincerity* on tap, a cover for some nameless fear?

Whatever the truth, it puts Betsy in another dimension, it makes my picture, however correct it once was, shallow in turn, shallow and mean. It is so easy, when you belong to the new poor, to despise the new rich. Then I remember the incident of Grandmama's ring and do not feel quite so wrong any more. But still sorry. And sorry about my facile image of Betsy as Dr Crump would find her, alone with the quiet servant opening Venetian blinds and collecting bottles under the couch, Betsy with the grubby chenille robe, the pink mules, the daisy-fresh face gone soft and puffy. ('Women are like fish,' Felix said cruelly once, 'if your fingers leave even a half-second's indentation, they are too old to eat.') And I wonder how much of it was Felix, whether Felix, as so often, was the catalyst, the push that sent poor Betsy over the brink. For no one who tangled with Felix was ever again quite the same.

XI

'Congratulate me, darling,' said Felix. 'I am getting married again. And you can have all the jewellery. You are the girl, it's only fair.'

'What little is left, you mean. Mama seems to have sold some more before she sold the house.'

We had both come home to deal with my mother's effects, and were having lunch in the *Bierstube* that Joshua had loved, a true stodgy Austrian lunch of *Knödel* and sauerkraut, which neither of us could resist.

'England hasn't changed you,' Felix answered cheerfully. 'You are just as much of a *Schwertgoschen* (a 'swordmouth') as you ever were. Just for that I might take the topaz for my fiancée. But Mama already gave her something, so I won't insist. The two amethysts, I know, are gone – she had them made into cuff-links for Krammel. A great pity, that. They should have stayed in the family. They were not meant for that little pig of a man to wear in his sleeves. Poor Mama. With men she really had no luck at all. Hey, you still have not congratulated me. You have not even asked me who I am marrying.'

'All right, all right. Who, then?'

Felix grinned, leaned over and whispered in my ear. 'Bavarian Edelbrau, the noble beer.'

'Edelbrau? You mean the beer heiress?'

'Yes, my angel.'

'Well,' I said, 'I hope you do better with beer than you did with dog food.'

'Oh, I think I will. Beer is a much more savoury product than something made of horse intestines. And I really get on with old Edel. He leans over backwards to be good to me. He's given me a very nice job in the sales department, and do you know, I quite enjoy it, as long as it doesn't get too arduous. I quite enjoy making money. Just to have it, of course, would be better, but I think I'd get bored, doing nothing in Ingrid's company. She's fine, but not the sort with whom you would want to play gentleman and retire to the family estate. Actually, I never *have* done nothing, you know, only so much of what I did met with everyone's disapproval. She's quite pretty, the little Edel. And a wonderful horsewoman. Almost made the Olympic team when she was nineteen. Such a little girl, and always on those big stallions . . .'

He paused, and smiled. In spite of all my contempt, I had to smile too. To recoup, I said, 'Yes, and you're already getting a slight beer-belly.'

'Am I? No, I can't be,' said Felix, appalled, immediately concentrating all his attention on his stomach. Again, I could not help smiling.

'Oh, Mitzi, how unkind you are. For a moment I thought – because you are always so truthful. It is an absolute sickness. No one else in this family seems to have caught it from you, though. No, but seriously, if there's anything I cannot bear it is a man who lets himself go. Or of course a woman. I exercise every day, swimming, tennis . . . No, there is nothing more terrible than those Bavarians with their great bellies spilling over their *Lederhosen*.'

'But why don't you tell me, Felix, more about your future wife? I mean not just about her fortune? What kind of a person is she? Is she like Betsy? Or at all like Juliette? Is there anything more to her than horsemanship and a pretty face? And why, I wonder, did they choose you? *They* will know you're not really a duke or a count – and with all that money she could have had one.'

'Oh well,' said Felix, a little uncomfortably, 'the famous titled grandmother does help, you know. Also you must re-member my usual magnetic effect. No, Mitzi, I really think this one is going to work. I am a realist now, not the romantic boy who married Juliette.'

'Nor, I suppose, the romantic boy who married Betsy.'

'That was romance of another kind. I was romantic enough

223

to think, for the sake of the brave new world, I could survive even Betsy's father with his homilies about clean country living and his giant futuristic machines digesting tripe.'

'Then you're really over Juliette.'

'No,' said Felix with a gravity I would have found touching and convincing in anyone else. 'I will never be over Juliette. Never. And that is one of the things that makes a *mariage de raison* actually so much easier now. I am no longer even pretending to look for love. You see, I'm actually like you, Mitzi. I cannot fall really in love more than once in my life. Perhaps it is a reaction to Grandmama, who was able to fall in love a record number of times.'

'I doubt she really did,' I answered, resenting his reference to Stefan but letting it pass. 'Except as one falls in love with a series of mirrors. Well, with all this splendid fortune, it's good you didn't kill yourself, as you threatened to do after losing Juliette.'

'Did I? Well I may have thought of something like that. One does mean these things, you know, at the time. Now, believe it or not, I'm even thinking of having a family. Actually, I never told you, but Juliette was pregnant once, only she lost the baby. That was why she went to that local doctor. And the reason she got so upset was because he accused her of losing the baby deliberately, of overexerting herself after he'd warned her to be careful.'

'Julie? She would never have done anything like that, she was so Catholic –'

'Oh, but at the time she was quite crazy. Completely paranoid. Said she did not want to bring my curse on future generations or something like that. Beautiful, but crazy, that girl. Anyway, I can never understand the English. Nor the French. I should have left her to her dancing.'

'You must have done something to make her paranoid.'

'Nothing, really. She was so pious, so proper, and I've never been at all like that . . . Julie couldn't bear it. She thought every woman she saw with me was my mistress, she hated my friends – all except Werner. I wish him joy of her.' He had completely forgotten his touching statement of a minute before. In fact he was, even for Felix, so erratic I began to wonder what he had been drinking, or taking, if there was something new wrong in his life and all the talk about marriage and bright prospects only a cover or another castle in the air. Still, he did have very expensive clothes, and he would not have used the name of Edel so blithely with no foundation. Let alone, I thought, give all the jewellery to me.

After lunch we came back to the little room my mother had occupied in Trudi and Berti's flat after she left Krammel – left him, the rumour was, because he had tried to install a younger mistress in the ground-floor flat of his own house. Trudi and Berti went out on the sled, as in old times, leaving us alone to sort out my mother's things. 'And please do not argue, children,' Trudi said, in parting, as though children we still were.

My mother had left her few possessions to be divided equally between us; or as equally as might be since Felix had had the lion's share long before. There was not much left that he wanted, so he made a great show of generosity. 'Take the miniature, Mitzi. It might fetch a good price. I know someone at Sotheby's who will look at it for you,' and other such pretentious, honeyed offers were showered upon me until finally I said, 'Felix, it's irrelevant, you know. The only thing I might really have wanted was the house.'

'Ah, the house. I am sorry about that. But you know, it *was* hers to do with as she chose. Let us not, Mitzi, rake up the past too much. Anyway, you never wanted to live there again, and you're not badly off yourself. You're doing very well at the university, I hear. Friends of mine have read your articles and say how good you are. But look, Mitzi, if it really has upset you that much one day I will make it up to you. Now that I am moving into a position . . . where I can say such things, and really mean them.'

'You are moving into a position of great pomposity, which does not become you at all.'

But as usual he was winning. I had meant to be totally distant, icy, brief. Instead I slid into my old ironies, which glanced off Felix's incorrigible egotism and became somehow featherlight, more like affectionate banter than mortal barbs. In vain I kept reminding myself of the house, of my mother, benighted and adoring to the last, of what he had told Juliette, what he had done to Juliette and to how many others. When he was there, I could never hate him entirely, even though the spark between us was gone. I could disbelieve his lies but I could not help being entertained. I was as weak as the others; I had had no right to blame my mother for selling the house. The tears I

225

had not shed for her death now came to my eyes at last, and they were also tears over the stones I had cast when my own walls were so patently made of glass. Now, perhaps, I could really have said to her, I forgive you, I love you – or at least, I will try to love you, the things that after Stefan I could never say. But as always it was too late. And in fact I knew quite well that if she had still been there, we would have fought again as bitterly as before.

Felix said, 'The poor old lady. I know,' and put an arm around my shoulders. 'Look, Mitzi, let's leave all this mess and go out for a drink before we get too depressed.'

I looked at the pile of books and music scores, the open cupboard from which clothes were trailing, the box of china and glass, the pile of photographs on the bed, a long kid glove dangling grotesquely from a drawer ... something of Grandmama's, no doubt; my mother had never had hands that thin and fine. I said, 'Yes, all right.' And then, without thinking, I picked up a photo, and Felix's hand tensed on my shoulder.

Wiping my tear-blurred eyes, I saw that it was a photo of Gordana and her son. Gordana and Joshua's son. Joshua's! The boy had Gordana's Slavic eyes, but he also had the high forehead, the arrogant sensuous mouth, the cleft chin of the Petrolinskis. I continued to stare at the photograph, wordless. Felix took his arm off my shoulder. For once, he too did not speak.

Finally I said, 'Now I understand why Joshua never asked me to visit, why he was so evasive when I wrote about studying in America. He wanted to keep the shame of this to himself. And in the end it was probably this that killed him. It wasn't enough that you gave him the forged letters. You also gave him your child.'

Felix, to my amazement, did not even try to deny that the child might be his. 'Oh, well – how much can you tell from a photograph? It could be Joshua's after all. Or mine. Or anyone's. I only slept with her once, when I came home very drunk and depressed.' Yes, I thought, much as you started sleeping with me. Felix went on, his tone deliberately light. 'Actually, those horse-faced women are often marvellous in bed. You know the phrase about thighs like a wild mare – well, maybe it's the ones who have faces like horses too. Sorry, Mitzi, I know I am being very vulgar, and not properly

226

serious. But if that is my son, it was one of those freak accidents, and I really do not feel responsible for it. Joshua didn't know about me, of course, but nor did I know about him. I never guessed she was pregnant until he offered to marry her, and the chances were probably much greater that the child was his. I didn't dream that it might be mine, until today when I found the picture. Gordana must have sent it to Mama behind Joshua's back, and Mama never said anything. Never.'

'Yes. All that is possible. It's also possible that Gordana told you she was pregnant, and that you told her to work on hooking Joshua, knowing what a pushover he was and that I did not want him.'

Felix's voice now was cold and very hard. 'You are always prepared to believe the worst, Mitzi, so believe what you like. But I will tell you something you may find even more surprising than this picture. The person your darling Joshua was in love with was me.'

'You'll say anything, won't you, anything at all to cover your tracks.'

'I'm not trying to cover them. I admit the boy could be mine. But just think about Joshua. How eager he was to do things for me, and how awkward with you. How he worshipped Grandmama, and his great friendship with our dear old lesbians, who know their own kind . . . It's all typical, isn't it? Oh, it was all repressed, of course. It was only once, when we got very drunk together, that he came close to declaring it. But it's why he wanted you, because you're my sister – not of course, Mitzi, that you are not desirable in your own right – and why in the end he married Gordana. He could never have borne a relationship with a woman who was really his equal. So you see, in a sense his marrying Gordana *was* my fault. But not a fault I could help, and not at all in the way you think.'

I tried to weigh what Felix had said. The terrible thing was that it *did* all make perfect sense, and that if it was not true, it was so plausible that I would never know. But it did not exclude the possibility of Felix having deliberately foisted Gordana on Joshua, and I told him so.

'I said, believe what you like. I still cannot take it all seriously. It's an old aristocratic tradition, the seduction of servants, and only in romantic novels that they are always beautiful. And we are a very traditional family, in our way.'

In spite of everything, my answer sounded like banter again.

'Yes, dear Felix, it's a tradition for a young boy to have his first experience with a maid. But this was hardly that.' Then I remembered when Felix *had* been that young, and I read the horror that must have shown on my face in the sudden fear on his own. I remembered him stammering, 'Grandmama – Grandmama says to look in the pond . . .' and thinking that *then* was the time I had seen Felix look afraid. Perhaps he had had the traditional first experience. With little Janka. And she, terrified of pregnancy or already pregnant, thinking that now she would surely be handed to the Gestapo, had, also in the tradition, the tradition of pregnant servant girls, thrown herself into the pond. When she disappeared, Felix, still young enough to be frightened, had confessed to Grandmama. And Grandmama had shielded him, as my mother had, as all of us had, even when he walked blithely over the dead.

I said at last, 'Felix, I do congratulate you now. I can find no words any more for what you have done and what you are. Why is it the innocents always, the most vulnerable – why Janka, why Joshua?'

'Because they are the innocents.' Felix, surprisingly, did not try to deny my suspicions about Janka either. 'That is the injustice of the world. Not my injustice. I am as I am, Mitzi. None of this is my fault except in eyes as blinded by absurd fanatical morality as yours.' But I saw that he was shaken; the episode of Janka, because it had been the first, was still the one he found hard to face.

I answered slowly, after a pause, 'I have tried to understand, Felix, the secret of your erratic but continuing success. I begin to think that maybe it is only your total availability. Which might be the secret of all Don Juans. Simply being there. Like a phallic idol, a blank erect figure on which we stupid women – I cannot exclude myself – paint our stupid fantasies.'

This one hit home. Felix did not like being referred to as blank. 'Ah, yes, Mitzi. But you could also say that I am simply a realist in a world of romantics. And you are the ultimate romantic, running away from the real. What is more of a blank figure than your gardener's boy, your Stefan, whom you hardly knew, a little cardboard figure with probably no brain at all, with nothing but a prick, on whom you painted all *your* fantasies for ever and ever, a cardboard figure for whom you sacrificed your life?'

There was only one way to go on from this point, and I

suppose I began it. I remember pulling out the drawer with the dangling glove and throwing it at his head. I think I might have killed him then if I could have, but the drawer missed and there seemed to be no better weapons, only shoes and hats and gloves and china and miniatures and photographs, and we pelted and struck at each other with anything that came to hand till the room was a mass of wreckage and through my tears I could see blood running down Felix's face. I thought with great satisfaction that it was I who had drawn the blood, after all. Then there were shrieks of horror, and Trudi and Berti, in ski-suits and dripping snow, charged into the room to separate us.

'It's all right,' said Felix calmly, casually wiping off the blood with some of the snow from Trudi's suit. 'It is an old aristocratic tradition to do this after funerals. It happens in all the best families. Only I'm afraid Mitzi and I have left a bit of a mess. Perhaps we should let you two do the dividing, eh, Mitzi? While there is anything at all left to divide. You were supposed to supervise it, anyway. Since we are such argumentative siblings, I don't know why you left us alone.'

As for me, I said nothing. When it came to choosing sides I knew they would always, in the end, choose him.

And the very last word was his too. We both left that evening, bandaged and subdued, having meekly listened to Trudi and Berti's lectures. 'Two adults who can behave like this! One is forced to believe the evil rumour that you descend from the stables,' etc., quite forgetting the insult this was to my grandmother and newly dead mother. Felix drove me to the station. There seemed no point in not accepting his offer to do so, but we both remained silent until the end of the drive. Then, as I got out of the car, I said, 'Now, at last and at least, there is one time and one person where you will not find forgiveness.' At which Felix smiled. 'Dear God, Mitzi – what would you all have done with your dreary lives, if you had not had me to forgive?'

XII

I was invited to Felix's wedding, and needless to say, did not
go. My next news, a year or so later, was not of Felix himself,
but a Sunday-paper story, about Mrs Ingrid von Lenauer,
née Edel, a story, spectacular enough to have been picked up
by the British press. Her mount had refused a jump in an
international competition, refused three times, disqualifying
her. Whereupon 'Mrs von Lenauer beat her horse so savagely
that attendants and spectators rushed to stop her. "Leave me
alone, you –" she was heard to shout. "It's my – horse, I can
beat him if I like. It's the only thing that makes the – go!"
And she threatened the horse's rescuers with her whip, until
the judge ordered her to dismount.'

I wondered if the quote was a rather free translation from
Ingrid's German. Whether it was or not, 'Mrs von Lenauer,
who had been given previous warnings and even prosecuted
on one occasion by the German Humane Society, was fined
and barred from show jumping for five years.' There were
pictures of Ingrid, flailing away with her crop at the hapless
horse's ears. Her fury-contorted face gave no idea of what she
might look like in repose. But she looked a lot bigger than I
imagined the 'little girl' Felix had called her. I wondered if it
was really the poor horse who had been the inspiration of so
much rage; and I wondered if Trudi and Berti, now my
mother was gone and after the last scene, would bail out Felix
yet again.

But three months after the newspaper story, it was on my
doorstep that Felix appeared.

*

He did not write, or phone. He was simply there, pacing in front of my little house when I came home from a late class, wearing a long Loden coat, the collar turned up. He had no umbrella, and his hair was dark and curled with rain. I knew at once what I should do; walk straight past him, go in and shut the door in his face. All the more, really, since my first sight of that Loden-coated figure in the mist had given me a crazy pang of hope – that even after all these years, against all odds, against all reason, it was someone else. And in spite of all that had happened, something of it lingered, something of that wild rush of buried love and longing stayed and stopped me, as if it were, a little of it, for Felix himself. Had there not, in the depths of my mind, been some such twisted identification all along – had I not already taken, in both senses, one for the other? So I let Felix in.

When we were inside, Felix turned his collar down, and I saw the two neat, new scars on his cheeks. 'My God,' I said, 'Was that your Ingrid?'

'I look like a university student from before the war,' said Felix grimly. 'It makes me feel young again. No. Actually it should make me feel old. I do feel old, Mitzi. I can no longer play these games quite as easily as I used to. Well, thank God she did that, so I had something to show in court. You should see the ones on my chest. Do you want to see the ones on my chest? And she – *she* was going to present herself as a battered wife. Less fortunately, she had a very cunning lawyer, and of course she – the family – pulls a great deal of weight. I did not, in all senses, come out of this one unscarred.'

'Felix – why did all this happen? What did *you* do? What did you do to her?'

'I? Believe it or not, nothing. Nothing yet. I had not even been unfaithful when it started. At least, not with anyone she could have found out about. Mitzi, it wasn't me – she *is* like that. Right now she is in a clinic, resting her so-called nerves. She is always in clinics except when she is in horse shows, and now it looks as if she will be in clinics a lot more. Unless one of her stallions tramples her, and nothing would please me better. When I married her I didn't know it, but I was supposed to play Petruchio in *The Taming of the Shrew*. Only it was not Shakespeare who wrote the script.'

'So, that was why they didn't mind her choosing you – a

231

penniless and dubious *von* . . .' I had to sit down, suddenly weak with laughter. 'Oh, my God, Felix, for once you've been trumped. It's better than the dog-food factory. It's better than anything.' Felix stood silently by while I shrieked and gasped, unable to stop myself. Once or twice, his mouth twitched, his arrogant, still-beautiful mouth, and I thought he was going to join my laughter, but he did not. Finally he said, 'Now that I have provided you with your evening's entertainment, do you think you could let me have some financial aid?'

That was Felix. He knew me better than to pretend he was here for any other reason, that he had come all the way to my meek terraced cottage in a sleepy English college town for comfort or nostalgia or friendship or love, or even that seemingly indissoluble tie of blood, which *he* had never really felt, any more than Grandmama. It was something the others of us felt, for them. He knew that any pretence would only harden me against him. His best chance, with me, was to show himself as shameless, and obviously desperate, as he was. He added, as if to underline it, 'You know how I am, Mitzi. You do not expect me to be any other way. I am not going to admire your decor, because I don't, nor say how good it is to see you, because neither of us can feel that now, though I have always had a weakness for you in spite of our differences. And you know that, too. So I am coming straight to the point. I am here because I need help. I am throwing myself on your mercy.'

'Oh, come now, Felix. If she was what you say, you can't have got out of the divorce as badly as that.'

'She was driving *me* mad. You don't know what my life was like at the end. I was desperate, and when I am desperate I tend to do . . . expensive things. I gambled, I ran up debts . . .'

'Is there no one else left, then? Have even Trudi and Berti refused you?'

'Trudi and Berti have already done what they can. There is no one left. I would not turn to you if there were. I know what you think about me.'

'Felix, look. You are a bottomless pit. And even if I were to say yes, I on my modest English salary could hardly give you more than you would get for the clothes on your back.'

'I'm not asking for anything out your modest salary. I am only asking you to let me have my half of the jewels back.

232

You remember, everything was to be divided, so half is legally mine anyhow. I know I said you could have them all but that was when I thought I was rich.'

'All! All eight pathetic pieces – or is it seven? And after you had the money for the house,' I said, and began to laugh again.

'I am glad I provide you with so much amusement.'

'You have already said that, Felix.'

'Yes. I know. But so much amusement ought to be paid for.' Suddenly he caught my wrist. 'Mitzi, get this through your head. I am desperate. I must have those jewels. I will pay you back as soon as I can, but I must have them. Tell me where they are.'

'They're not anywhere. Go ahead, search the place, wreck it as you wreck everything. I sold them to buy this little house. And now I want you to get out of it.' My voice was level, but for a moment I was really afraid.

Felix let go of me, and some of the darkness went out of his eyes. 'Oh, well then,' he said, and he sounded, curiously, almost relieved. 'Well then, of course, it's too late. I can hardly ask you to sell your house too. All right, Mitzi, I will go. It's a shame we have to part again on such terms but I really am in a situation which leaves me no time for tender family scenes. Even if you should want one.'

'Felix – just out of idle curiosity – what sort of trouble are you in this time, really? I mean, other than the divorce.'

'It is nothing that you would find enlightening to hear, or that it would improve my situation to tell you.'

'Felix, I can lend you – give you – a bit of money. At least the fare –'

'That is *grandieuse* of you, Mitzi, but not necessary. We are not yet at the stage where one sells the coat off one's back, as you so wisely pointed out I could do.'

I smiled, in spite of myself again more amused than afraid, and I let him kiss me goodbye, wanting no final altercation to slow his departure. He said one last thing to me, as if it were truly important to him that I should believe it, though he must have known I would not. 'Mitzi, whatever else, the letters were real. Read the last letter from Handelbein, the one he wrote when he was dying, just before the beginning of the first war, and think very hard whether that letter could possibly have been written by anyone else.'

233

'I will,' I said, 'I will.' I locked the door behind him, drew the curtains, and took Maria Aurora's last brooches and bracelet and ear-rings out of my jewellery box and buried them in the flour bin. Then I sat down dutifully with Joshua's book and re-read the last Handelbein letter; but when I had read it, I still did not see why, for all its passion, it was more convincing, or less, than any of the others.

My dearest Mitzi,

Yes, it is grave. I had not told you how grave it is. I can say this now, I must say this now, because this letter may be the last I will write you. It is at my wish that you are not with me. I could not bear to have you see me as I have become. There is no one else; I will have no one else near me. In the last months, the whole of humanity has become for me like uninvited visitors who will not leave; a paradox, since it is I who am leaving. But would you, who are so vital, so undivided, so unafraid, understand if I said it is not only myself I am afraid for, that I have a sense of the whirlwind coming out of a darkness infinitely vaster than my own? There are a million hands building the city of my fear, a city that has grown overnight from such harmless, such rural beginnings, an enormous city in which unspeakable enormities are done.

Oh, Mitzi, you can live without me, as I could not live without you; I would never have the effrontery, the vulgarity, to ask you to live for me, but I do ask you to live, to live as I will not, to be well, to be happy, to live until the end. And all this in face of a raging egotism that warns me to warn you again not to come, even should you (as you will not) be able to come in time. For were you here, I might even, in a last great surge of lust and despair, kill you to take you with me into the dust. I can leave everything else, Mitzi. The unbearable is to let you go.

The next day, looking over my shoulder all the time like one hunted, I dug the jewels up again and deposited them in a safe in my bank. It was paranoid and hysterical but I was almost sure that he would come back; that he, Felix, could never be so naïve as to think me as incapable of lying as he himself was incapable of truth. But Felix did not come back. And two weeks later his Aston-Martin – which he had surprisingly not yet sold, or rather, as it turned out, not yet paid for – missed a curve and smashed into a lorry just outside Trieste, at over a hundred miles an hour. It was one of those accidents which can hardly be called suicide, especially as

Felix always drove suicidally, but which in their timing leave a lingering suspicion of at least unconscious intent.

No one knew, or ever will, why Felix was heading for Trieste, as no one will ever know half of what Felix did or intended. Felix, like Grandmama, was material for a legend, but his was not the sort that relatives are usually anxious to preserve. And Felix himself, who took such pains to provide the documentation for one family history, took equal pains to see there was none to document his own. I have pondered, for a long time, if he told me to read the Handelbein letter because there was in it some cryptic message for me. I have come to no conclusion. Except that a legacy of bewilderment is just what Felix would want to leave.

And now, since this is in its way a confession – I suppose these things, however they begin, can end no other way, the narrator becoming too involved to escape – I will admit what I felt about Felix's death. Not grief, no; though grief and guilt is what the clichés of psychology would have it that I felt. To truly grieve for Felix one would need to be blind and in love with him, as a good many people were. (I actually received several indignant letters from women not invited to his funeral; I had decided not to hold one, and have what little was left of him buried near where it was found. I suspect these women would have liked a funeral partly to see who their rivals were, and the battle royal Felix and I myself staged after my mother died might have been nothing to what would have ensued if I had indulged them.)

Nor did I feel that idiotic sense of waste which seems to invade mourners of charming and beautiful villains (though God knows most villains are neither), the sentiment that makes them sigh deeply and say, 'What he might have been if only he had used his talents for something constructive!' Felix had no talents, except for what he did, and he did it superbly, until the end. That he rose only to fall again was what made him superb. The rogue who succeeds, who becomes a fixture in high places and covers his tracks, as many do, is the worst of rogues and the least entertaining, a pompous bore with all the vices and none of the virtues of respectability.

But I am digressing, procrastinating. I have said that I felt no grief. But I did feel an acute empty space, the presence of absence. And I felt release. Not from my bondage to Felix.

My bondage to Stefan. Do not ask me to explain this; I cannot. It was as if Felix's death had snapped the last link with my youth, with the love I had thought would dominate me forever. And I knew then that if there had been someone else after Stefan, later, when I was stronger, if Felix had not been the first, my life might have taken a different course. It was simply another of the many devastating effects of Felix's careless self-indulgence, effects that seemed almost inevitable. Though Felix was perhaps not evil in the grim Biblical sense in which we use that word, if we use it at all, though he did not actually delight in pain and corruption, it was as if some destructive principle worked through him. Just as some great creative principle, as well as the same destructive one, at least for weaker spirits, worked through the Maria Aurora of the letters. But with these Joshuan peregrinations I may slide into doing for Felix a little of what he did for Maria Aurora; and that I have no intention of doing at all.

Not grief, then; no. But I am making myself sound colder than I was. The space left empty was not small. I was free, but it was too late. Of the rest of *my* life, my classes, my articles, my shorings up of Joshua's by now monstrous baroque edifice, I will tell nothing because there is nothing of interest to tell.

I have said that there is a truth, but it is not for us; and still I have tried to come as close to it as I can. It is not my fault that life so consistently imitates not art but pulp romance gone awry; nor that what the old Russians would have made high tragedy becomes comic opera on the banks of the Danube. We are too jaded, too polyglot, too sensual and ironic. Our most desperate situations are never entirely serious.

Today Sir Henry phoned me again. I was prepared to say no; then I thought of Dr Dawn Crump, still not quite deflected, and Perdita Blank, and I said yes. This memoir I will put in a trunk, for some future Joshua to discover – if there are future Joshuas, or indeed a future. By then it will be too long ago for anyone to untangle myth from reality, even the little I have been able to myself.